The Urbana Free Library

To renew: call **217-367-4057**
or go to **urbanafreelibrary.org**
and select **My Account**

The Reporter's Kitchen

The Reporter's Kitchen

JANE KRAMER

St. Martin's Press ❦ New York

www.stmartins.com

Designed by Donna Sinisgalli Noetzel

The material in this book, with the exception of
the Introduction and "Rites, Rituals, and Celebrations," originally appeared in *The New Yorker*.

The Library of Congress Cataloging-in-Publication
Data is available upon request.

ISBN 978-1-250-07437-9 (hardcover)
ISBN 978-1-4668-8598-1 (ebook)

Our books may be purchased in bulk for promo-
tional, educational, or business use. Please contact
your local bookseller or the Macmillan Corporate
and Premium Sales Department at 1-800-221-
7945, extension 5442, or by email at
MacmillanSpecialMarkets@macmillan.com.

First Edition: November 2017

10 9 8 7 6 5 4 3 2 1

For Wicky

Contents

INTRODUCTION

Right now I'm trying to decide what to cook for dinner. Yesterday I finished revising the last chapter of this collection, and whenever I finish a book—or a long piece of reporting or even a tough review—I take a few days off and celebrate by getting reacquainted with my kitchen, my husband, my family, and my dog. This is not to say that I've neglected any of them, and certainly not my kitchen, only that, as my daughter, Aleksandra, complained when she was a child in Paris, still answering to her baby nickname, Wicky, "Mommy, you're here, but you're *not* here." She meant, of course, that wherever *we* were, a good part of my head was still at my desk, locked in a battle with words, a battle I occasionally won by plunging into a magic circle of concentration, which in those days was bounded by a pack of Marlboro Lights on one side of my computer and a bag of chili taco chips on the other, with me in easy reach of them all. The cigarettes are long gone from my life, the taco chips, too. And mirabile dictu, Aleksandra Crapanzano grew up to become a writer herself. A screenwriter and a food writer. A multitasker, as her generation of brainy, beautiful Brooklyn women call themselves (I call them "jugglers"), always on deadline with a screenplay, plus a weekly food column in *The Wall Street Journal* and a second cookbook in the works, not to mention materfamilias to a household, with a husband and an eleven-year-old boy of her own, and even a dog like the Bouvier des Flanders she got for Christmas, in Paris, when she was her son's age. More to the point, we have finally made peace in the kitchen—where she had glowered through an adolescence of scullery (I prefer "sous-chef") servitude to a mother referred to in her stove mode as "the Fürher" or on the good days, merely "Sergeant Kramer." I knew she was trying to outcook me, which is to say outclass me, in my own—well, our—kitchen, and to suggest that we were anything less than fiercely territorial about our rights at the stove would be, *pace* Kellyanne Conway, an "alternative fact."

Wicky bided her time. She was thirteen when the moment came. I was stuck in Germany on a story, my plane canceled, and, without a word to her father, she took over the kitchen and went to work preparing an exceedingly elaborate meal for him and the two friends from Stockbridge whom I'd invited to dinner, thinking I'd be back. By all reports, he came home from work ready to make his excuses and order in, only to discover the dining room table set with our best china and wedding silver, and our daughter in the kitchen, macerating mangoes and strawberries, à la Marcella Hazan, in an exceedingly pricey bottle of Sauternes that she had talked our local wine store into delivering by calling up and pretending to be me. There was an asparagus soup from Simone Beck's *Simca's Cuisine*, with tarragon simmered in white wine, waiting on the stove; a salad of Bibb lettuce in a champagne vinegar dressing on the counter; and in the oven, a roulade of chicken from an old copy of *Gourmet*—a truly complex dish involving boneless chicken pounded thin and rolled around

alternating layers of spinach and bell pepper purée to produce, when sliced, a beautiful swirl of white, red, and
green. Thus, on my return from Germany, we entered the
second phase of our competitive cooking life. Call it the wary
collaborative phase. Or Venus and Serena.

It didn't take long for Wicky to morph into Aleksandra
or to claim parity in the kitchen. For one thing, she baked.
She loved baking and was never daunted by the timing and
precision involved in making a perfect cake or a flaky, buttery crust that didn't stick to some impossibly fluted baking
dish, whereas I have only recently mastered the task of rolling a sheet of frozen puff pastry for a potpie, and my go-to
cakes tend to be Ballymaloe's Tunisian orange cake, where
bread crumbs and ground almonds are as close as you get to
flour, or the River Café's pistachio loaf cake, where the addition of ground pistachios obviates even the need for crumbs.
What's more, while my daughter can often be right up there
on what you could call the anxiety meter ("Mommy, remember to phone as soon as you arrive," she says whenever her
father and I take a trip, meaning anything from the nine-and-
a-half-hour flight from Kennedy to Fiumicino to twenty-five
minutes on the F and C trains from Boerum Hill to Central
Park West), she is remarkably serene in the kitchen, where
my anxiety spikes but hers dissolves into a kind of blissful
and commanding competence that can always stretch a meal
to include anyone who happens to call on a Sunday morning
when she is at the stove, with eggs scrambling on one burner,
pancakes on another, bacon on a third, and therefore a couple
of burners still available for a pot or pan. I have been to known
to panic at the thought of just a few unexpected guests, except in Italy in the summer, where my hospitality is relative
to the capacity of my pasta pots—and mine are big.

There is a deep pleasure in seeing your child sneak up behind you, match you, and stride right past you, the way my daughter has. As anyone who reads this book will learn, my mother couldn't cook and *her* mother couldn't, either. In those days, there was no glamour in cooking if you didn't have to, especially in New England, where the idea of "luscious" was close enough to "lust" to be far more shocking than inspiring. It amuses me now to see Providence—where generations of my mother's family were born and raised on what was known generically (whoever you were) as "Protestant food"—referred to as a hot culinary destination. But if it's true that certain gifts—cooking, gardening, music, to name a few—tend to skip a generation, then it stands to reason that if they skip two, the next two generations get to make up for it. My daughter and I are doing that now. We cook together on holidays and have come to terms on the subject of who does what best. She brines and roasts the crispest, juiciest, most tender Thanksgiving turkey I have ever eaten, the most ambrosial cranberry sauce and pies; I am the secret twelve-ingredient cornbread stuffing chef, and, I have to admit, produce a delicious bones-to-bourbon gravy. On Christmas, the baby Brussels sprouts with shallots, pancetta, and balsamic vinegar and, clearly, the bûche de Noël are hers to make. The Yorkshire pudding, parsnip purée, and rib roast with horseradish sauce are mine. We have not done battle in the kitchen for years. She still calls me Mommy. Her father and I still call her Wicky. Her husband (and friends and colleagues) call her Aleksandra. Her son calls her Mommy, Mom, Mother, Aleksandra, Wicky, or Woman, depending on the message he wants to send.

This book is for her, with love and pride. As for dinner tonight, I am still deciding what to make.

PART I

The Reporter's Kitchen

THE REPORTER'S KITCHEN

AUGUST 2002

The kitchen where I'm making dinner is a New York kitchen. Nice light, way too small, nowhere to put anything unless the stove goes. My stove is huge, but it will never go. My stove is where my head clears, my impressions settle, my reporter's life gets folded into *my* life, and whatever I've just learned, or think I've learned—whatever it was, out there in the world, that had seemed so different and surprising—bubbles away in the very small pot of what I think I know and, if I'm lucky, produces something like perspective. A few years ago, I had a chance to interview Brenda Milner, the neuropsychologist who helped trace the process by which the brain turns information into memory, and memory into the particular consciousness called a life, or, you could say, into the signature of the person. Professor Milner was nearly eighty when I met her, in Montreal, at the neurological institute at McGill University, where she'd worked for close to fifty years, and one of the things we talked about was how some people, even at her great age, persist in "seeing" memory the way children do—as a cupboard or a drawer or a box of treasures underneath the bed, a box that gets full and has to be cleaned out every now and then to make room for the new treasures they collect. Professor Milner wasn't one of those people, but I am. The memory I "see" is a kind of kitchen, where the thoughts and characters I bring home go straight into a stockpot on my big stove, reducing old flavors, distilling new ones, making a soup that never tastes the same as it did the day before, and feeds the voice that, for better or worse, is me writing, and not some woman from another kitchen.

I knew nothing about stockpots as a child. My mother was an awful cook, or more accurately, she didn't cook, since in her day it was fashionable not to go anywhere near a kitchen if you didn't have to. Her one creation, apart from a fluffy spinach soufflé that for some reason always appeared with the overcooked turkey when she made Thanksgiving dinner (a task she undertook mainly to avoid sitting in the cold with the rest of us at the Brown Thanksgiving Day home football game), would probably count today as haute-fusion family cooking: matzo-meal-and-Rhode-Island-johnnycake-mix pancakes, topped with thick bacon, sour cream, and maple syrup. Not even our housekeeper and occasional cook could cook—beyond a tepid sherried stew that was always presented at parties, grandly, as lobster thermidor, and a passable apple filling that you could spoon out, undetected, through the large steam holes of an otherwise tasteless pie. I don't think I ever saw my father cook anything, unless you can call sprinkling sugar on a grapefruit or boiling syringes in an enamel pan, the way doctors did in those days, cooking. (I use the pan now for roasting chickens.) The only man in my family with a recipe of his own was my brother Bob, who had mastered a pretty dessert called pumpkin chiffon while courting an Amish girl who liked pumpkins. My own experience in the kitchen was pretty much limited to reheating the Sunday-night Chinese takeout early on Monday mornings, before anyone else was awake to eat it first.

I started cooking when I started writing. My first dish was tuna curry (a can of Bumble Bee, a can of Campbell's Cream of Mushroom Soup, a big spoonful of Durkee Curry Powder, and a cup of instant Carolina rice), and the recipe, such as it was, came from my friend Mary Clay, who claimed to have got it directly from the cook at her family's Kentucky farm. It counted for me as triply exotic, being at once the product of a New York supermarket chain, the bluegrass South, and India. And never mind that the stove I cooked on then was tiny, or that "dining" meant a couple of plates and a candle on my old toy chest, transformed into the coffee table of a graduate-school rental, near Columbia; the feeling was high sixties, meaning that a nice girl from Providence could look forward to enjoying literature, sex, and cooking in the space of a single day. I don't remember whom I was making the curry for, though I must have liked him, because I raced home from Frederick Dupee's famous lecture on symbolism in *Light in August* to make it. What I do remember is how comforting it was to be standing at that tiny stove, pinched into a merry widow and stirring yellow powder into Campbell's soup, when I might have been pacing the stacks at Butler Library, trying to resolve the very serious question of whether, after Dupee on Faulkner, there was anything left to say about literature, and, more precisely, the question of whether I'd find anything to say in a review—one of my first assignments in the real world—of a book of poems written by Norman Mailer on the occasion of having stabbed his second wife. I remember this because, as I stood there, stirring powder and a soupçon of Acapulco Gold into my tuna curry, I began to accept that, while whatever I did say wasn't going to be the last word on the poetics of domestic violence, it would be my word, a lot of Rhode Island still in it, a little New York, and to my real surprise, a couple of certainties: I was angry at Norman Mailer; I was twenty-one and didn't think that you should stab your wife. Mailer, on the other hand, had produced some very good lines of poetry. He must have been happy (or startled) to be taken for a poet at all, because a few weeks after my review ran—in a neighbor-hood paper you could pick up free in apartment-house lobbies—his friend Dan Wolf, the editor of what was then a twelve-page downtown alternative weekly called *The Village Voice*, phoned to offer me a job.

I bought a madeleine mold, at a kitchen shop near the old *Voice* offices, on Sheridan Square. It was my first purchase as a reporter who cooked—a long, narrow pan of shallow, ridged shells, waiting to produce a Proust—but though I liked madeleines, they didn't collect my world in a mouth-ful, the way the taste of warm apples, licked from the cool tingle of a silver spoon, still does, or for that matter, the way the terrible chicken curry at the old brasserie La Coupole in Paris always reminded me of Norman Mailer's wife. The mold sat in my various kitchens for twelve years before I moved to the kitchen I cook in now and tried madeleines again, and discovered that, for me, they were just another cookie— which is to say, not the kind of cookie that belonged in the ritual that for years has kept me commuting between my study and my stove, stirring or beating or chopping or sift-ing my way through false starts and strained transitions and sticky sentences.

The cookies I like to make when I'm writing are called

"dream cookies." I made my first batch in my friend John Tillinger's kitchen in Roxbury, Connecticut, at one in the morning, in a mood perhaps best described by the fact that I'd just been awakened by the weight of a large cat settling on my head. The cookies were a kind of sand tart. They had a dry, gritty, burned-butter taste, and I must have associated them with the taste of deliverance from sweet, smooth, treacherous things like purring cats. I say this because a few years later I found myself making them again, in North Africa, in the middle of reporting a story about a tribal feud that involved a Berber wedding and was encrypted—at least for me—in platters of syrupy honeyed pastries, sugared couscous, and sweet mint tea.

At the time, my kitchen was in the Moroccan city of Meknes, where my husband was doing ethnographic research, but my story took me to a village a couple of hours up into the foothills of the Middle Atlas Mountains. It was a wild, unpleasant place. Even today, some thirty years, a couple of wars and revolutions, and an assortment of arguably more unpleasant places later, I would call it scary. The wedding in question, a three-day, her-house-to-his-house traveling celebration, was about to begin in the bride's village—which had every reason to celebrate, having already provided the groom's village with a large number of pretty virgins and, in the process, profited considerably from the bride-prices those virgins had commanded: goats, chickens, silver necklaces, brass plates, and simple, practical, hard cash, some of it in negotiable European currencies. The problem was that none of the young men in the bride's village were at all interested in the virgins available in the groom's village, whose own supply of goats, chickens, necklaces, plates, and money was consequently quite depleted. All that village had was an abundance of homely daughters—or, you could say, the bad end of the balance of trade in brides. As a result, the men in the groom's village were getting ready to fight the men in the bride's village, a situation that left the women in both villages cooking day and night, in a frantic effort to turn their enemies into guests.

By then I was close to being an enemy myself, having already broken one serious taboo: I had asked the name of somebody's aunt in a conversation where the naming of paternal aunts in the company of certain female relatives was tantamount to calling catastrophe down on the entire family, and the women had had to abandon their cooking in order to purge the premises, which they did by circling the village, ululating loudly, while I sat there in the blazing sun, under strict orders to keep the flies off a platter of dripping honey cakes. It hadn't helped any that, in a spirit of apology (or perhaps it was malice), I then invited the villagers to Meknes and served them my special Julia Child's bœuf bourguignon, which made them all quite ill. A few days later, I went to the medina and bought some almonds for dream cookies. I don't know why I did it. Maybe I was homesick. Certainly I was being spoiled, knowing that Malika, the young Arab woman who worked for me and had become my friend, would grind those almonds into a sandy paste as quickly as she had just peeled peaches for my breakfast—which is to say, in less time than it took me to check for scorpions underneath the two cushions and copper tray that were then my dining room. But I think now that I was mainly trying to find my voice in a country where some women couldn't mention an aunt to a relative—where the voices of most women, in fact, were confined to their ululations. Once I heard that same shrill, fluty cry coming from my own kitchen and rushed in to find Malika shaking with pain and bleeding; she was sixteen, and had taken something or done something to herself to end a pregnancy that I had never even suspected. After that, I would sometimes hear the cry again and find her huddled in a corner of the room, struck with a terror she could not describe. No one had ever asked her to describe it, not even the man she'd married when, by her own reckoning, she was twelve years old.

I never finished the story about the Berber bride. I was a bride myself, and this posed something of a problem for my erstwhile village friends, who had wanted to find me a husband from the tribe and thus assure themselves of the continued use of, if not actually the title to, my new Volkswagen. In the event, one night, after we'd been trading recipes, the women sent me home with a complicated (and fairly revolting) "love recipe" to try out on the husband I already had, and it turned out—at least according to the neighbors who warned me not to make it—to be a bit of black magic whose purpose was, to put it discreetly, less amorous than incapacitating. I took this as a sign that it was time to come down from the mountains. I wrote a book about an Arab wedding instead, and I waited until I was back in my study in New York to finish it. The lesson for me, as a writer, was that I had to burrow back into my own life before I could even start thinking clearly about someone else's, or come to terms with the kinds of violence that are part of any reporter's working life, or with the tangles of outrage that women reporters almost inevitably carry home with their notes.

In New York, I cook a lot of Moroccan food. I keep a tagine on the shelf that used to hold the madeleine mold, and then the Swedish pancake skillet and the French crêpe pan and the Swiss fondue set and the electric wok that my husband's secretary sent for Christmas during a year when I was stir-frying everything in sesame oil—something I gave up because stir-frying was always over in a few fraught seconds and did nothing at all for my writing. The cooking that helps my writing is slow cooking, the kind of cooking where you take control of your ingredients so that whatever it is you're making doesn't run away with you, the way words can run away with you in a muddled or unruly sentence. Cooking like that—nudging my disordered thoughts into the stately measure of, say, a good risotto simmering slowly in a homemade broth—gives me confidence and at least the illusion of clarity. And I find that for clarity, the kind that actually lasts until I'm back at my desk, poised over a sentence with my red marker, there is nothing to equal a couscous steaming in its colander pot, with the smell of cumin and coriander rising with the steam. That's when the words I was sure I'd lost come slipping into my head, one by one, and with them, even the courage to dip my fingers in and separate the grains.

Some of the food I learned to cook in Morocco didn't translate to New York. I have yet to find a hen in New York with fertilized eggs still inside it—a delicacy that the Meknasi would produce for their guests in moments of truly serious hospitality—not at the halal markets on Atlantic Avenue or even at International Poultry on Fifty-fourth Street, poulterer to the Orthodox carriage trade. I cannot imagine slaughtering a goat on Central Park West and then skinning it on the sidewalk, if for no reason other than that I'm an ocean away from the old f'qi who could take that skin before it stiffened and stretch it into a nearly transparent head for a clay drum with a personal prayer baked into it. I have never again squatted on my heels, knees apart and back straight, for the hours it takes to sift wheat through a wooden sieve and then slap water into it for a flat-bread dough, though in the course of various assignments I have made chapati with Ugandan Asian immigrants in London, stirred mealie-mealie with Bushmen in Botswana, and rolled pâte feuilletée with Slovenian autoworkers in the projects of Södertälje, Sweden. And I am still waiting for permission to dig a charcoal pit in Central Park for the baby lamb that I will then smother in mint and cumin, cover with earth, and bake to such tenderness that you could scoop it out and eat it with your fingers.

But when I'm starting a piece about politics, especially French politics, I will often begin by preserving the lemons for a chicken tagine, perhaps because a forkful of good tagine inevitably takes me back to the home of the French-speaking sheikh whose wives taught me how to make it (to the sound of Tom Jones singing "Delilah" on a shortwave radio), and from there to the small restaurant in Paris where I ate my first tagine outside Morocco, and from there to the flat of a surly French politician named Jean-Pierre Chevènement, who lived near the restaurant, and who unnerved me entirely during our one interview by balancing cups of espresso on the breasts of a hideous brass coffee table that appeared to be cast as a woman's torso, while barking at me about French nuclear policy. Similarly, I make choucroute whenever I'm starting a piece that has to do with music, because my first proper choucroute—the kind where you put fresh sauerkraut through five changes of cold water, squeeze it dry, strand by strand, and then braise it in gin and homemade stock, with a ham hock and smoked pork and sausages buried inside it—was a labor of love for the eightieth birthday of the composer George Perle; and since then the smell of sausage, gin, and sauerkraut mingling in my oven has always reminded me of the impossible art of composition, and set my standards at the level of his luminous wind quintets.

On the other hand, when I write about art I like to cook a rabbit. My first rabbit was also, unhappily, my daughter's pet rabbit, and I cooked it with understandable misgiving, one summer in the Vaucluse, after an old peasant sorcerer who used to come over during the full moon to do the ironing took it from its hutch and presented it to her, freshly slaughtered and stuffed with rosemary, on the morning of her first birthday, saying that once she ate it, she would have her friend with her "forever." We had named the rabbit Julien Nibble, in honor of our summer neighbor Julien Levy, a man otherwise known as the dealer who had introduced Max Ernst and Arshile Gorky and most of the great Dadaists and Surrealists to New York, and my daughter, who is thirty-one now, has refused to eat rabbit since we told her the story, when she was six or seven. But I have kept on cooking rabbit, changing recipes as the art world changes, and always asking myself what Julien would have made of those changes, and of course whether he would have liked the dinner. There was the saddle of rabbit in a cognac-cream sauce that smoothed out my clotted thoughts about a middle-aged Italian painter with what I'd called "an unrequited sense of history." There was the *lapin niçoise*, with olives, garlic, and tomatoes, that saw me through the first paragraphs of a story about the politics of public sculpture in the South Bronx. There was the rich, bitter rabbit ragout—a recipe from the Croatian grandmother of the Berlin artist Renata Stih—that got me started after a couple of earthquakes hit Assisi, shattering the frescoes on the ceiling of San Francesco into a million pieces. Dishes like these become invocations, little rituals you invent for yourself, in the hope that your life and your work will eventually taste the same.

Good cooking is much easier to master than good writing. But great cooking is something different, and during the years that I've stood at my stove, stirring and sprinkling and tasting, waiting for a sauce to thicken and a drab sentence to settle—if not precisely into echoing, Wordsworthian chords, at least into a turn of phrase that will tell you something you didn't already know about Gerhard Schröder, say, or Silvio Berlusconi—my cooking has leaped ahead by several stars, leaving my writing in the shade. Some dishes have disappeared from my repertoire; tuna curry, for example, has been replaced by the crab-and-spun-coconut-cream curry I first tasted in Hong Kong in 1990 and have been working on ever since, and never mind that the crab in Hong Kong turned out to be doctored tofu, while mine arrives from a Broadway fishmonger with its claws scissoring through the paper bag. Some dishes I've sampled in the course (and cause) of duty are memorable mainly because I've tried so hard to forget them. For one, the crudités I managed to get down at Jean-Marie Le Pen's gaudy and heavily guarded Saint-Cloud villa, with M. Le Pen spinning an outsize plastic globe that held a barely concealed tape recorder, and a couple of Dobermans sniffing at my plate. For another, the rat stew I was served in the Guyana jungle by a visibly unstable interior minister, who had accompanied me there (en route to a "model farm" hacked out of the clearing that had once been Jonestown) in a battered Britten-Norman Islander with no radar or landing lights and a thirteen-year-old Air Force colonel for a pilot. Some dishes I've repressed, like the cauliflower soup that was ladled into my plate in the dining room of a Belfast hotel just as a terrorist's bomb went off and a wing of the building crumbled, leaving me, the friend whose couch I'd been using for the past week, and a couple of other diners perched in the middle of the sky—"like saints on poles," a man at the next table said, returning to his smoked salmon. Some dishes I've loved but would not risk trying myself, like the pork roast with crackling that Pat Hume, the wife of the politician and soon-to-be Nobel Peace laureate John Hume, was in the process of carving, one Sunday lunch in Derry, when a stray bullet shattered the window and lodged in the wall behind her; she didn't stop carving or even pause in her conversation, which, as I remember, had to do with whether the New York subways were so dangerous as to preclude her visiting with the children while John was in Washington, advising Teddy Kennedy on how to get through a family crisis.

Some dishes I've left in better hands. It's clear to me that I'm no match for the sausage vendor at the Frankfurt Hauptbahnhof when it comes to grilling a bratwurst to precisely that stage where the skin is charred and just greasy enough to hold the mustard, and then stuffing the bratwurst into just enough roll to get a grip on, but not so much roll that you miss the sport of trying to eat it with anything fewer than four paper napkins and the business section of the *Frankfurter Allgemeine Zeitung*. In the same way, I know that I will never equal my friend Duke, a Herero tribesman known from the Kalahari Desert to the Okavango Delta by his *Dukes of Hazzard* T-shirt, in the art of thickening a sauce for a guinea fowl or a spur-winged goose in the absence of anything resembling flour. Duke was the cook at my fly camp when I was out in the delta researching a piece about "bush housekeeping," and he thickened his sauces there by grating roots he called desert potatoes into boiling fat. But the secret was how many potatoes and, indeed, how to distinguish those potatoes from all the other roots that looked like potatoes but were something you'd rather not ingest. I never found out, because the day we'd planned to fly to the desert to dig some up, a tourist camping on a nearby game preserve was eaten by a lion, and my pilot volunteered to collect the bones. Food like that is, as they say in the art world, site-specific.

Take the dish I have called Canard sauvage rue du Cherche Midi. I cooked my first wild duck in a kitchen on Cherche Midi in 1982, and during the seventeen years that I lived between Paris and New York, I honed the recipe to what my friends assured me was perfection. But it has never produced the same frisson at my New York dinner table that it did at the picnic table in my Paris garden, if for no reason other than that my neighbors across the court in New York do not punctuate my dinner parties with well-aimed rotten eggs, accompanied by shouts of "*Sauvages!*," the way one of my Paris neighbors—a local crank by the name of Jude—always did, and that consequently my New York guests know nothing of the pleasure that comes from pausing between bites of a perfect duck in order to turn a hose full blast on the open window of someone who dislikes them.

Some dishes just don't travel, no matter how obvious or easy they seem. I know this because I tried for a year to duplicate the magical fried chicken known to aficionados as Fernand Point's Poulet Américain—a recipe so simple in itself that no one since that legendary Vienne chef has ever dared to put it on a menu. I have never even attempted to duplicate the spicy chicken stew that the actor Michael Goldman heats up on a Sterno stove in his damp, smelly Paris cave, surrounded by the moldy bottles of Lafite and Yquem and Grands Échézeaux that you know he's planning to open as the night wears on. Nor have I attempted the Indonesian rijsttafel—which is basically just a platter of rice with little bowls of condiments and sauces—that my late friend George Hoff, a Dutch kendo master and nightclub bouncer, tossed off one night in London after a long and strenuous demonstration that involved raising a long pole and slamming it down to within a centimeter of my husband's head. Or the fish grilled by a group of young Portuguese commandos in the early summer of 1974—I was covering their revolution; they were taking a break from it—over a campfire on a deserted Cabo de São Vicente beach. Or for that matter, the s'mores my favorite counselor roasted over a campfire at Camp Fernwood, in Poland, Maine (and never mind that I hated Camp Fernwood). Or even popcorn at the movies.

But most things do travel, if you know the secret. A lot of cooks don't share their secrets, or more often lie, the way my mother-in-law lied about the proportion of flour to chocolate in her famous "yum-yum cake," thereby ending whatever relationship we had. My best secret dates from a dinner party at Gracie Mansion when Ed Koch was the mayor of New York. I had known Koch from his Village Independent Democrat days, when he pretty much starved unless his mother fed him. But now that he was Hizzoner the Mayor of New York City, he could, as he repeatedly told his guests, order anything he wanted to eat, no matter what the hour or the season or the inconvenience to a staff best trained in trimming the crusts off tea sandwiches. The dinner in question got off to an awkward start—"You're Puerto Rican? You don't look Puerto Rican" is how, if I remember correctly, he greeted the beautiful curator of the Museo del Barrio—and it was frequently interrupted by phone calls from his relatives, who seemed to be having some sort of business crisis.

But everybody agreed that the food was delicious. It wasn't elaborate food, or even much different from what you'd cook for yourself on a rainy night at home: pasta in a tomato sauce, good steaks, and hot chocolate sundaes for dessert. But the meal itself was so uncommonly tasty that I went back to the kitchen afterward and asked the cook how he'd made it, and he told me, "Whatever Ed likes, whatever he says he never got as a kid, I double the quantity. I doubled the Parmesan on the pasta. I tripled the hot chocolate sauce on the ice cream." Ed's principle was "More is more."

It's not a principle I would apply to writing, but it's definitely the one I cook by now, on my way from excess in the kitchen to a manuscript where less is more. If my couscous is now the best couscous on the Upper West Side, it's because, with a nod to Ed, I take my favorite ingredients from every couscous I've ever eaten—the chickpeas and raisins and turnips and carrots and almonds and prunes—double the quantity, toss them into the broth, and then go back to my desk and cut some adverbs. I put too many eggs in my matzo balls, too much basil in my pesto, too much saffron in my paella. I have no patience with the kind of recipe that says "1/4 teaspoon thyme" or "2 ounces chopped pancetta." I drown my carrots in chervil, because I like the way chervil sweetens carrots. I even drown my halibut in chervil, because I like what it does to the reduction of wine and cream in a white fish sauce—though, now that I think of it, when I'm on a bandwagon, when I'm really mad at the world I'm writing about and the people in it, I will usually switch to sorrel.

The first time I cooked halibut on a bed of sorrel, I was in New York, laboring over a long piece about liberation theology in South America and, in particular, about a young priest whose parish was in a favela with the unlikely name of Campos Elísios, about an hour north of Rio de Janeiro. I wasn't mad at my Brazilian priest—I loved the priest. I was mad at the bishop of Rio, who was on the priest's back for ignoring orders to keep his parishioners out of politics. At first I thought I could solve the problem by taking the afternoon off to make moqueca, which was not only my favorite Brazilian dish but, in my experience, an immensely soothing one—a gratin of rice, shrimp, lime, and coconut cream, served with (and this is essential, if you're serious) a sprinkling of toasted manioc flour—which provides the comforts of a brandade without the terrible nursery taste of cod and potatoes mushed together. I made moqueca a lot in Rio, because I was angry a lot in Rio. Angry at the poverty, at the politics, at the easy brutality of people in power and the desperate brutality of people without it. But it's hard to make my moqueca in New York unless you have a source of manioc flour, and the closest I came to that was the seven-foot-long flexible straw funnel leaning against a beam in my living room—an object devised by the Amerindians, centuries ago, to squeeze the poison out of manioc so that they wouldn't die eating it. I had wasted the better part of the afternoon on Amsterdam Avenue, searching for manioc flour, when I happened to pass a greengrocer with a special on sorrel. I bought him out, and a couple of hours later I discovered that the patient preparation of sorrel—the blanching and chopping and puréeing and braising in butter—had taken the diatribe in my head and turned it into a story I could tell.

There are, of course, moments in writing when even the most devoted cook stops cooking. Those are the moments that, in sex, are called "transporting," but in journalism are known as an empty fridge, an irritable family, and the beginnings of a first-name friendship with the woman who answers the phone at Shun Lee West. When I am lost in one of those moments, I subsist on takeout and jasmine tea, or if takeout is truly beyond me—the doorbell, the change, the tip, the mismatched chopsticks, the arguments when I won't share—on chili tortilla chips and Diet Coke. If the hour is decent, I'll mix a bloody mary or a caipirinha like the ones that the priest and I used to sneak in the kitchen of the parish house of Campos Elísios on evenings when the Seventh-day Adventists would arrive at the favela in force, pitch a tent in a field, and call the poor to salvation through amps rented by the hour from a Copacabana beach band. But moments like those are rare.

My normal state when beginning a piece is panic, and by now my friends and family are able to gauge that panic by the food I feed them. This past spring, in the course of a few weeks of serious fretting over the lead of a story about an Afghan refugee, I cooked a small Thanksgiving turkey, two Christmas rib roasts, and an Easter lamb. I cooked them with all the fixings, from the cornbread-and-sausage stuffing to the Yorkshire pudding and horseradish cream—though I stopped short of the Greek Easter cheesecake that three cookbooks assured me had to be made in a clean flowerpot. My excuse was that I'd worked through Thanksgiving and been snowbound in Berlin through Christmas, and of course it was nearly Easter when I began my holiday cooking. Easter, actually, went well. No one mentioned the fact that we were celebrating it on a Saturday night, or for that matter, that at noon on Sunday we were due, as always, for our annual Easter lunch at the home of some old friends. But Thanksgiving in April brought strained smiles all around, especially since my next-door neighbor had already cooked a lovely

Thanksgiving dinner for me in February. And while my first April Christmas was a big success—one of the guests brought presents and a box of chocolate mushrooms left over from a bûche de Noël—my second Christmas, a few days later, ended badly, when my daughter suggested that I "see someone" to discuss my block, my husband announced to a room full of people that I was "poisoning" him with saturated fats, and my son-in-law accused me of neglecting the dog. But I did end up with a paragraph. In fact, I thought it was a pretty good paragraph. And I finished the piece the way I usually finish pieces, with notes and cookbooks piled on the floor, working for a few hours, sorting the Post-its on my desk into meaningless neat stacks, and then heading for my big stove to do more cooking—in this case, to add the tomatoes to a Bolognese sauce, because my last paragraph was too tricky to handle without a slow, comfortable Italian sauce, and I'd been using Bolognese for tricky characters since I first tackled the subject of François Mitterrand, in a story on his inauguration in 1981.

It seems to me that there is something very sensible about keeping your memories in the kitchen with the pots and the spices, especially in New York. They take up no space; they do not crash with your computer; and they collect the voice that you can't quite hear—in tastes and smells and small gestures that, with any luck, will eventually start to sound like you. I'm not in New York right now. The dinner I was cooking a few pages ago—the clam-and-pork stew with plenty of garlic and piri piri peppers that I first ate in a Portuguese fishermen's tavern near Salem, the day I tacked wrong and sailed my boyfriend's sixteen-footer into a very big ketch and broke his mast and, with it, whatever interest he had in me—is not the dinner I am cooking today, at a farmhouse in

Umbria. My stove is smaller here (though my pots are bigger). I do not write easily about myself. I am not as tasty or exotic as the characters I usually choose. My first attempt at anything like autobiography was a thinly disguised short story, and it was returned with the gentle suggestion that I replace myself with someone "a little less like the kind of person we know everything about already." But twenty years later I did manage to produce a reminiscence of sorts. It was about my mother and my daughter and about being a feminist, and it ended where I am writing now, in Umbria, looking across my pond to a field of wheat and watching a family of pheasants cross my garden. It occurred to me, worrying over this ending—not quite a panic but enough of a problem to have already produced a Sardinian saffron-and-sausage pasta, a cold pepper soup with garlic croutons, nightly platters of chicken-liver-and-anchovy bruschetta, pressed through my grandmother's hand mill, and twenty jars of brandied apricot jam—that I might possibly solve the problem by cooking the same dinner that I'd cooked then. It turns out to be one meal I can't remember.

PART II

Profiles

THE HUNGRY TRAVELERS

⤜

NOVEMBER 2008

In the fall of 1985, a few months after China opened the Tibetan border, Jeffrey Alford from Laramie, Wyoming, met Naomi Duguid from Toronto on the roof of a hotel dormitory for foreigners in Lhasa. It was ten at night, and since there were no lights on the roof to see by, they sat in the dark, listening to the sound of chimes and chanting, and began to talk—which turns out to have been the best way to get acquainted. They had this in common: they were restless; they were at home in strange and forbidding places; they were attached to the early albums of Herbie Hancock; and they liked to eat. But it was hard to imagine them getting acquainted in what you would call the real world—let alone getting married, writing cookbooks, and ending up members in high standing of a small scholarly circle of food writers whose work leaves the rest of the food world far behind, collecting recipes.

Duguid, known to her friends as Nom, was a tall, streaky-blond, hazel-eyed lawyer of thirty-five, with a house and a boyfriend at home, and she was traveling through Asia on a five-month work sabbatical, hoping to resolve the question of why the offer of a partnership in the Toronto firm where she had labored happily for nearly five years had made her want to flee. Alford was thirty-one, a tall, skinny, ponytailed seeker of truth with a master's degree in creative writing, a passion for the East, a light heroin habit, and a reputation for supporting his wanderlust with tag sales in his parents' front yard—his father was a vice-president of the University of Wyoming—and with odd jobs as a gold and cash courier on the South Asia smuggling circuit. At the time, he and five recruits were getting ready to cross the Himalayas, from Lhasa to Kathmandu, on mountain bikes, for a magazine called *Bicycle Rider*, which was planning to run a piece by Alford about cycling in Tibet. Duguid was traveling with the eighty-two-year-old Swiss writer Ella Maillart, a legendary adventurer whose letters Nehru once claimed had saved his sanity in prison, and whom Duguid had met for the first time that September in another foreigners' dorm, in Kunming. "Nom always meets everybody," Alford says. "Even me."

The logistics of love are daunting at twelve thousand feet—Alford describes their attempt at a kiss as "two sheets of sandpaper scraping"—but not, as it were, insurmountable. Ten days later, Duguid wrote a letter of resignation to her law firm—"Dear guys, It's not the altitude, but I'm not coming back"—placed an awkward call to her boyfriend, and set out to explore Nepal with a couple of anthropologists she had just met, while Alford finished his assignment. She wasn't worried about their future, because they had already covered all the big, important "life things." Did they want a family? Could they have one and keep traveling? How would they pay for "a life open to the world"? By November, they had made their way south to Thailand and were camped on an island beach, where Alford started to withdraw. ("I had scored this big hit in Hong Kong. I gave it away. But I had thought, 'How do I explain this part of my life to Nom?' She was great.") It took four days, and they got through them talking about all the places that were left to see and how to get there.

A month later, they flew home. Alford met Duguid's friends, including her old law-firm colleagues at Sack, Charney, Goldblatt & Mitchell, whose view of her defection, as she describes it, ran from disbelief to "we're sorry for us but exhilarated for you." Duguid met Alford's friends and got to know his family. Her own family—her father, a navigational engineer; her mother, a physiotherapist for disabled children; and her only brother—had died by the time she was twenty-seven, and she told the Alfords that until Jeff "so much loss" had kept her running from anything like a settled life. A few months later, they were married and back in Asia, crossing the Pamir and Karakoram mountains—from Kashgar, in the Turkic province of Xinjiang, to Gilgit, in Pakistan—on a pair of red mountain bikes.

They began writing together about biking together, perhaps because in those days Duguid was better on a bike than in the kitchen, where long workdays had left her pretty much limited to baking bread—something her mother had taught her—and boiling pasta. But Alford, by his account, was already obsessed with food. He had cooked his way through his mother's *Joy of Cooking* by the age of twenty, worked as "the sauté guy" at a fancy Laramie restaurant as a University of Wyoming undergraduate, and learned the rudiments of Thai cooking from a student from Bangkok who worked there with him. He was also passionate about baking. When he wrote his master's thesis—his adviser, the novelist John

Edgar Wideman, had told him, "Write me a story about the things you know"—he called it "Bread, Travel, and Drugs," which just about covered nine months he had just spent in a cottage-cum-student crash pad on the Dingle Peninsula, hiking, smoking pot, and perfecting his landlady's recipe for Irish soda bread. "I love utilitarian things," he says. "I loved being in that kitchen, I loved the smell of the bread and the steamy windows and my sour-green-apple jam sitting on the sill." After a month in the Pamirs—in the course of which he tasted "some amazing flatbreads," and confessed to Duguid that he wanted to write a flatbread book—he started looking through food magazines and said to her, "Wait a minute, I can do this. I know more about food than anything." Their first food article, "Delicious Asian Flatbreads," appeared in *Bon Appétit* in 1988. (They got a thousand dollars for it, or about what Duguid would have been bringing in for a day's work as a partner at Sack, Charney.) A year later, they published a piece on Thai drinking food—the tapas of Southeast Asia—in *Food & Wine*, which discreetly called it "Be Cool . . . with Spicy Thai Salads." "We write to travel" is how Duguid describes their life since then. "It was never the other way around."

By now, Alford and Duguid have raised two sons and written six books. And while their books are undeniably cookbooks (two James Beard Awards for Cookbook of the Year, for a start), they are also cultural encounters—travel journals, stories, history lessons, and photographic essays that, taken together, explore the imagination and the exigencies that produce a cuisine and in many ways define the people who create it. The couple have been called culinary anthropologists, but culinary geographers is at least as accurate. They prefer "friendly amateurs." Ann Bramson, their editor and publisher at Artisan Books in New York—who inherited their first manuscript in the mid-nineties, languishing neglected at another press, and has been shepherding their books since then—says that she recognized them right away as "prodigious readers and unaccredited scholars," and was determined to do justice to them with books that were serious enough to accommodate their field photographs and uncommon texts and at the same time striking enough to make you stop, look, read, and reflect on your way to a recipe that you might otherwise never think of trying. (Duguid, an accomplished photographer, "does people," and Alford, who has turned himself into one, does the mise-en-scène, a job he more or less described this way: "I'm not a ruin kind of guy, but there were these ruins, so I took the picture.") A few critics have found them too striking or, as Mark Bittman in the *Times* once put it, would have preferred more recipes. James Oseland, the editor of *Saveur*, disagreed. "People pick up a book of Nom and Jeff's, and they know that it's something else, something more than a cookbook," he told me after a lecture they gave at the Asia Society in New York. "It's their overriding sense of humanity that sets them apart from the flock. They're taking the exotic out of the everyday in every sense, not simply the recipe sense. They're telling you, 'It's just the world. The world won't hurt you. Don't be scared.'"

That world has nothing to do with states and borders. They write about foods, like grains or rice, that nearly everyone cultivates and, in one form or another, eats—their first book, *Flatbreads & Flavors: A Baker's Atlas*, took them to four continents in six years—and, most often, about the kind of cooking that defines what they call the "real regions," which are ethnic or even tribal and topographical and ignore the boundaries of nation-states to form culinary countries of their own. *Hot Sour Salty Sweet*, their third book, was about the food cooked by the peoples of the Mekong Valley, and for it, they followed the river from near its source, high on the Tibetan plateau, through China, Burma, Laos, Thailand, and Cambodia, and down to the delta in Vietnam where it meets the South China Sea. *Beyond the Great Wall*, their sixth, was a culinary tour through the hinterland cultures of "the other China"—cultures beyond the pale of the country's insistent Han identity—and took the Alford-Duguids from Tibet to the Xinjiang-Kazakh border, and from the grasslands of Inner Mongolia to the rice terraces of southern Yunnan. Alford calls it a book about survival.

They travel light, on anything headed in the right direction—a riverboat, a mountain bus, a truck that stops for them on an empty road, a train with a thousand people hanging out the windows. When nothing shows up, they hitchhike or rent a bike or walk. Duguid, who on one trip to China rode from a Dong village in Guizhou to a bus stop near the Guangxi border "strapped onto the back of someone's motorcycle with my backpack, my camera pack, my tripod, and three Guizhou stools," calls this "staying vulnerable" to the people, the place, and the possibility of a new taste wherever they get dropped off. "They still travel the way I did when I was twenty and backpacking through Europe, going where the wind blew me," Tina Ujlaki, the food editor at *Food & Wine*, says. "They talk about arriving in a place and having no idea of what they'll find there. The awe that comes with that—it's always present."

Alford once told me that his father's idea of travel was to cajole one of his three boys into the family Rambler—Jeff was the most willing—and drive to Colorado to play the dog races. "We'd sleep in the car and in the morning head for the truck stop with the best cinnamon rolls," he said, sending me back to Alford and Duguid's fourth cookbook—*Home Baking: The Artful Mix of Flour and Tradition Around the World*—for the recipe: yeast, water, oil, salt, brown sugar, cinnamon, and thirteen cups of flour make a dozen rolls, and you won't need anything else on the ride home. The first real traveling that Alford did was a bicycle trip through Wales, the summer after his freshman year in college, and he describes it this way: "I was sooooo lonesome. I missed my parents. I wanted to go home."

Duguid, however, had been traveling since childhood—first with her family, and then as a student after her father died, on a legacy from a great-aunt who "saw to it that I didn't owe." By the time she finished college—she read geography at Queen's University in Ontario, with a year abroad at the London School of Economics—she had already seen "some nice bits" of Africa. By the end of law school, she knew India and Nepal. Two years after getting her degree, she was back in India. She calls that trip an experiment in "living undefended, unintroduced, and depending on serendipity." She was also, by all accounts, a brilliant lawyer. She had what her college roommate and University of Toronto law-school classmate Trisha Jackson calls "that special combination of intellect and intuition and engagement." But she had no interest in a white-shoe practice. At law school, she had volunteered to work with immigrants at a legal-aid clinic. As a lawyer, she specialized in labor arbitration, "always for the labor side." She was a radical in a suit. She loved immigrant Toronto and rented an apartment in a house on Henry Street, just around the corner from the ethnic olio of food stores known in the city as Kensington Market. (The year before she left for Tibet, she bought a house of her own on the same block.) She wanted to know where everybody came from, what their families did, and what their lives had been like in, say, India or China. And whenever she could, she went back to Asia.

Alford began what he calls his "Asia adventures" in 1977. He says that, unlike Duguid, who is instantly at ease with strangers, he was "too shy" for conversation and would simply dig in wherever he landed for a couple of months, not saying much until people got used to him. He was able to live in Asia on very little money, and when he ran out, he usually found a way to make more. (His brother Jim, who is an artist in Santa Fe, told me, "He left on that first trip with twelve hundred dollars, and he came home two years later with twelve hundred dollars, and I didn't ask.") He bought clove oil in Sri Lanka and sold it to Ayurvedics in India, and then he bought Indian saris to sell in Sri Lanka. He bought jewelry in Thailand and Nepal, hawked it at his Laramie yard sales, and paid for his next plane ticket with the profits. His days as a smugglers' courier began in 1981, and they took him from Hong Kong to Kathmandu (where the airport metal detectors were always broken) with, as he usually describes it, "five pounds of gold up my bum." He made eight hundred dollars for every flight, with two hundred more thrown in for the flight back, which involved the arguably easier job of carrying twenty thousand dollars in a money belt. He could live for a year on a thousand dollars. That was his life until he decided to write a story about bicycling across the Himalayas and met Duguid on a roof in Lhasa. "Here was my vagabond brother, moving into her life," Jim Alford told me. "It took a lot of courage, maybe even more for him than for her."

One of the things that Alford and Duguid decided, early on in Lhasa, was that any children they had should travel with them—which means that for the better part of fifteen years they packed up their boys in November, along with the books and the homework, the Beanie Babies and the Legos, and deposited them back in their classrooms at the end of January. Dominic—a senior at the University of Toronto now—rode from Cholon to Saigon on the back of a motorcycle at the age of two; Tashi, a Toronto freshman, started walking at one, in Tafraout. Neither seems to have suffered from his peripatetic life, or in fact to have found it at all unusual. (It lasted until Dom's eleventh-grade French teacher started giving him zeros for incomplete assignments.) Sometimes they missed the sandwiches—bread by Duguid—in their school lunch boxes, or at least preferred them to some of the food they tasted traveling; Tash hates onions, garlic, scallions, chives, and "every other oniony thing," and Dom's view of seafood is "I have trouble being at the same table with a fish." But Tash talks casually about the day he ran off a path in Laos—he was eight then—hoping to climb the biggest funeral jar in the Plain of Jars, and had to be rescued from a minefield. And Dom includes in his list of "fun times" the night a plane taking the family from Rangoon to Mandalay made a mysterious stop and left them stranded on a darkened airstrip outside Taunggyi, the capital of Burma's dissident Shan State; they ended up in a hotel room with one bed and a television set and got to watch the playoffs between the Denver Broncos and the Pittsburgh Steelers. (He was eleven when that happened.) Between them, the boys can name twenty-five or thirty countries where they have traveled. When I asked Dom if they were ever scared, he said, "Why? Nom and Jeff were with us."

Tash describes his parents' way of working abroad like this: "When we traveled, I was always very confused. We'd

eat somewhere, leave, go back to the same place, eat more.
I'd say, 'Guys, call back! Get the recipe!' But they didn't need
to. They 'see' recipes." Alford and Duguid's methods are, by
their own admission, odd. "We don't 'do' interviews," Duguid
says. "We don't take notes unless we're asked to. We engage.
We appreciate. We're there to learn." (They don't use trans-
lators, either; they figure that by now, between them, they
can get by in about a dozen languages.) Even the diaries
they keep at night on the road are sketchy. Mainly they
depend on the photographs they take—at last count, an
archive of more than a hundred thousand color slides—as
aides-mémoire and on the kind of confidence that comes
from months spent watching and tasting and listening, or as
Alford calls it, "hanging out."

They also rely on Duguid's prodigious memory. She remembers everything—from the date she sailed to Europe
with her parents on the *Empress of England* (May 12, 1961)
to the minutiae of cases she argued twenty-five years ago to
the names and smells and colors and textures of foods she
sampled months before in a Tajik yurt near the Khunjerab
Pass or at a stand in a market in northern Laos, and the order
in which different cooks put those foods in the pot, and
even the shape of the pot. Alford, for his part, absorbs what
could be called the praxis of a particular place: the way a fire
is tended in Tibet, where even a cup of tea can take an hour
to heat; the way the spices are ground and roasted separately
for a coconut-chicken curry in Kandy; the way a mound of
sticky dough turns into a five-foot strand of "flung noodles"
when a burly Uighur grabs each end and, with a flick of his
wrists, sends it looping through the air—a process that he
and Duguid describe in *Beyond the Great Wall* and admit to
never having mastered.

Sometimes they miss something or remember wrong. (The "spicy chickpea fritters," from their fifth book, *Mangoes & Curry Leaves: Culinary Travels Through the Great Subcontinent*, will fall apart unless you think to beat a couple of eggs and add them.) Sometimes their recipes are more interesting than appealing; it is hard to imagine working up an appetite for Tibetan bone broth, even if you take their advice and substitute oxtails or beef shanks for the yak. But most of the time they send you straight to the kitchen. I've cooked from their books since *Hot Sour Salty Sweet* came out, in 2000, and I made an instantly addictive Thai soup—the one with, among other good things, wild lime leaves, bird chilies, oyster mushrooms, lemongrass, and a lot of fresh shrimp. James Oseland from *Saveur* told me, "The difference between Nom and Jeff is precisely what makes them complementary as observers. Nom is the person reaching out, leaning over, looking into the pot of that soup lady in Thailand and finding out how many kids she has, and Jeff is the one who is there, quiet, filing away the information in his head, processing it, and someday they will use it together."

Duguid and Alford live with their sons in the house on Henry Street that Duguid bought the year before she went to Tibet—a brick Victorian row house with a garden in back and a small carriage house off the alley behind it. They have not changed much in twenty-three years, though Duguid's idea of a great suit now is apt to involve an antique Akha tribal jacket from a Laotian flea market and a pair of jeans, and Alford's ponytail has long been replaced by short, if unruly, gray hair, trimmed at home by a hairdresser he met in the park one day; she told him that he "needed work." But the house has changed. It is stuffed with memories of travel, in the form of fabrics, hangings, bowls, pots, posters, jewelry, and a lot of unidentifiable objects that Duguid refers to generically as "rescued stuff." It is also where they write their books, reconstruct the flavors they carry home in their heads from halfway around the world, and consult a food and travel library that over the years has spilled out of the big study they share on the second floor up to the door of the master bedroom, on the third, and down to the workshop in the basement where Alford listens to world music, restores whatever "useful" (or possible) furniture he finds, discarded, on Toronto's sidewalks—the family eats at a big open maple counter that was once a length of floorboards in the local Chinese Methodist church—and mends old bicycles, including the two red mountain bikes that saw them safely from Kashgar to Gilgit in 1986.

When the Alford-Duguids work on a book at home, they divide the recipes between them, cook something, and then see if the other eats it or thinks it's "right." Duguid describes the testing they do as a kind of translation, because they cook in a simple hand-me-down Western kitchen, with ingredients that any of their neighbors would be able to find, albeit with some effort, in an Asian market. She says that they test "by taste," though this is a term that for her can include the smells from the brazier in a tribal kitchen and even the stories the women cooking in it tell. They are less interested in accuracy than in authenticity. (The exception, of course, is baking.) Call it the evocation of a world on a plate. I spent a couple of weeks with them in Toronto, and on my first day in their kitchen Duguid told me to stop worrying about what their recipes said, because "our whole point is that you're not a cookbook, you're in your own kitchen with your own pots and pans: relax, go to the market, think 'yummy,' and use what's there." She and Alford are splendid cooks—which

doesn't always follow from being splendid cookbook writers—
but if dinner on Henry Street is "less good" sometimes, she
says, "it's not the end of everything."

Alford likes his recipes simple. "Pure" and "cheap" is the
way he describes his style. Their friend Ethan Poskanzer, who
claims the distinction of knowing the Alford-Duguids before
they knew each other—he crashed (and cooked) with Alford
in Ireland as a student, and a few years later turned up at law
school in Toronto with Duguid and then at the same law
firm—told me that "if there are only three ingredients in one
of Jeff and Nom's recipes I know the influence is his." Today
I read their cookbooks with this in mind. The Hani pork
jerky in *Beyond the Great Wall*, which came from a sidewalk
vendor in Jiangcheng, near the Laos border, is unmistakably
Alford's—pork butt, coarse salt, black pepper—and so is the
story of how he came to eat it: "I was feeling a little let down
by Jiangcheng the next morning as I waited for the bus. Then
I spotted a Hani woman with a woven basket sitting on the
sidewalk . . . everything got better from there on." Duguid,
on the other hand, likes her food "bountifully simple," to
which she often adds "soft" and "maybe a little sweet." Her
stir-fry with pork and chives, on the facing page, starts with
red chilies, minced garlic, and thin slices of cornstarch-coated
pork loin, each seared in a little peanut oil and then combined and enriched with a new taste or texture every minute
or two: salt and chives, then broth, then soy sauce, and at the
end, a sprinkling of fresh coriander. In the book, she describes
the effect this way: "This pork stir-fry from Yunnan uses
chives for flavor and color. The strands of green are very
pretty among the strips of pork. You can substitute garlic
shoots if you wish, or else scallions, cut into ribbons."

A few days before I left Toronto, Alford and Duguid

decided to have a dinner party—meaning that whenever a friend called that morning Duguid, who is irrepressibly hospitable, said "Come." At noon, with the guest list at ten and growing, she told me, "Well, do we want to muddle along today, stretch some Kazakh noodles, or seize the day with marketing," and the three of us headed to Kensington Market to shop. Alford markets the way he cooks: he buys just what he needs and nothing more, and if something is missing, he makes do. But Duguid markets the way she cooks; whatever she sees that pleases her goes into her shopping bag. (Alford, who had been thinking of a "simple feast," maybe some noodle soup and grilled boar, quickly headed off to a music store, saying he couldn't bear to watch.) We came home with rhubarb, ginger, and asparagus from a Tamil organic grocer called Potz; coconut milk, pickled mustard greens, and chili-bean paste from the Hua Sheng Chinese Supermarket; rice flour and mung dal from the Indians at House of Spice; pressed tofu from the Vietnamese "tofu lady" at Fong On; and limes and celery root from the Portuguese greengrocer. Duguid used it all.

The asparagus and the limes ended up in a Thai chicken and vegetable salad. The rhubarb topped an "anyday skillet cake" from *Home Baking*. ("I do my grandmother's thing," she said, plunging the stalks into hot and then cold water three times. "Rhubarb leaves fuzzies in your mouth usually, but not this way.") She minced the ginger with garlic, shook them into some hot peanut oil in her favorite wok, stirred for a minute, added the chili-bean paste, stirred some more, added the celery root, peeled and sliced, and a little soy sauce, tasted it, sprinkled salt, stirred again, and simmered it all in boiling water. Meanwhile, she had started the dal—a Henry Street staple—sniffed it, thought for a bit, and tossed in a handful of the mustard greens. While the dal cooked, we dry-roasted some Ethiopian coffee beans, wolfed down a lunch of pickled-vegetable and pork-pâté sandwiches from the local Vietnamese takeout, and tried the tofu. The phone rang, and with the receiver scrunched to her ear, she talked a Washington food reporter through a recipe for Tibetan stew while measuring the water for a pot of Asian rice (place the tip of your index finger on the rice; stop pouring when you get to the first knuckle).

Forty minutes into these whirlwind preparations, she instructed me on the essentials of a Thai beef salad, somewhat embellished since it first appeared in *Seductions of Rice*, their second book, but still the recipe everyone mentions as the one they can almost taste, just by reading the ingredients: rare sliced sirloin, lettuce, cabbage, shallots, cucumber, dandelion vinegar, fresh coriander, pepper, minced hot chili, lime juice, and "whatever else looks good," as long as it's laced with Thai fish sauce, preferably the kind with the picture of a squid on the bottle. When she finished the list, she laughed and said, "How good is that!"

Alford, meanwhile, had been rolling cracker dough with a French pin—a long narrow walnut cylinder that he had dug out of a drawer full of flatbread stamps and rolling pins, many of them tin chapati pins that they bought in India in 2004, researching *Mangoes & Curry Leaves*. Alford controls the production of all things dry, flat, and salty on Henry Street (and Duguid the production of loaf breads and most of the cakes), and he is passionate and precise about his crackers (a teaspoon of salt and a cup of "warmish" water to every two cups of organic whole-wheat flour in the food processor). He rolls his dough to the kind of paper thinness that bakes in a minute or two and breaks into hot, crisp chips. "Push from the body, not the arms," he kept telling me when I tried the pin. He sprinkled the first few batches of dough with Parmesan, stopped for a short argument with Duguid, who loathes Parmesan crackers—"The cheese burns and everything turns bitter and it's like the terrible crunch of burnt toast in your mouth," she says—and put the cheese down after she started tossing coriander leaves into a pot of pristine chicken soup (chicken and water) that he had simmering on the stove. Dom, who was home by then, told me that his parents rarely fought, but that they did have "some intense discussions" about food.

Alford had promised me a lesson in making the Kazakh soup noodles from *Beyond the Great Wall*—flour, salt, and water, stretched by thumb and, in his kitchen, dried on a rack that had started life as a neighbor's deck chair—so we slapped together some batter, with the help of a friend who had come early for a lesson, too, and had been waylaid slicing celery root. When the rack was full, we switched to hand-rolled Guizhou rice noodles, which you shape into balls between the palms of your hands and then flatten into pointy ovals by rubbing the palms together. (It's harder than it sounds.) They felt gummy, so we dropped a few into Alford's broth. Duguid tried one, pronounced it "tough"—it was—checked the label on the sack she had just bought, and said, "Aha, a rice-flour issue! This comes from India. It should have been Chinese flour. Much finer."

By then the house was full of people. (The youngest was two.) They sniffed the pots, said "ummm" or "cool"— the one prerequisite for food and friendship at the Alford-Duguids is a healthy contempt for the rhetoric of culinary appreciation—poured some wine from an assortment of bottles and Tetra Pak cartons, and settled down on the garden steps to watch Alford feed charcoal into an old Weber for a roast of rubbed wild boar. (His rub is Thai fish sauce and a lot of pepper: "accessible home cooking," as he describes it.) Dina Fayerman, a high school English teacher and cookbook collector who met the couple at a concert of "two-headed Ethiopian lutes" in 1992 and quickly became their bottom-line taster and grammarian, sat down next to me, and we began to talk. A few days earlier, I had asked Fayerman to describe them, from her point of view as a Jewish intellectual who could tell a Montreal bagel from a Toronto bagel in a blind tasting. "They have that Wasp virtue of not being sheeted and compressed, that pioneer thing that drives people to repudiate expectations," she told me. "I've watched them making sausage. They have no casing. Nom cuts the ends off a big plastic tonic bottle, pushes the meat in one end and out the other, and it's a sausage. Jeff does the same thing with one clean sock, and saves the mate. They mesh with each other because they're so completely different."

We served ourselves at the kitchen counter and ate in the garden. Nobody talked about food then. A television producer named Anne Mackenzie told me a funny story about trying to talk the CBC into a cooking show with the Alford-Duguids called *Eyes Wide Open*. ("Forget the movie," she said. "It's the way they travel around the world. And besides, it sounded cheaper to do than Nom's title, *A Travelers' Kitchen*.") Dom, who is thinking about a doctorate in analytic philosophy, showed me his reading list. Tash emerged from a laptop session on the living room couch to announce that reticulated pythons were thirty-seven feet long. Duguid, who just that week had spotted the first lilies of the valley of the season coming up nicely a few feet from the front steps, wondered aloud if her delphiniums were doing as well at the family's farm—ninety acres of fields and woods outside the town of Durham, a couple of hours northwest of Toronto, where the Alford-Duguids spend their summers and weekends. She was worried about skunks digging up her beds for grubs. Alford was worried about groundhogs—"my Moby-Dick"—digging up his fields. It was a warm night. We looked at the stars and ate. Everything was delicious. Toward ten, Fayerman held up her empty plate, shook her head, and said, "What do I need to cook for when I've got Nom and Jeff living down the street?"

Duguid likes cooking with friends around. She likes the conversation, the gossip, the chance to hear a good story. She takes her time, and she isn't bothered when dishes pile up in the sink. She says, "Friends in the kitchen? What could be more communal than that?" Alford likes cooking alone—the concentration, the economy of thought and gesture. "Nom will take an interest in what I'm cooking—she's more experimental, she has such an active head," he says. "But I have zero desire to hear her suggestions for change." He washes the pots and the plates he uses as he goes along and "all the surfaces, then the fridge." By dinnertime, the floor is mopped and the kitchen is clean. "For me, it's a kind of meditation," he told me. "Like building our barn at the farm or making a stone wall or quilting. It's all the same." (Alford learned quilting from his mother; he makes quilts, mends quilts, and will happily spend "more money than I ever spend on anything" if he comes across a nineteenth-century double pink at a flea market.) Duguid likes the buzz of Toronto life—dim sum with friends, a morning at the museum, her weekly belly-dance classes, the pleasure of being anonymous in a big city. Alford, whose concession to city life mainly involves a morning trip to the corner Starbucks for a cup of coffee, prefers the farm—a day on his John Deere tractor or out in the woods, hacking paths, while Duguid gardens or drives to the shape-note group she sings with.

Duguid likes the party they throw in Toronto in December, the night before New Year's Eve, with the house so crowded and toasty and the kitchen so full of good smells. Alford prefers the party they throw at the farm in July, although he complains afterward about the lawyers who drive up from the city in "a stream of BMWs." He says that the lawyers intimidate him. (Duguid tells him, "Phooey, it's you who intimidate them. Get over it. Preserve the harmony.") The party at the farm lasts all weekend. Alford keeps a wood fire going in the grilling pit that he put together with rocks from the farm and rebar grating from a local hardware store. People pitch tents, and if it's chilly at night, they grab some padding from a pile of down jackets that he and Duguid buy by the armful at a Toronto resale establishment called the Pound, where two dollars buys a pound of clothes. They hold figure-eight bicycle races. They dance to a DJ's track and to Alford's remix disks in the big barn that the family has been rebuilding since 2000—the year after they bought the farm and started stripping the farmhouse—with the help of a local writer, barn scholar, and shiitake farmer by the name of Jon Radojkovic. Radojkovic, who has since become Alford's closest friend, told me that there were "two Jeffs": the Jeff from Toronto, who doesn't answer the phone, and the Jeff from Durham, who farms all day and talks by the fire all night.

Last summer, Alford and Duguid decided that the time had come to take on separate projects. They were at an impasse on the research for a new book, about Celtic cooking. Duguid had flown to Galicia and Asturias in November, to see what remained of traditional Celtic food in fusion Spain, and hadn't found much besides spelt bread. Alford had flown to Wales and found some, but most of the people cooking it were rich Londoners in weekend cottages. ("The best thing I learned in Wales was when I passed this guy, way out on the Llŷn Peninsula, who was building stone walls," he says. "I pulled over. He taught me so much about walls!") In the end, they were relieved to stop. Duguid, who has always thought of herself as "a photographer first and a food writer second," wanted to put together a book of her own—a book of photographs and maybe an exhibit to go with it—about "how humankind has fed itself, but without being geeky." The title she had in mind was *Food Everywhere* ("from planting and threshing to herding and marketing and cooking," she said), and she had already started taking pictures for it, on a trip to Ethiopia last spring. "There was an aroma of butter and woodsmoke in the air—I thought of Tibet," she told me. "And the people? They were ecstatic, they were kissing their churches, they were melding with the walls!"

Alford, for his part, was thinking about some time on his own in Thailand. He had fallen in love with Thailand in the seventies, on his first trip—with the food, the language, the music, the dancing that starts in the bars at midnight and goes on till five in the morning—and since then had managed to get back nearly every year. Three years ago, he and Duguid bought an apartment on the "liveliest, tastiest street" in Chiang Mai, sixty miles from the Burma border; he calls Chiang Mai "the city where I belong." ("People are so much their jobs in Toronto," he told me, "but in Chiang Mai I'm the one with more of a job than anybody.") Last fall, writing there every day, he finished his first novel—a "love story" about four young junkies hanging on to each other and to their tattered lives in a Kathmandu flophouse called the Bluebird Lodge. He wanted to go back and begin a new one: "I'm thinking, it's about northern Thailand, a year in the same place, some food in it, with me as the fly on the wall."

There was nothing to stop them. The boys were in college, the world would survive for a while longer without Celtic recipes, and as Duguid said, they never compete for space; they cede it. Alford put it this way: "We're massive talkers, we negotiate." But a few months later, to no one's surprise but theirs, they set those plans aside and called Ann Bramson about a new cookbook they were going to write together. "It was a Saturday, but we were so excited, we called her cell phone and caught her in the middle of brunch with friends," Duguid wrote to me that week. The book was going to be "Burma-focused," because Burma, with its variety of tribal peoples, "closes the loop of food cultures" between the Indian subcontinent and Southeast Asia, and because "the situation in Burma makes it all the more obvious and necessary to go"—and of course because the food there is spectacularly interesting. They were going to base themselves in Chiang Mai. Alford could start his new novel, and since they would both be there, why not hold a series of Chiang Mai cooking classes, featuring their local street vendors? Alford, in his own letter, called it "a chance to do something, workwise, to help make money for people we know who are struggling to survive." They plan to leave this winter, right after their Toronto party. As Duguid says, "How good is that!"

Naomi Duguid and Jeffrey Alford separated and divorced in 2009. Since then, Alford has lived and cooked with a Thai woman in a Khmer village near the

Cambodia border, and has produced a book about the food there. Duguid has spent much of the last ten years in exhaustive culinary commutes, first from Toronto to Burma—as a food scholar, she was one of the only Westerners allowed to travel freely there—and then to Iran and the four neighboring states of what she calls the Persian culinary region. The books she produced in those years, *Burma: Rivers of Flavor* and *Taste of Persia*, were instant classics.

SPICE ROUTES

꧁

O ne day some years ago, Claudia Roden was walking down the hall of an apartment house in North London, on her way to a friend's, when she smelled a soup that reminded her of home. Roden was born in Cairo. She has lived in London for more than fifty years, and she carries a British passport, holds respectably British left-wing views, owns a big house in Hampstead Garden Suburb, and has written ten cookbooks in the English language, including *A Book of Middle Eastern Food* and *The Book of Jewish Food*, and is finishing an eleventh, about the food of Spain. But if you ask where she's from she says "Cairo," and if you ask her about the soup she says, "Melokhia, a soup no one but we Egyptians like"—which, she also says, is why she followed the smell to a stranger's door that day, rang the bell, introduced herself to the Egyptians inside (they were not at all surprised), and was promptly invited in for lunch. She describes the soup in a discouraging, or perhaps proprietary, way: "It's made with a dark-green leaf, like a gelatinous spinach. You find it in all the Egyptian tombs, and now, through DNA, in the mummies' stomachs." But she's wrong about no one except Egyptians liking it. I tried my first melokhia at a wonderful London restaurant called Moro, in Exmouth Market, and it was so good that I nearly canceled the rest of dinner and ordered more. "The melokhia? That's Claudia," Samantha Clark, who, with her husband, Samuel, cooks the food at Moro, told me. "Her *Middle Eastern Food*—when we opened the restaurant, we soaked it up like sponges. There was so much there, and we wanted to learn as much as possible from it. Some of our first menus were written with Claudia in mind, and the soup stayed."

Roden, at seventy, is one of the most revered writers in what the British call "cookery." She is the youngest and last of a triumvirate of hungry, highly literate, and ethnographically indefatigable women who helped transform how Britain cooked and what it cooked, persuading the domestically challenged bourgeoisie of the postwar years that the taste of a good soup held a world of history and culture, and that the pleasures of the table did not stop at the shores of Albion but, in all likelihood, began there. The first of those women was the well-born, flagrantly libertine Elizabeth David, who had discovered the South in the course of a peripatetic wartime love affair, and then, with her books on French and Mediterranean food, produced a culinary revolution in a country where the sale of olive oil was mainly confined to pharmacies, as a balm for earaches, and where saffron, eggplant, and zucchini blossoms had barely entered the vocabulary, let alone anybody's local market. The second woman was Jane Grigson, a modest, amiable translator who had studied at Cambridge and, with her husband, the poet Geoffrey Grigson, spent her summers in a village in the Loire Valley. She put the flair of the French into English cooking, and under her gentle instruction the overcooked Sunday joint became a juicy, garlicky leg of lamb and the leached vegetables got back their flavor. But Roden didn't have to discover the South. She was born to it, at the heady end-of-empire moment when the British controlled Egypt but the markets of Alexandria and Cairo belonged to the Arabs, Greeks, Turks, Armenians, Copts, and Jews who lived there, and meals, for the upper classes, were a serious, almost erotically exhausting pleasure. She left Egypt at fifteen, for a boarding school in Paris, and after a few years of returning for summer holidays, didn't eat in Cairo again for a quarter century.

Most people meeting Roden for the first time would find her very British. She has peachy skin and a smooth high brow, and at home she wears good, comfortable English country clothes: floppy skirts, pastel cashmere cardigans looped over her shoulders, and sensible shoes. But she is often told that she has an "Egyptian face," and when you look closely you begin to see the East in the upturned curve of her smile and in the dark hair falling from a center part and in the almond eyes. When she is dressed for a party, wrapped in the silky rich blues and reds and purples of her evening clothes, Egypt is unmistakable. Everyone notices her eyes then, because they are rimmed with kohl. She can tell you how the women in the Middle East prepare their kohl. ("In Morocco, you burn a cloth with oil and keep the soot that collects" is one recipe.) But, like her recent attachment to vacuum-packed fish stock and frozen artichoke hearts, her own kohl recipe is updated and efficient. "I turn a Pyrex dish over a candle flame," she says, "and within fifteen minutes I have enough soot for a year of powder."

She comes, in fact, from an old Syrian Jewish merchant family, or more accurately, from two old Syrian Jewish merchant families, the Doueks (her father, Cesar) and the Sassoons (her mother, Nelly), who had moved their operations to Cairo in the 1890s, following the cotton trade that opened with the Suez Canal. Two generations later, Nasser seized the canal and began expelling Jews and foreigners. The family today is scattered through Europe and the Americas. The Doueks and the Sassoons, like many Jewish traders in the Middle East, had grown prosperous over the centuries by dispatching their sons to the caravan stops of the silk and spice routes and the shipping ports of India and the Far East; and the most successful had kept their money (and their debts) in the family by marrying off their daughters if not to a cousin or an uncle, then to the sons of like-minded and equally prosperous Jewish merchants. The family's business base and, you could say, its reproductive center was Aleppo, where, as Roden will tell you with a sweet smile, "there have been Jews since Abraham came through Syria with his sheep." Her paternal great-grandfather was the chief rabbi of Aleppo during the last half century of Ottoman rule and, in line with his status and his family responsibilities, had sired an enormous brood—twenty-six children—most of whom multiplied as energetically as he had. Roden has hundreds of cousins and appears to know them all. Her daughter Nadia, an artist and a maker of animated films who lives in New York, says that the three Roden children grew up convinced that everyone they met besides their classmates and teachers was a relative, or might marry a relative and become one.

Nelly and Cesar Douek arrived in London in 1956 (after a year in Sudan, whose only tangible benefit to the family was an excellent new recipe for tahini-lemon-and-yogurt cream). Claudia and her two brothers had already been in the city for two years, studying, and on Friday nights the Doueks' house in Golders Green would fill with people of all ages passing through London on their way from Paris or Milan or Geneva to Mexico City or Los Angeles or Barranquilla—wherever the émigrés of the latest Sephardic diaspora had chosen to restart their lives. They spoke French— the language of choice among the Cairene bourgeoisie— slipping in and out of Arabic or English or Italian, depending on where they had lived, and where they were living now. Some of the old women spoke Ladino, the Hebrew-Castilian language of the Spanish Jews at the time of the expulsion of 1492. ("Sefarad" means Spain, in Hebrew, and originally referred only to Jews of Spanish and Portuguese origin.) Roden calls it "the language of women's secrets."

The women, without servants to cook for them, would sit and gossip in Nelly Douek's kitchen, and Roden began to watch and listen. She says that the first thing one woman would ask another was: What recipes do you have? They exchanged recipes, and sometimes argued about recipes. Was the kibbeh better in Aleppo or Damascus? Were the pastries better in Alexandria or Cairo? Roden had no interest in cooking then, but it was clear to her that families like hers, who had left their lives behind in the Middle East, had managed to carry one thing to the West with them—and that was the taste of the food they ate at home. The historian Donald Sassoon, a younger cousin of Roden's and one of her closest friends, describes it this way: "At Claudia's parents', I was captured by a nostalgia that I didn't even feel myself. The house would be full of exiles, going on and on about Egypt. 'Oh, Nelly, the rugs, the jewels, the servants we used to have,' they'd say—though the truth was we didn't have such great carpets in Egypt, and the servants cost nothing, everybody had them. But we hadn't lost our food. Our food was what made us different from the others, it was a way to distinguish ourselves without having to pay the price of 'difference.' Nelly, all those women—they cooked to re-create the Egypt of their youth."

Roden started writing down their recipes. "Even now, whenever I cook I think about how I got the recipe, who gave me the recipe, what their story was," she says. Her "famous orange cake"—a rich Sephardic confection of eggs, sugar, oranges, and ground almonds that has been appropriated by so many other cookbook writers since she included it in *Middle Eastern Food* that she has lost count—was "Iris Galante's, one of the Aleppo Galantes. She was the grandmother of my brother Ellis's first wife, visiting from Italy. I watched her cook—she had a little handwritten book, and I said, 'Can you give me a recipe?' I got a *windfall*. The first recipe was pastellicos, from Salonika. That's a little pie, with minced meat or cheese and onions. The French writer Edgar Morin called it the heart of the heart of Salonika. After Iris, I talked to everyone who came to the house. I started with the people from Egypt, and then with my parents' friends from Turkey and Iran. 'How much flour do you use?' I'd ask them. The best answer came from Istanbul, or perhaps it was Izmir: 'Press your earlobe. See how it feels. When the dough feels like your earlobe, it's the right consistency.'"

For Roden, it was an unexpected preoccupation. "In London, I had been free for the first time," she says. "I was a Marxist—of course, I had never *read* Marx—and I went on marches and joined the New Left Club and went to art school at Saint Martin's. I was going to be a painter, a muralist like Diego Rivera, or a filmmaker—which horrified my parents. Now suddenly I was under their jurisdiction again. I lived at home. I took a job, but they hated that. I was in reservations at Alitalia, and you could see me through the windows. My father was so ashamed. He wanted me in the house. 'Why do we have girls?' he said. 'Because they're the sunshine of the family.' Whenever Egyptian friends came, he would tell me to call in sick—because for a daughter of the house not to be home when friends came! So suddenly I was embraced by the émigré world, submerged in it. I was researching my book without even knowing it was a book."

The Doueks thought of their daughter, at twenty-two, as stubbornly close to spinsterhood, having offered her one very eligible cousin to consider, before she was fifteen, and not long afterward, a "really ugly" businessman from India—both of whom she refused. But one day in 1958 she presented them with a nice young man who, they were somewhat scandalized to learn, had been sharing her table at a café down the street from Alitalia. A year later, she was married. Paul Roden was a self-made businessman from a family of Russian Jewish immigrants. He had gone to work at the age of sixteen, when his father died, and Cesar Douek liked him for that. The family welcomed him, to Claudia's great relief, because for most Sephardic émigrés the Ashkenazi of Northern and Eastern Europe were an almost mythically bewildering people—"peasants" who raised carp in bathtubs for a tasteless dish called gefilte fish and didn't know a cardamom pod from a coriander seed, or worse, the sort of intellectuals who had brought Zionism to a Middle East where, in the émigrés' wishful imagination, everybody had got along. (Their view of Ashkenazi intellectuals was summed up admirably by Claudia's great-uncle Moussa Douek: "Read and write? I have people who read and write for me.")

The marriage lasted for fifteen years, produced two girls

and a boy, and gave Roden back a measure of independence. (She never married again, although by all accounts she was much courted.) More to the point, she had her own kitchen. She learned to cook, and spent the first ten years of her married life collecting and testing the recipes that became *A Book of Middle Eastern Food.* "I worked with Jane Grigson and Elizabeth David in mind," she told me. "I had found a melokhia recipe in Elizabeth's book on Mediterranean food, then a few more Middle Eastern recipes she had collected. She said, 'This is the tip of the iceberg. Somebody has to take this much further.' So I went to the British Library. 'Are there any Arab cookery books?' I asked. There were not. I wrote to Muslim friends in Egypt and asked *them.* The only cookery book they could find in Cairo was an old British quartermaster's book from the Second World War, and it was all cauliflower and cheese, macaroni and cheese. So I went to the embassies here and talked to the people waiting. I sat in the Iranian embassy. They asked me, 'Do you want a visa or a passport?' and I said, 'No, I'm here for recipes.' I'd go to the big carpet warehouse on the Thames. The men were Iraqis. I would ask for their wives' recipes. All through the sixties, I did that. I was raising a family and trying to paint—I painted the rabbis of Jerba; you can see them at the Spanish and Portuguese synagogue, in Maida Vale—and I even wrote a play about the false messiah Sabbatai Zevi. But mainly I was home taking care of the children or I was looking for recipes."

She turned out to be a natural scholar, despite an almost insistently idyllic vision of (pre-Israel) Middle Eastern life that, forty years later and to the despair of her friends, remains untempered by reality. ("Of course I have an attachment to that life," one of them told me. "It was a colonial and cosmopolitan world—that's what made it attractive—but I'm more cynical than Claudia. I have bitter memories.") Simon Schama once wrote that "Claudia Roden is no more a simple cookbook writer than Marcel Proust was a biscuit baker." Her Middle East is an act of imagination, a kind of domestication of memory, and to create it she prowled the stacks of obscure archives. She read historians, anthropologists, Arabists, folklorists, philosophers, and poets, hoping for information and inspiration. She spent a year testing a book of thirteenth-century Baghdad court recipes that had been unearthed and translated by an Arabist in Cambridge. She made friends with the French Marxist scholar and Muhammad biographer Maxime Rodinson, who had written his doctoral dissertation on a culinary manuscript from medieval Damascus. "I just got so interested in the history of food, and I was making all those medieval dishes, and it blew my mind—the idea that through food you could describe or reconstruct a world," she says. She ended up reconstructing several worlds—eight hundred recipes, and a trove of folktales, proverbs, stories, poetry, and local history—and when she finally sat down to write, it was in a clear, humorous, elegant voice that she hadn't known she had, a voice that could keep you up, nights, reading.

When the book was finished, she went to Foyles and copied the name and address of every cookbook publisher in sight. It was 1967, the year of the Six-Day War, and the Middle East, as she puts it, "was not at all popular just then." She ended up at a small house with an editor who, she was delighted to discover, had been born in Turkey. The book was a sleeper. Its reputation spread in England—"People here were completely bouleversés by those tastes," Tom Jaine, at the food journal *Petits Propos Culinaires*, told me—and then to the Middle East, where there were soon so many pirated printings of *Middle Eastern Food* that you could find it in kitchens from Cairo to Beirut and Damascus, and even Riyadh. By the end of 1970, Jill Norman, the cookbook editor at Penguin, had bought the rights to *Middle Eastern Food* and published a paperback edition. ("It walked off the shelves," she told me.) Two years later, her American counterpart, Judith Jones, the editor who discovered Julia Child, published it at Knopf. Roden today counts both women among her best friends, though at the time they were put through their paces at her family dinners (Claudia cooked; Nelly "supervised"), swore to a passion for minced lamb, bulgur wheat, and honey-drenched pastry, and were pronounced relatives. "Nelly was something of a drama queen," Norman told me, "and the food was very grand."

Roden was famous much sooner than she was solvent. Penguins, in those days, sold for a few shillings a copy—which is to say it was not much money for a woman paying the mortgage on a big North London house and trying to raise three children on her own. For two years after her separation in 1974, Roden gave cooking classes at home, an experience that her son, Simon, describes as six or seven middle-aged English ladies up to their wrists in Iranian rice pudding or Lebanese meatballs, making a mess of the kitchen. The children were alternately amused, irritated (they did the washing up), and impressed by Roden's foray into the world of business stationery and flyers. Simon, a London architect with a wife and two boys, told me, "After my dad left, he went bankrupt. We were on our own. We'd have these guys at the door, like bailiffs, trying to take the TV, but my mom was tough. She shouted them down." His sister Anna, a financial manager with a husband and three girls, says, "Mom could make a piece of broccoli on a plate look lovely, but it was so horrible, that worry." She thinks that even today, ten books and considerable celebrity down the line (a James Beard Award for Cookbook of the Year; six Glenfiddich awards; and in Holland, the Prince Claus Fund Award for cultural achievement, the first ever given to a food writer), Roden is marked by those lean years. "If I had one word for my mom, it would be 'martyr.' She won't willingly take a taxi. She refuses to have a housekeeper. Last year she finally replaced the upstairs carpeting. It took us thirty years to persuade her."

Roden's kitchen remains resolutely unchanged. She calls it "my seventies kitchen," because that was when she put in the countertops and the cabinets and bought the stove and the yellow-and-blue Portuguese splatter tiles and the long table where she spreads whatever recipes she is testing, and does her chopping and peeling and a lot of her entertaining. There are always garden roses and a bowl of mangoes on the table. When a friend stops by, Roden reaches into the bowl, the way another woman might reach for knitting, feels for the ripest fruit, and starts slicing and peeling while they talk. When she is ready to eat, she simply pushes everything aside, gets some plates, and brings out a loaf of bread, a package of Serrano ham, and maybe some good Spanish anchovies, a dish of roasted peppers, and a bottle of whatever wine she has opened a day or two before. She knows good wine; she is delighted to be served it, but she rarely buys it. She carries the notion of simple table wine to a Mediterranean extreme. Her sink is usually piled with pots and dishes, waiting their turn in the backup dishwasher in her laundry room—an open, converted pantry where every surface is covered with sacks and tins and bottles of the beans, oils, peppers, fish, and spices that she is using to test recipes for her book about Spanish food. A second pantry is entirely given over to the grains and preserves and flower waters that she keeps in stock for Middle Eastern meals. (Her latest, and perhaps most inventive, book, *Arabesque*, is devoted to the food of Morocco, Lebanon, and Turkey. She had hoped to include Iran and Syria, and when that was vetoed, she threatened, only half in jest, to produce a sequel called "The Food of the Axis of Evil.")

On Sundays, Roden has the family to lunch. In spring and summer, they eat in a big garden off the kitchen, where the older grandchildren can kick a soccer ball while the younger ones poke through a tangle of overgrown hedges, hoping to catch a glimpse of the two prize pigs that the BBC presenter who lives next door is raising as family pets. Roden uses those lunches to test and retest her most problematic recipes, like the one for slow-roasted Andalusian lamb where the lamb ended up swimming in a thin puddle of honey, white wine, and rendered fat. (Her son-in-law, who may have been forewarned, arrived that day with a bag of bread, cookies, and cold cuts from the nearest Marks & Spencer.) "She'll call, she'll say, 'I made it again,'" Anna told me. "We are the 'taste it again' people." Roden presides over the tastings with an indulgent, if somewhat distracted, calm. "You can see why I can't let anyone clean here," she said one afternoon when I was helping unload the dishwashers and discovered that some of the wooden spoons went into a basket on the kitchen sideboard, and others went into the dining room, thirty feet away; and that the silverware was divided according to some obscure logic among three far-flung drawers. "You see, everything has settled into different drawers and places. You can't put it away. Everything would end up in the wrong place. I would never find it."

In 1980, Roden began thinking about her book on Jewish food. By then she was finishing two more books: a short history of coffee and a pleasant, idiosyncratic foray into alfresco food called *Picnic*, which ran the gamut from Hong Kong barbecue to Glyndebourne on the grass. She was in demand on the lecture circuit and the conference circuit and the cooking-demonstration circuit, and she was writing about food for most of the best British papers. But *The Book of Jewish Food* was a singularly daunting project—a history of Jewish life and settlement, told through the story of what Jews ate and where and why, and how they made it. Jill Norman—the idea for the book was hers—had urged Roden to sign a contract; Judith Jones, who edited the book, had called it her "logical, natural next step"; and Jane Grigson had been encouraging her to write it. Even so, she was reluctant to take it on, and even more reluctant to finish once she did. It absorbed her for the next sixteen years, and staked a claim on whatever diffidence as a writer she still had. "Sixteen years, and I just couldn't let go," she told me. "My friends thought it would be published posthumously."

Hampstead Garden Suburb is part of a Northwest London catchment area where so many Jews have settled over the last century that the government was finally persuaded to turn it into an eruv—an area circled by a string wire in which Orthodox Jews can push a baby carriage or carry keys on the Sabbath, enjoying a state of exemption from their own rules. Roden herself is devotedly secular. She says that her parents left Orthodoxy behind when they moved to a mixed Cairo neighborhood and developed a taste for seafood—"I asked my father what he liked best on a night out; he said, 'Prawns and beer'"—and for the ham at Groppi, the famous old Cairo café. But she is attached to her London neighborhood, in part because so many Middle Easterners work nearby. When she was writing *Middle Eastern Food* and *Arabesque*, she could get in her car and in a few minutes be at the Hormuz market, on Finchley Road, shopping for dried Iranian limes and Lebanese rosewater and even melokhia, from Egypt. Now, testing recipes for *Jewish Food*, she could go to Frohwein's Kosher Butchers, or to the Indian super-market with a "Jewish floor," or in an emergency—she swears that she never had one—to one of the halal butchers in the neighborhood. "Well, in Cairo my grandfather once saw the kosher butcher buying from the Muslim butcher" is how she puts it. (Either way, it was a trial for Roden, since the meat that Muslims and Orthodox Jews eat, which is ritually drained of blood, loses much of its flavor in the process.) When the subject was fish, she could go to the fishmonger in Golders Green who kept a list of the "forbidden fish"—anything without scales—in his window. She remembers the excitement, in the richer precincts of Northwest London, when a board of rabbis announced the discovery of a vesti-gial scale on a baby sturgeon, and caviar went on sale.

Two-thirds of the three hundred thousand Jews in Great Britain (and 90 percent of the world's Jews) are said to trace their origin to Eastern Europe, and it is safe to say that they were never known for the delicacy of their cuisine. Bagels and matzo balls aside, it's hard to think of an Ashkenazi contri-bution to the British diet. Not even the fish in fish and chips, long attributed to a nineteenth-century Eastern European immigrant (and East End restaurateur) named Joseph Ma-lin, is Ashkenazi. Malin's recipe for deep-fried cod—served with a side of fries, and now consumed by Brits to the tune of two hundred and fifty million orders a year—was in fact carried to England by sixteenth-century Portuguese Marranos, or you could say, by ur-Sephardic Jews. (According to Thomas Jefferson, who tried it, it was known as "fried fish in the Jewish fashion.") Roden, growing up, had rarely tasted Ashkenazi food, and had since managed to avoid it (most publicly, at a conference in Jerusalem called "Gefilte Fish or Couscous," which included a cook-off between the Sephardic and Ashkenazi guests, and which she describes this way: "None of us went to the Ashkenazi side to taste, but all the Ashkenazi came to ours"). She was not enthusiastic about starting now. "I don't feel British," she told me. "I don't consider myself like one of the Eastern European Jews. We have nothing in common with those Jews. We lived in a Muslim world, they live in a Christian world. They are not me."

There was, of course, no way to write the story of Jewish food without including the food that most Jews in the world once ate, and many still eat. Jill Norman told her to remember that those people knew nothing about Sephardic food— that the contrast was what was interesting. "Little by little, I got interested," Roden says. She told the story of Ashkenazi settlement as it moved eastward from Germany through Poland and into Russia, and then turned back across what Auden once called beer-and-potato-culture Europe, with its joyless, wintery kitchens. And in the process she managed to collect some three hundred surprisingly good Ashkenazi recipes. A few—her Shavuot cheese blintzes; her Hungarian-Jewish goulash—could even be considered worthy of a Sephardic kitchen. And never mind that she failed spectacularly with matzo balls. (She left out the chicken fat and the seltzer, separated the eggs, and then beat the whites, as if she were planning to float *oeufs à la neige* in her chicken soup.) When I asked how she came by such a peculiar recipe—"America," she said—she admitted to having been less than discerning when it came to some of the Ashkenazi dishes, matzo balls being the first, gefilte fish the second, and a cake called lekach, which she actually liked, the third. A day later, she said that I shouldn't really count the lekach, because the problem had to do with a slip in her metric-to-imperial-cup conversions and she corrected that in the next edition, and besides, the recipe was now famous and has won many awards.

But the heart of her story belongs to the Sephardim. Two-thirds of the recipes are Sephardic—"Just the opposite of the population figures," she likes to say—and they describe a world that once stretched from Spain to China, and now reached westward to the Pacific. (Israeli reviewers called the book "the Sephardic revenge.") Roden says that she worked like a sleuth on the Sephardic chapters. "It was like writing a mystery," she told me. "The Jews of the Sephardic diaspora—well, in those days you couldn't Google and find them. And in a way I'm glad, because it made the work sort of exciting. My parents had had this thing, when they traveled, of looking for Jews. I became like them. My cousin Eric, in Paris"—Eric Rouleau, *Le Monde*'s former Middle East correspondent, who was the French ambassador to Tunisia and Turkey during those years—"said, 'Claudia, when are you going to stop looking for Jews?'"

In the end, Roden went to fifteen countries looking for Jews, and nearly as many countries where she wasn't looking but found them anyway. She told me, "It proves that when Jewish people are there, and you meet them, there is always a cuisine." She financed the first of these trips by writing two more cookbooks, in the late eighties; they became best-sellers, to no one's surprise but hers. (The first, *Mediterranean*

Cookery, grew out of a television series that she was putting together for the BBC. The second, *The Food of Italy*, began as a year of region-by-region pieces for the London *Sunday Times Magazine:* "I was in Turin. I was in a hotel. I knew no one. So I opened the phone book and started calling the numbers on the page.") The rest of her trips, which took her through the early nineties, were in large part sponsored by the *Telegraph*. "I was writing a monthly column," as she tells the story. "Whenever I tried to stop, the paper said, 'We'll send you. Go for us, and then take a day or two off and look for Jews.' Which is what I did."

She still talks about the Jews she didn't meet. She missed the Surinam Jews—which is to say their recipe for a Surinamese root vegetable called pom. (She has it now.) She missed the Falasha from Ethiopia; they lived in Israel by then, but none of them ever showed up when she arranged meetings. And she never got to China, to look for traces of the old Jewish settlement in Kaifeng—"Muslims with blue *kipas*," the Chinese called them—which in all likelihood had once supplied local agents to the Baghdad branch of her mother's far-flung Sassoon family. (Today those Jews are indistinguishable from everyone else in Kaifeng, and are said to know nothing about Judaism, let alone about Jewish Chinese food.) But those, arguably, were all she missed.

It may have been just as well, because, as she often says, there is no such thing as one Sephardic recipe for anything. There are Sephardic *recipes*, as particular to the places where Jews lived, and the people they lived with, as an Arab couscous from Morocco or Algeria. The Iraqi Jews didn't like the food of the Syrian Jews; they called the Syrians "cows," because they ate too much parsley. The Syrians didn't like the Iraqis' food, because it had too much fat and meat. Then,

there were the Iraqis in Iran, who united the Jews of Lebanon
and Syria against them by putting beetroot in their kibbeh.
The Sabbath stew of the Livorno Jews, from Portugal and
Spain, was nothing like the stews of the Jews in Rome—or
even of the Jews in Venice, many of whom came from Sicily
and Turkey. The almond pastries of the Comtat Jews, who
had lived in Provence under the protection of the Avignon
popes, were nothing like the pastries other Sephardim ate.
There were the Izmir Jews, whose food was different from
the food of the Istanbul Jews; the Jews of Bombay, whose food
was different from the food of their cousins in Calcutta, or
Goa or Cochin. And, of course, there were the Jews of
Aleppo, like the Doueks, who wouldn't dream of making Damascus dishes, though they ate them happily enough at the
parties of Damascene friends in Cairo.

The book is a kind of archive. People look to it for the
"authentic" recipes of Jewish settlement, and Roden tends to
believe in the idea of authenticity. *The Wall Street Journal
Europe* arts and food writer Paul Levy, Roden's co-chairman
at the yearly Oxford Symposium on Food & Cookery, told
me, "Claudia is a wonderful cook, but you have to remember
that her kitchen is a place of exploration. She's impelled to
codify. That's good. It means that she is not distracted by
the lack of success of a dish. What is this *supposed* to taste
like? That's her most important question. She has that impossible anthropological goal." And her old friend Sami
Zubaida, an Iraqi Jew who taught politics and sociology at
the University of London for more than thirty years, said,
"She is on a hunt for the correct version. Her book is enor-
mously attractive for her empathy, but her argument tends
to be that if the Jews ate it, then it's authentic Jewish food.
Some of the Arabs who read the book were outraged. They

thought it was *their* food. They said, 'The food is the same, the difference is in the word for it.'" Nigella Lawson, who is an ardent fan, put it this way: "Things change, products change, and you can have a huge argument about how something should be cooked. When you do an awful lot of research, like Claudia, you have to stand back sometimes and ask, 'Do I really want to eat this?'"

One afternoon in late May, I asked Roden what she meant by "authenticity." It was a day of tasting recipes. We were about to leave for Asturias, one of the provinces she had yet to visit for her book on Spanish food, and were sitting at her kitchen table, debating the relative merits of five or six scribbled recipes for a Catalan romesco sauce (a rich purée of almonds, hazelnuts, tomatoes, sweet dried Spanish peppers, garlic, bread, and saffron) while waiting for the beans to cook for an Asturian fabada (white beans, chorizos, blood sausages, and saffron) and for the squid to defrost for a Catalan chipirónes en su tinta con fideos (squid, vermicelli, onions, garlic, white wine, parsley, and tomatoes). I wanted to know which of the romesco recipes looked to Roden to be the most authentic. They were all from good Catalan cooks, cooks she knew and trusted, and yet they were quite different. One recipe said to use one tomato, another said ten. One recipe said to fry the peppers and garlic, another said not to. In the end, Roden chose the recipe with the most nuts, adjusted it slightly, turned on the food processor, tasted the result, and pronounced it "my best so far." To me, it was perfect. "Most good things just happen," she said. "I don't proceed in a very organized way. I choose what I like, I trust my taste. I tell people, 'Well, what else do you trust but your own taste.'" For Roden, the word "authentic" is very simple: it means that "you can't invent with new ingredients"—unless, like some of the diaspora Jews, new ingredients are all you have. She thinks that cookbook critics (she has had her share) tend to forget that between the "big change" of the 1500s, when the produce and animals of the Americas first reached Europe and the Middle East, and the revolution in transportation, travel, and communication of the postwar years, there was very little variation in the food that ordinary people—people rooted in one place—ate, and in the way they prepared it.

Roden has been traveling to Spain for the past two and a half years, and one of the things she likes about the country is that the food is still so regional and the culinary history so particular—"a little Visigoth, and then the Moors and the Jews and the Catholic clergy and the French, and of course the New World, and what the rich took from it, the chocolate, the game, and what the poor took, the vegetables and the beans and the corn." In the food of Andalusia, where the Moors ruled for eight hundred years, you can still taste Spanish Islam. In the food of Aragon and Castile, where the courtiers in Ferdinand's entourage were as often as not Catholic converts, or conversos, you can still taste Spanish Judaism. Roden told me that before the Inquisition the Jews in Spain used olive oil for cooking, the Muslims used clarified butter, and the Christians used pork fat. After the expulsion, everyone switched to fat, and the conversos hung hams in their houses the way they hung crucifixes and rosaries—conspicuously, fearfully, hoping to convince Inquisitors on the prowl that Spain belonged entirely to Christ. She discovered that Sephardic desserts, like her orange-and-almond cake, had survived in Spanish convents, brought by novices from converso families, and that the rice puddings of the Middle East—she has three rice pudding recipes in *Middle*

Eastern Food, including one with anise, to which I am addicted—had somehow, over the centuries, made their way to northern Spain, and even to Asturias, which had been effectively cut off from the rest of the country, by the Picos de Europa range, until the 1960s. She wanted to ask Asturians for their mothers' pudding recipes.

Roden's reputation preceded her to Asturias. We were met at the airport near Oviedo and invited to beautiful restaurants where the rice pudding was "deconstructed" (rice on the bottom, caramel in the middle, and a froth of milk on top) and the lamb chops served in a sauce of baby snails, the young chefs of northern Spain being much under the influence of Ferran Adrià, the Catalan kitchen impresario who had taken the French idea of "creator cuisine" and elaborated on it to the point where you couldn't tell if the foam you were spooning was asparagus or trout. Roden had expected simple food in what is still a largely undiscovered region of green fields and streams running from mountain caves (where the shepherds smoke a sharp local blue cheese called Cabrales) to the fishing villages of the Atlantic coast. She cheerfully ate her way through ten-course nueva cocina dinners, but the things she asked about and jotted down in the outsize flowered folder—"Gauguin, from the National Gallery"—that she carried everywhere with her were the best of the local foods: the beans and sausages; the fresh anchovies, marinated in an escabeche that could easily have come from Persia; the morning's dorade, baked in white wine, shellfish stock, and a simple sofrito of onion, garlic, saffron, and smoked paprika, and finished with a splash of cognac. ("This will go in my book," she said after her first forkful.)

She has a horror of fusion food, "on principle," though she

allowed that nothing she ate in Asturias was quite so "fusion" as the dish called "Egyptian sushi bottarga" that she was served on her last trip to Cairo, in 2003. ("I was giving seminars to Egyptian chefs," she said. "I told them, 'You've got to have *your* food. At the time of the Mamluks, you had three hundred recipes; now you make only four. Don't do fusion. Please!'") Pepe Iglesias, a local food writer who was Roden's touchstone on the Asturian trip, had told her that there were now twenty-five serious young fusion chefs in Asturias, and after a few days' eating she ventured the opinion that that was perhaps more "creators" than a barely touristed province of a million people needed. ("When I travel now, I'm so used to being looked after," she said later. "I'm used to accepting what happens, but no one can control what I do or think.") What interested her more was the history of Asturian food. She was curious about the influence of the local monasteries, because Spain's religious orders had been in large part responsible for the development and refinement of traditional Spanish cuisine—much more so than the aristocracy or the upper classes, which had been eating "Bourbon food" since Philip V inherited the Spanish throne, in 1700, and moved from Versailles to Madrid. ("The monasteries were the centers of gastronomy here," she told me. "They had money and land and their own peasants. Some of the great Lenten recipes came from them.") She was curious about the influence of the "Indianos"—poor Asturians who had sailed to the Americas, made fortunes in tobacco, sent their brides to cooking school in Paris, and come home at the turn of the twentieth century with a taste for big painted Mexican villas, Cuban rum, and French crêpes. By then we had been to Casa Fermín, the great traditional restaurant of Oviedo, eaten its best dishes, and talked recipes with the chef. Now she wanted to talk to ordinary people, who lived from the sea and the land, about what they cooked at home.

On our last night in Spain, we drove into the Picos, to an old farmhouse near a cluster of villages where the family of a forty-year-old Asturian named Jaime Rodriguez has farmed for generations. We had met Rodriguez by chance, coming out of a shop in the town of Cangas de Onís that specialized in Asturian beans, and he had invited us home. For Roden, he was one of the "good things that just happen" when she cooks or travels. He was personable, articulate, intelligent, and, it turned out, an enthusiast of Asturian food, someone who had leaped through centuries, going from "two pigs, some sheep, and a cow" to university in Barcelona and on to a good government job—after which he and his wife had added a wing to their farmhouse and turned the rest into a bed-and-breakfast, where people hiking or fishing in the Picos could stay and, if they were hungry, eat. His mother-in-law made supper for the guests that night: vegetable soup from the garden and a tuna loaf, made with eggs, onions, and red peppers, called *rollo de bonito*, "from the part of the tuna that rich people don't like." While she was cooking, Roden took out her folder, settled into an armchair by the television, turned to Rodriguez, and started asking questions.

"What is the food of the mountains?"

"White beans. Not the biggest, they're too expensive. We eat green beans sometimes, in expensive restaurants, with crab or lobster or langoustines. But for everyday, we eat small white beans. My parents grow four kinds. We eat fabada all the time."

"How many times a week?"

"At least four times, always with pork, but not necessarily with chorizos. We also eat cornmeal, eggs, onions, and bacon."

"When did the corn and beans come?"

"In 1546."

"And are eggs important?"

"Eggs, meat, beans—those are the most important."

"And fresh vegetables?"

"We eat very few fresh vegetables in Asturias. The beans, some peppers, potatoes, and peas. This is a region of meat eaters. The sea is a small slice of it. We eat a lot of game: rabbit, boar, deer, birds, wild goat."

"What else is traditional here?"

"Crêpes, with sugar or honey and apples. And of course sidra—hard cider."

"How many families make their own cider?"

"In my village, two."

"What are the local tapas?"

"Croquetas. Chorizos with sidra. Big blood sausages—you boil them, slice them, and then fry them. Pork tripe. Pork cheeks. And fresh bacon, boiled and served with potatoes."

"And for a wedding?"

"Baby goat, and especially lamb. Inside, you fry the lamb with onions and white wine, and then you stew it. Outside, you use burning embers."

"What do you eat for dessert?"

"We have apple cake and flan. The flan is traditional. My mother makes it only with eggs and sugar, not milk."

"And how does she make it?"

"Over a corncob fire. The first layer is caramelized sugar. Then she adds the sugar and eggs, and then she covers the lid with charcoal from the corncobs. Every few minutes she stirs the flan and adds more charcoal."

"Is the flan creamy?"

"No, it's very dense. We eat it a lot—it's very common. For special occasions, we make rice pudding."

"Rice pudding? With anise? With butter and milk?"

"Not with butter. With rice, milk, cinnamon, sugar, lemon rind, and yes, anise or a little cognac."

"Do you think I could get the recipe?"

Claudia Roden's masterly compendium of Iberian culinary arts and history, *The Food of Spain*, was published in 2011. She remains, at eighty, the president of the Oxford Symposium on Food & Cookery.

THE PHILOSOPHER CHEF

❧

In 1997, in Amsterdam, Yotam Ottolenghi finished writing the last chapter of his master's thesis on the ontological status of the photographic image in aesthetic and analytic philosophy, rode his bicycle to the post office, and sent copies of the manuscript home to Israel. It was his second year away. He was twenty-nine, and nearing the end of an adventure in indecision that began a few months after he had completed the coursework for a fast-track interdisciplinary bachelor's and graduate degree at Tel Aviv University—known among students as "the genius program," because only fifteen freshmen a year were admitted—and decamped with his boyfriend to sample the famously accessible offerings of the city of marijuana cafés, Ecstasy raves, and breakfast hams. When he wasn't celebrating his release from school, he worked. He edited the Hebrew pages of a Dutch-Jewish weekly known by the acronym *NIW*, plowed through the essays of Ernst Gombrich, passed the qualifying exams for a doctorate in the United States—he was thinking comparative literature at Yale—sat through long nights as a desk clerk at the kind of hotel he wouldn't recommend, and wrote his thesis. "I'm incredibly self-disciplined," he says. "I never would have not written it."

One copy went to his thesis adviser in Tel Aviv, and another to Yehuda Elkana, the philosopher who created the genius program. A third copy—"the one I dreaded sending"— went to his parents in Jerusalem, where his father was a chemistry professor at Hebrew University and his mother, a former teacher and herself the daughter of a professor, was at the Education Ministry, running the country's high schools. It was a moment of truth, Ottolenghi says. He slipped a note into the envelope—"actually, buried it in the manuscript"—which read, "Here is my dissertation. I've decided to take a break from academia and go to cooking school." A few months later, he was in London, rolling puff pastry at the Cordon Bleu.

The moral is that smart people can be masters of many trades, though Ottolenghi claims that it took him a lot longer to "really experience pastry with my hands" (six months) than to make his way through Hegel (an excruciating few weeks). At forty-three, he is not much changed from the recovering geek of his Amsterdam years—lanky, loping, and quite tall, with the same short, sticking-up dark hair and fashionably stubbled chin, and even a version of the same black-rimmed student glasses. The difference is that today he wears the happy smile of a man who has left behind *The Phenomenology of Mind* for baked eggplants with lemon thyme, za'atar, pomegranate seeds, and buttermilk-yogurt sauce—and in the process become the pen, prime mover, and public face of a partnership of four close colleagues who have quietly changed the way people in Britain shop and cook and eat.

At last count, his eponymous reach extended to two

hugely popular London restaurants, the flagship Ottolenghi in Islington, and in Soho, NOPI (for North of Piccadilly, but known to foodies as "Yotam's new place"), as well as three packed gourmet delis, in Notting Hill, Kensington, and Belgravia, which are never without his favorite pastries and his signature platters of butternut-squash salad, roasted aubergine with yogurt topping, grilled broccoli with chili and fried garlic, and fresh green beans. The delis, along with the Islington restaurant, also provide a catering service that will deliver a dinner party to your door or, if you happen to be the queen, put together a groaning board of snacks (as in "golden and candy beetroot, orange, and olive salad with goat's cheese, red onion, mint, pumpkin seeds, and orange blossom dressing") for the eight hundred and fifty people sipping champagne at your jubilee party at the Royal Academy of Arts.

Ottolenghi himself is the author of a weekly food-and-recipe column in *The Guardian* and a visually irresistible vegetable cookbook called *Plenty*—proof that an education in aesthetics is never wasted—and with Sami Tamimi, his Palestinian executive chef and one of the early Ottolenghi partners, the coauthor of two other cookbooks, the latest of which, *Jerusalem*, is about the food of their hometown and the rich symbiosis of Arab and Jewish culinary traditions that survives in the markets and kitchens of an otherwise fractured city. (The book came out in Britain and America this fall, but the British got a preview late last year, when Ottolenghi became the peripatetic guide and narrator of a BBC documentary about his research, *Jerusalem on a Plate*.)

No one who has grown up in the Mediterranean Middle East can really live without the colors and textures and tastes of home. The food that Ottolenghi serves and writes about often includes them all, but it isn't ethnic cooking grounded in one tradition, and it certainly isn't fusion cooking or its muddled suburban hybrids. He uses the fish and meat and produce that everyone in Britain eats, and then, he says, "borrows from here and there" the tastes that will produce a recipe he likes. His instincts are collaborative and practical. When he started the column in *The Guardian* six years ago, he wanted to create recipes that a home cook could pretty much put together from the shelves of a decent supermarket. (At first he sent them to friends to test. His bottom line: a harried childminder in Hackney, with two children of her own to feed.) He was wrong about supermarkets. But his column was so successful that the chain Waitrose began to stock his favorite condiments and spices. And he eventually launched an extensive online catalogue, in the hope of restoring domestic calm to readers like the woman who wanted to make his whitefish-grapefruit-and-fennel seviche. She ignored his advice about the quarter teaspoon of dried fennel pollen—"Don't worry if you can't get it, though. This cured fish dish will still taste great"—and wrote to the paper, "I'm a bit of a Yotam fan, but his mere mention fills my husband (who does most of the shopping) with dread. This week's 'dried fennel pollen' might send him over the edge."

Ottolenghi's first word was "ma." He didn't mean "mama," and he didn't mean *marak*, which is soup in Hebrew. He meant the croutons that his mother scattered on the tray of his high chair while the soup was simmering. ("Store-bought croutons," he maintains.) He can still name everything his parents cooked, from his mother's beef curry, stuffed red peppers, and gazpacho to his father's polpettone and polenta. His older sister, Tirza Florentin—a businesswoman who lives in Tel Aviv with her family—says that as a boy in Jerusalem, he was "very passionate about food," but much more interested in talking about what he ate and where it came from than in actually cooking any. It was a household of cosmopolitan tastes and backgrounds. Ottolenghi's mother, who comes from a Berlin Jewish academic family (her uncle was the modernist architect and critic Julius Posener), had arrived in Palestine via Sweden, where she was born, in 1938, the same year that his father's Florentine merchant family arrived from Italy. Two prominent secular Zionist clans had pulled up stakes in the wake of the Hitler-Mussolini military pact and, with it, the certainty of disaster.

Ottolenghi calls them a strong-minded and resilient people—smart (one grandfather started the mathematics department at Tel Aviv University) and, like him, masters of many trades (one grandmother worked for Mossad, forging documents for the agents who, most famously, captured Adolf Eichmann in Buenos Aires and delivered him to an Israeli prison). His sister calls it a family of high unstated expectations "that were simply something we grew into." The burden of them fell on Yotam when he was twenty-three, and his younger brother, Yiftach, was killed by friendly fire during field exercises toward the end of his military service. "For Yotam, I think it was a tragedy on top of a tragedy," Florentin says. "Yiftach had been the star; he was outspoken, charming, always in trouble—making us laugh—and very bright. Yotam was the reserved one then. And like me, he was in a kind of under-the-surface competition with our brother. He wanted to find his niche. When Yiftach died, we were very concerned about how my father would get through the loss. He was a conservative person, which made it terrible for Yotam. Not talking to him about being gay—that was the price he had to pay for a long time."

Every Israeli boy spends three years immediately after high school in the Israel Defense Forces. (Girls spend two.) Ottolenghi had studied Arabic in school—in part, in the hope of avoiding assignment to a fighting unit. He succeeded and went to army intelligence headquarters instead. "Otherwise, I was a conformist boy," he says. "I studied physics and math because my best friend was good at that, but I was really much more interested in literature. I read a lot in the army. I had a good time and made lots of friends and went home at night for dinner." A few months before his discharge, he fell in love with a twenty-five-year-old Tel Aviv psychology student named Noam Bar, and that fall—after a summer in Berlin, learning German—he moved to Tel Aviv, started college, and began experimenting with his father's Florentine pasta sauces. (Bar did the dishes.) He also managed to land a part-time job on the news desk at *Haaretz*. "I'd arrive at four-thirty in the afternoon, when the news was coming in fast," he says. "It was very exhilarating—everybody was young, everybody smoked. I was going to become a journalist if not a chef." His parents were still thinking "a professor." Four years later, with a thesis to write, he left for Amsterdam with Bar. "We arrived the month of the Rabin assassination and joined the demonstration," he says. "That death was the end of a moment of high optimism at home. Israel became a very closed culture again, living according to its own rules. There was a desire growing in me to live somewhere else."

In Amsterdam, he began to cook in earnest. He prowled the fishmongers for mackerel and herring. He stopped at the butchers he passed for bones, and made his own stocks. He roasted, sautéed, and baked his way through Julia Child, started ordering from Books for Cooks, and "cooked for everyone who asked." So many people did ask that at dinnertime, his walk-up, on Herengracht, turned into an open house. "We were his guinea pigs," a Tel Aviv friend named Ilan Safit, who was studying in Amsterdam at the time, told me. "I had a Dutch girlfriend. We were living practically hand to mouth, but even after we got married we must have eaten at Yotam's every other night. He loved the kitchen. He was obviously an intellectual—a first-class intellectual—but he wasn't happy writing philosophy in his study. He was happy feeding people. He said, 'Ilan, I don't want to go back to academia, I don't want to live with books.'"

His father was shocked. "This is not a very good idea" was his reply to the note buried in Ottolenghi's thesis. His adviser, Ruth Ronen, puts it this way: "Cooking? It was like a metamorphosis, it was so extreme. His thesis was excellent, very thoughtful and intriguing. He had a natural inclination to philosophy—you could feel the urge—and the world of cooking was so far from that; I couldn't even see the connection. Was I disappointed? In a way, yes." But his sister told him, "This is the coolest thing." His mother wanted to see him happy. And his old mentor, Yehuda Elkana (who died in Jerusalem this fall), even claimed some credit for the change. "We had hundreds of candidates for the program," he told me. "We were looking for the few who had an original attitude to something in life. It could be anything. How you made love, how you made bread, how you 'made' philosophy. Yotam had that curiosity and enthusiasm. He would come to my home, and I'd cook for him. I'm a very good cook, so I may have had an influence. Even then, he was proof that the division academics make between 'cognitive' and 'emotional' is bullshit."

Ottolenghi still makes the puff pastry that he learned at the Cordon Bleu. He loved the pastry part of his cooking course; he found the "physicality of pastry" soothing. But he found the savory part—which, in the hierarchy of professional kitchens, is called "cuisine"—so pressured and unnerving that it nearly ended his new career. "I thought, 'This will only get worse,'" he says, and it did. His first cooking job was a trial run at a London restaurant called the Capital. He spent three mind-numbing months whipping egg whites for the pastry chef to fold, and then was promoted to full time in the cold-starter section. "On my first day, the sous-chef said, 'Okay, now make me a lobster bisque and an amuse-bouche.' It was terrifying. I couldn't sleep all night, and by the middle of the next day I was so exhausted that I took my scooter and went home and never went back. I said to Noam, 'This is not a normal job.'"

He was rescued by the well-known London chef Rowley Leigh—an experience on the order of starting out in New York with, say, Daniel Boulud ("Not charitable, but sweet," Ottolenghi describes him. "I doubt if he likes my food."). Leigh placed him at a small restaurant that he had opened in Kensington called Launceston Place, where he quickly became the pastry chef. "I could do what I did best, and I was really teaching myself, because the menu was basically French-English, and French pastry wasn't my thing. I wanted the vibrancy and freshness of California pastry"—the Ottolenghis had spent a sabbatical year in Mill Valley, when Yotam was ten—"so I bought Alice Waters, and Emily Luchetti's *Stars Desserts*. I made fresh-fruit galettes and meringue pies. I stayed a year and got a lot of confidence. You can do that with pastry; you learn a certain range of processes, and it's very contained. I began to think that maybe I had a pastry talent and should get a pâtisserie job—see how it all worked, napoleons, pâté à choux, crème pâtisserie."

He went to work for a chain of bakeries—a franchise spinoff of the entrepreneurial restaurateur Raymond Blanc. The bakery turned out to be a factory, where the crème pâtisserie came out of a machine. Plus, it was freezing. "Fifteen degrees," Ottolenghi says. "The guy next to me said we'd be warmer driving a minicab. I did twenty-five shifts, and on the one where I worked a machine that poured chocolate mousse into sponge cake, I decided that this was not what I needed to know to further my career." A few days later, he got on his scooter and rode up and down the streets of central London, "searching for bakeries that looked exciting." On a quiet street in Knightsbridge, he spotted a small traiteur called Baker & Spice, peered through the window, and ran in. "It was completely magical," he says. "I saw all these walls and counters covered with a marvelous mix of food. There were Middle Eastern salads, Italian caprese salads, rotisserie chickens, even char-grilled broccoli, and you could see into a small kitchen open to a mews garden, full of light. You could even see Ringo Starr's house." A young chef, about his own age, came out of the kitchen and said, "I'm Sami. I'm from Tel Aviv." Ottolenghi said, "Me, too."

Sami Tamimi was seventeen when he moved out of his father's house, in the Old City of East Jerusalem. It wasn't entirely his decision. "My family was a very traditional Muslim house," he told me one day in Acton, in West London, where he lives with an English property-research analyst named Jeremy Kelly, his partner of eight years. We were in the kitchen. I had found him making a cheesecake for us to have with coffee; the cake was from a television recipe he had just downloaded, but the gesture of hospitality was timeless, tacit, and very Arab. "I had six siblings and five step-siblings; every time I came home, there was another baby born. And when the whole sexual thing came up—well, in Palestine you can't tell anyone how you really feel. I was fifteen when I left school; I always knew there was something else in life." At the time, Tamimi was working at the Mount Zion, a West Jerusalem hotel whose German chef, seeing the makings of a cook, had promoted him from kitchen porter to "head breakfast chef," a job Tamimi describes as an education in scrambled eggs. Three years later, he said goodbye to his friends and left for Tel Aviv.

He says that he could "breathe" in Tel Aviv, a city as open then as Jerusalem was staid. He acquired an Anglo-Israeli boyfriend and a decent restaurant job, discovered his talent for catering home-cooked food ("After all those years of dreaming about European food, I realized that the food I grew up with was the food I did best"), and settled into the kind of "good" neighborhood that he describes drily as "quite unusual for an Arab living in Tel Aviv." He stayed for the next twelve years. He liked the city—the freedom he'd felt at first, the European cafés and restaurants, and, above all, the chef's job that he eventually found at Lilith, a fashionable new brasserie whose owner, a transplanted American, served an eclectic "California-Mediterranean" mix of grilled meats and vegetables that was, in many ways, a version of the kind of food Tamimi cooks now. One night a woman visiting from England ate at Lilith and asked to meet him. She said that she loved his food, and that there would always be a job waiting for him with her in London. In 1997, he called the woman, got on a plane, and started working at Baker & Spice—"creating the concept" that made Ottolenghi stop his scooter, on a spring day two years later, and run in, asking for a job.

"We clicked as friends, right away," Tamimi says. "It was an 'everything' mesh. We came from the same place, we tasted food in the same way. And of course our cooking was very similar. We both wanted to surprise, but we also wanted our food to taste 'comfortable.' Our feeling was: pick good ingredients and let them speak." They worked together in Knightsbridge for about two years—with Tamimi running savory and Ottolenghi eventually running pastry—and talked, from time to time, about someday opening a place together. In the fall of 2001, Ottolenghi left to find one. Tamimi stayed. "For months, I was thinking yes, no, yes, no," he says. "Then Yotam asked me to join him, and a few weeks later it was yes." The Notting Hill deli opened with a bright-red OTTOLENGHI painted in block letters above the door. I asked Tamimi if he thought it should have had his name, too, and he shook his head: "It was Yotam's vision and his dream. The work was his. The stake was his. I didn't have money to invest. He risked everything he had. A few years later, I became a partner, but regardless of the cookbooks we do, regardless of our friendship, I'm still working for Yotam. He's my boss."

Tamimi writes poetry in Arabic, and paints. There is a haunting gouache on his living room wall—lines of script painted over with bright-yellow flowers and green leaves. The poem, he told me, is "about the things you're supposed to remember and the things you have to forget"; the flowers are "the way I felt after it was written." There are layers of irony (or innocence) in a lot of what Tamimi says, and perhaps because of this, he stays away from the kind of exposure that Ottolenghi is able to embrace—and weather. When they

worked on *Jerusalem*, it was Ottolenghi who did the traveling, the interviewing, and nearly all the writing, but it was
Tamimi who in many ways talked him through the experience. "We'd sit down and think about little things we'd done
as children—things associated with a recipe," Tamimi says.
"We'd tell stories. We'd compare the smells and tastes and
sounds that were our memories of food. It was mind-blowing,
for me, to be re-created through that book." This fall, he
went with Ottolenghi on two *Jerusalem* book tours—first in
England, then in Canada and the United States—and admits
to having enjoyed them both. He discovered two nephews
looking for him on Facebook, and even talked by phone to a
brother who hadn't spoken to him since the day that as a gay
man, he became unwelcome in their father's house. He and
Kelly are going to East Jerusalem for a week at Christmas—
his first trip to Israel in nine years. (He had told me that after
the second intifada started, in 2000, visiting "became un-
bearable; the hatred on both sides was too intense.") "I don't
know what will happen, but I'm going," he says. "We'll see."

In Acton that day, he said, "I'm very private. I don't think
I'm built to be Yotam's sort of famous person." Ottolenghi—
who stopped cooking at the restaurant and deli kitchens
when he took on the column and, with it, the job of creating, testing, and writing new recipes each week—still visits
them almost every day, to check out the food and talk to the
chefs and the staff. The customers recognize him. They stop
him to say hello. They ask about recipes. Some take out their
smartphones and ask him to pose with them for pictures.
(He obliges). Tamimi never leaves the kitchen if he can help
it, and he shoos away any customer (including me) who in-
vades his space during lunch or dinner service, hoping to
watch him work. "I'm happy in our kitchens," he told me. "I

divide my week between them, working with the chefs all day, and you can't do that and have a public image. It would be easy for me to visit a kitchen, taste, and leave, but my idea of teaching our chefs is to work with them, to work as hard as they work—to compete. They're young, they respect that, and I like passing what I know to other generations. I have so much knowledge in my head that it just comes out. You spend your life learning, and a time comes when you want to share it."

Ottolenghi likes to write. "He wasn't interested in sports," his mother says. "He was interested in trying his hand at a short story." He expects that one day he will produce a book about food that isn't a cookbook—something literary, maybe a memoir full of experiences and ideas. *Jerusalem* includes his nimble, often eloquent evocations of the city and its multitude of different peoples, and of the helplessness both he and Tamimi feel as "that elusive dream of peace in the Middle East" fades. He put it this way: "It takes a giant leap of faith, but we are happy to take it—what have we got to lose?—to imagine that hummus will eventually bring Jerusalemites together, if nothing else will."

In the fall of 2004, a literary agent named Felicity Rubinstein, who lived a few blocks from the Notting Hill deli, suggested that Ottolenghi write a cookbook. She wasn't thinking about literature. "I wanted the recipes," she says. "I was shopping at Yotam's all the time—the food was different from anything I'd ever eaten—but I was spending a lot of money there. I thought, I could do this myself if I had a book." At the time, Ottolenghi had only one deli, and the Islington restaurant had just opened. He was working at both kitchens with Tamimi, doing pastry or savory or both, as the need arose. They were absorbing each other's recipes and techniques. His ideas for a book were perhaps still more philosophical than gastronomic. "I heard back that it was 'maybe no recipes, maybe no paper,'" Rubinstein says. She told him to think again.

A year later, with the Kensington deli open, he was ready. By then he had established a name, and also what in the restaurant trade is called a look—thanks, in large part, to a commuting Israeli architect and friend named Alex Meitlis, whom he credits with the clean white laid-back elegance that all the Ottolenghis share, from the red logo on their white menus to the chairs and countertops and tables. (Meitlis told me, "Yotam has absolutely no ego when it comes to how much of the aesthetic success is his.") His one problem was the limited reach of his reputation. He had a big following in the trendy boroughs of central London, but not much farther, and to fast-track that to a good book deal, as they would have said in the genius program, his choice was apparently between flinging pots and flipping fritters, as a wannabe television-chef celebrity, and producing a weekly column in the kind of national newspaper whose readers would like his butternut-squash salads and his green beans. *The Guardian* was "inevitable," Rubinstein says.

Ottolenghi isn't a vegetarian. He once told me that he hadn't left the country of "no seafood, no pork" in order to cook for people who wouldn't eat anything but plants. But many of the customers who ate his beans and salads assumed that he was one of those people—and as it turned out, the only available space in *The Guardian*'s overflowing food pages was the "vegetarian slot." The slot had for years been filled by Rose Elliot, an ardent herbivore and astrologer with an army of sandal-wearing fans, who had departed the paper with an MBE and the royalties from more than fifty books waiting in the bank.

At first Ottolenghi thought he should refuse the column. He said this to me one night at NOPI, as we were sitting down to a carnivore's feast of sharing dishes that began with gurnard, a fish from the Celtic Sea, which the chef, Ramael Scully (born in Malaysia, raised in Australia), had filleted into a beautiful chunk of white flesh, marinated in a complex curry-lime-and-coconut paste, wrapped in a pandan leaf, steamed, and served with a pineapple sambal. (Not for the home cook.) Ottolenghi, who has a huge appetite, had ordered half the dishes on the menu. We finished the fish, cleaned a plate of zucchini-and-manouri-cheese fritters with lime yogurt, and moved on to a baby chicken—simmered for an hour, marinated overnight in Asian wine and spices, then flash-fried crisp—so tender that you could munch the bones. We washed them down with a good light Austrian white, and I asked him what changed his mind. "My agent," he said. "She told me, 'Yotam, beggars can't be choosers. The day you take that column, you'll get a book deal.'" He took the column, and three months later he had the deal. His first recipe was for "seriously zesty bread salad," which appeared with the addendum: "Will taste amazing alongside a piece of slightly charred meat from the barbecue." There were so many letters that week from angry readers that, despite his frequent pleas "to get my brief expanded," he had to swear off any mention of flesh until the fall of 2010, when Merope Mills, the editor of *The Guardian Weekend* and a "big Yotam advocate," called to say, "The shackles have lifted—write anything you want."

By then, of course, he was seriously into vegetables, and

today at least one recipe of the two or three in each of his columns remains a vegetable dish. "I found it appealing—the idea of celebrating vegetables or pulses without making them taste like meat, or as complements to meat, but to be what they are," he says. "It does no favor to vegetarians, making vegetables second best." In his first cookbook, *Ottolenghi*, vegetable dishes were often spiked with a bit of meat: try the caramelized endive, smothered in bread crumbs, Parmesan, thyme, and cream, and roasted with a topping of serrano ham. With *Plenty*—a collection, for the most part, of his favorite vegetarian columns—the vegetables stood alone, their ontological status deliciously revealed. The book, which sold nearly half a million copies in Britain, became a bestseller in Germany, Holland, and America. A Russian translation is on the way.

Noam Bar, who moved to London with Ottolenghi in 1997, doesn't cook. Nor, in fact, was he still living with Ottolenghi when the Notting Hill deli opened, five years later. But he had remained Ottolenghi's closest friend—"the one person in the world who I knew would never let me down," Ottolenghi says—and had also become his business partner, the éminence grise of the operation. "Our MBA," Ottolenghi calls him. "He put the company together." It was Bar who pushed Ottolenghi to open his own place, searched with him for the *right place*, structured a backers' prospectus that would spread the risk among small investors (who are "more than satisfied," he says), and over the years, has sat at the negotiating table for every one of Ottolenghi's contracts. "Noam's the one who rattles the cage," Ottolenghi told me. Rubinstein put it this way: "He's more abrasive than Yotam, but he's much softer than he appears, and Yotam is much steelier than he seems."

Bar is another polymath. He grew up in Haifa, where his father—a Polish Jew and Holocaust survivor—was a chemical engineer and his mother taught literature and Bible studies at a junior high school. "I had a problem with Haifa," he said in the middle of a conversation one morning at his house in Hammersmith. "I couldn't express myself in that middle-class city. Actually, I couldn't express myself in Israel. It was opera seria then. Today it takes a lot out of me just to be there." He has not stopped running since he left. In Amsterdam, he started a company that offered "premium-line telephone services" (horoscopes, dating, and the weather). The Internet killed it. In London, he went back to school for his business degree, and in 2000, when he and Ottolenghi ended their nine-year affair—a parting that left them both shattered—he flew to Dharamsala to meditate and study Tibetan medicine. A year later, he was back in London, getting a degree in homeopathy, which he still practices, in Marylebone, twice a week. When he can get away, he flies to Tanzania and volunteers with a homeopathic project that provides supportive treatment to AIDS victims. The rest of his time is spent keeping the Ottolenghi brand current—*Jerusalem* was originally his idea—profitable, and realistic. Meitlis calls him "the wind behind everybody's wings."

"My job at Ottolenghi is asking the 'now what, now where' question—it's about strategy, about keeping an edge," Bar told me. "Food is not my passion. Nothing infuriates Yotam more than me in the kitchen, making comments about the food. My passion is the organism—it's about people working together with a sense of movement and purpose." He says of Ottolenghi and Tamimi, "Yotam is inventive; he has the ultimate, the most discerning, palate. Sami is more traditional, but he's the kitchen authority; his hand goes into the salt, and his fingers know it's the right amount."

And he says of himself, "I'm the one who's either solving problems or looking for the next new thing. The fact is that most restaurants fail. You have to stay one step ahead. We were fine in Notting Hill for a while, but the back room was always too small. Then there was Islington. We know how to fix things now, but in 2004, when we bought Islington, we didn't know what we were doing with a restaurant. It's been a big success, but at the beginning, I'd go for dinner, there would be eight people. Maybe. I'd want to slit my wrists. And Belgravia? We opened Belgravia in 2007, and it was another catchment. We're still working on a hot breakfast there. Last year, the problem was NOPI, because Soho is *definitely* another catchment. You can't do an Islington there." He meant that a couple of North London literati looking to sample and share, in Islington, after the curtain falls across the street at the Almeida, is not the same as a couple of testy businessmen walking a few blocks from their offices to SoHo, looking to seal a deal. "We had to reinvent the wheel at every level, without making the mistake of surprising at every level."

Bar thrives on his intimations of disaster. "You have ten minutes of Noam, maximum," their general manager and fourth partner, Cornelia Staeubli, says. "He gets bored, and he's on another planet—or another problem that nobody else has seen. He loves change, and Yotam doesn't. We will sometimes do Noam's idea just to prove him wrong." Bar says that their arguments are "loud but never personal. It was never difficult, working with Yotam on a new basis. We were always more than lovers. We had that deep trust; we broke

up, I went to India, and a year later we had new lives, but
we still had it. We're very complementary. Yotam is measured. I'm forward-looking, always pushing. Yotam says, 'Stop!
Let's wait and think.' I say, 'Let's do it now!' A restaurant is
like a bicycle—if it stops moving, it has no life."

The partners call themselves a family. They eat at one another's houses, take vacations together, and occasionally
even rent a house in the country together for a weekend, to
reconnect—or, as Meitlis puts it, "to celebrate their different obsessions." "Three gay guys and a mother hen" is how
their friends describe them, which isn't entirely accurate,
since the family now includes their lovers and spouses and
parents and brothers and sisters and nieces and nephews, and
the list goes on. Staeubli, a blue-eyed Swiss beauty of forty-
four, is de facto the mother hen. Bar calls her "the foreman,"
and says he can see her "moving armies around in World War
Two, calm and energized in a crisis." Ottolenghi says, "She
makes everything work." She shares *his* obsession with the
"context of food," with the balance of buzz and quiet in a
restaurant, and especially with the way the mood and clarity of its spaces can anticipate and echo the look and taste of
the food in front of you on the table. "She's tough, too," he
told me. "She'll spot the one speck of dirt on the floor—the
way I'll see the one tart that's badly displayed—and stand
there until it's gone. But there's the other side. I've seen her
go out and buy a sleeping bag for a waitress who didn't have
a bed. She looks after a staff of two hundred people. She
takes care of us all."

Staeubli comes from Goldau, a mountain town in the
canton of Schwyz so remote that, when she left it at nine-
teen, for an au pair job in America, it had "maybe a thousand people, just like me." She still talks about the thrill of

landing at JFK: "The smells, the elbows out, I loved it all. I loved that there were so many nationalities in those visa lines, everyone with the same goal—to start their lives." (In her best of all possible worlds, she would open a New York Ottolenghi, "big, like Eataly.") Her job turned out to be in a New Jersey suburb. The family was rich, the children spoiled, and after three months she decided that she was "not an au pair person" and fled to the Lower East Side, where she waitressed happily until her visa expired and she had to go back to Switzerland. She stayed there for ten years, and at thirty-two, quit the last of a series of dull office jobs and set off to see the world. She flew to Southeast Asia, and eventually on to Sydney in the middle of a winter so cold that she got on a bus for Queensland. The trip took forty-eight hours, and at the end of it she fell in love with a backpacking Englishman who had boarded along the way. They spent a week together in the sun, on Airlie Beach. Three months later, she arrived at Heathrow to the same multicultural mix of people that had delighted her in New York, and she and the man from the bus—a journalist named Peter Lowe, who is now the managing editor at Sky News—got married.

Nine years ago, Staeubli sold her half of a small Internet café-cum-restaurant that she and a friend had opened in Putney a year earlier, and went out looking for a job closer to the Notting Hill apartment where she and Lowe then lived. She passed a SALES ASSISTANT WANTED sign in the window of the Notting Hill deli, met Ottolenghi, and started working the next day. "I came home that night crying," she told me late one afternoon, over tea at their apartment. "I said to Peter, 'I can't do it, it's too chaotic there.' He said, 'Try till Christmas.'" By April, she was managing the store. A year later, she was managing managers, and doing it so efficiently and agreeably that she was invited into the business. "I know I'm the mother hen," she said. "I don't have children of my own, so I like that. But I don't mother them. I *love* them. I do the hiring, the staff, the managers, and the chefs. I fill in when someone on the staff's away. My job is to make everything okay." She spends her days whizzing around London, from deli to restaurant to the next deli, and knows before anyone else when something's wrong.

I asked her what exactly the problem had been at NOPI, which opened in February last year and is now arguably one of the city's hottest restaurants, and she said, "At first it was all sharing plates, like Islington. I told Yotam, 'We haven't got the right customers here yet. We've got your most boring fans, the food bloggers and the ladies over fifty who sit with a glass of water and talk about your beautiful salads, and then order a single plate to share.' Sharing is fine at night, but the rich guys we need for lunch in Soho, the ones with offices in the neighborhood, don't want to be disturbed or distracted by the food. They don't want a cluttered table. They want a main dish, fish or meat, and if they get that they'll order a nice expensive wine to wash it down. Yotam got that wrong." (She meant he was nervous about diluting the Ottolenghi signature.) "But Noam and I fixed it. It didn't take long. You can share tastes or you can dig into your own big steak. We're *very* popular now."

On my last night in London, a Friday, Ottolenghi and I cooked from *Jerusalem* in the Notting Hill apartment that he shares with Karl Allen, a quirky and quietly impressive Northern Irishman whom he met at the gym twelve years ago—and married in September in Massachusetts, where gay marriage has been legal for eight years. Allen, who is a law graduate, a former British Airways flight attendant, and a keen-eyed collector of vintage fifties antiques—he found the outsize cabbage-leaf chandelier that hangs like a flashy hat above the receptionist's stand at NOPI—has been managing the company's Kensington deli since it opened, in 2005. ("You function at 80 percent when you fly," he says. "You don't realize it until you've spent a week in one time zone. I met Yotam and I wanted that.") His plan is to quit Kensington "when the first baby arrives" and become a house parent, eventually selling antiques or designing interiors from home. With family in mind, they have bought a large house on a quiet street in Camden—a short walk from Ottolenghi's test kitchen, in an old building under the Camden railway arches, and the adjoining prep kitchen, where the bread for his restaurants and delis is now baked and the pastry is prepared for on-site finishing. "Pretty, respectable, and bourgeois" is how Ottolenghi happily describes the house. It has five bedrooms, a deep garden, and a proper kitchen to replace the one he cooks in now, which is minuscule, or as he put it when I walked in, "a case of the cobbler goes barefoot." Every inch was taken.

Ottolenghi cleared some space for us on a serving counter above a shelf of tottering pots and bowls and unpacked the fixings, which in keeping with his "any decent supermarket" home-recipe rule, he had just picked up at the local Waitrose. He tweeted a picture of the radishes he'd bought, glistening in the sink, "because they look so fresh," and then a message to say that regrettably they were tasteless—after which we took a break, opened some white wine, and stepped onto a narrow balcony off the kitchen for a clandestine cigarette. Ottolenghi rarely smokes. His real vice is drugstore candy, which he keeps stashed in the glove compartment of an eight-year-old Prius, and dips into on his daily rounds. He is almost preternaturally energetic, perhaps because of the sugar but more likely because of the Pilates classes he takes twice a week and never misses. He started Pilates twelve years ago, with a terrible "bending-over-the-stove" backache. Eight years later, he qualified as an instructor—something he hopes will come in handy on the off chance that London ever stops eating Ottolenghi.

My first job that night was to help assemble a "one-pot Sephardic hybrid" inspired by a dish called plov—a barberry, cardamom, onion, chicken, and rice concoction, originally hours in preparation, that Bukharan Jews introduced to Jerusalem and still serve in one form or another at celebrations. "You have to remember that for Jews, Jerusalem was never an affluent town," Ottolenghi told me. "It was different for Palestinians. The Arab middle class was affluent. But for most Jews it was a poor immigrant town. They cooked with what they had. There is no one recipe. In fact, we never replicate recipes. We replicate the *idea* of a dish. We replicated the idea of plov." The barberries—a sour dried berry from Iran—went into an infusion of water and sugar to plump and sweeten. The chicken thighs went into a marinade of olive oil, green cardamom pods, cinnamon sticks, and cloves, along with salt and pepper. Sliced onions slowly caramelized in a frying pan, and we began chopping herbs and tearing lettuces for a raw cauliflower salad. I looked at my watch: we'd been back in the kitchen less than twenty minutes, and talking all the time. Ottolenghi had been so carefree and relaxed, juggling pots and pans in that ridiculous space, that it was impossible to imagine him as the panicked apprentice who had once fled on a moped from the cold starter station of a London restaurant.

He consulted his list—he is a compulsive list maker—and

announced that dessert was next, whereupon he opened two
packages of phyllo pastry, melted a good third of a pound of
butter, brushed some onto a baking tray, and began layering
the tray with sheets of buttered phyllo. The name of the dish
was mutabbaq. It was Palestinian, and was traditionally filled
with "hard-core" goat or ewe cheese, which, Ottolenghi
allowed, was an acquired taste. He and Tamimi had decided
instead on the combination of ricotta and soft white goat
cheese that he now mixed together with a fork and spread
over half the phyllo sheets, leaving me to cover the mixture
with the rest. It took me seven sheets, but the last one looked
respectable. He checked it out. "Phyllo masks all mistakes,"
he said, reaching around me for a small pot to hold the sugar,
lemon juice, and water for a pastry syrup. While the syrup
boiled, he tackled the bowl of chicken. Soon the spicy smell
of the thighs, browned with the cloves and cardamom pods of
the marinade sticking to their skin, was mingling with the
sour-sweet smell of barberries and caramelized onions in a
pot of simmering basmati rice. We opened another bottle of
wine, filled a dish with some olives left over from the cauliflower salad, and crashed.

It had been what his friends call "a Yotam week." He had
worked mornings at the test kitchen with his assistant, Sarah
Stephens, a young Tasmanian chef of surpassing patience
whose job, at the moment, was to produce a large number
of interesting, attractive dishes for the British food photographer Jonathan Lovekin, who had taken the pictures for
Plenty and whom I met that Monday, waiting in a patch of
light by the front door, to start taking them for *Jerusalem*.
(We ate the morning's offerings for lunch.) He had visited
the prep bakeries next door, where the pastry chef (Lebanese-
Brazilian) taught me how to work the dough laminator (think

of an old-fashioned clothes wringer, only horizontal and sleek steel) and to hand-roll croissants (so addictive it was hard to stop), and a staff of sous-chefs from Australia, Poland, and Brazil fed me leftover crackers, smothered in salt caramel and chocolate, which they called "brittle." He had played the fall guy in an interview routine at a cabaret in Soho, appearing between a campy stand-up comedy act and a famous cross-dressing singer; agreed to four more television hours, this time for Channel 4, which would take him from Morocco to Tunisia, Turkey, and back to Israel by the end of the summer (and be ready to air this month); met for a long Islington breakfast with a group of American women (chefs, food writers, and their friends) on an eating spree in London and Paris; hosted a butchery demonstration at NOPI; endured a humorless session with a group of Dutch students, who were horrified to learn that he ate meat, shopped occasionally at a supermarket, and stretched his carbon footprint by importing his pomegranate molasses from Beirut; prepared for the class that he and Tamimi teach on alternate Saturdays at Leiths cookery school, in West London; written three columns; and made time for countless hours eating and talking with me.

Ottolenghi works hard, and the challenge for him is long-term: how to maintain the Ottolenghi signature and, at the same time, not exhaust its appeal in a notoriously trendy and capricious city. NOPI was an attempt at both. It tastes different—more Asian and exotic—and looks different, with a gleaming brass counter and brass tabletops and fixtures replacing the pristine Corian white of Islington and the delis. "We wanted a brasserie feel, something fresh," Meitlis told me. "So we kept the white walls but made it as mellow and deep as possible, and let the brass shine." Ottolenghi admits that it looks terrific. Whatever hesitations he had at first are long resolved. "We wanted to get everything right—right away," he says. "It's not easy to keep on reinventing." He worries (or, more accurately, Bar and Staeubli worry for him) about the downside of so much success—about the gorgeous Ottolenghi-catered buffet becoming the ubiquitous Ottolenghi buffet. One writer recently grumbled about walking into an Ottolenghi dinner party and wondering what had happened to serious English food, served in the proper English dinner order. Another quoted his wife saying that 94 percent of the DNA in every Ottolenghi dish is identical—arguably a case more of expectation than of reality. Ottolenghi experiments all the time. Lately he has been incorporating tastes he discovered this year in Turkey into recipes at his test kitchen. Tamimi, who loves Japan—he says that "taste is a part of me, it's why I travel"—has been working with Asian seaweeds and vinegars. As for me, I would be hard put to explain what, genomically speaking, the Malaysian-spiced gurnard I sampled at NOPI had in common with the Turkish-inspired zucchini fritters I also ate that night—beyond the fact that they were both good, in an unmistakable Ottolenghi way.

At seven, Allen came home from the Kensington deli and took a Friday-night nap on the living room couch. When he and Ottolenghi met, Allen was in the habit of driving to Gloucestershire on Fridays, to work on an old cottage that he had bought to sell. "I grew up in the countryside," he told me. "I can rough it in a sleeping bag. But Yotam? It would have killed him. Luckily, it was sold." The phone woke him. Bar, who was coming to dinner with his boyfriend of four years, Garry Chang—a young Taiwanese doctor with the National Health Service—had called to say they were running late. We turned off the pot, and I peeked in. The plov was as beautiful as it smelled. "The senses are not so separate," Ottolenghi had said one day in Camden, en route to a High Street diner for a quick lunch. "They're synesthetic. They need to work together." He called this his aesthetic. The word at work is "smiling." Staeubli, who coined the expression, says, "Sami can make food smile," and Allen swears that he has seen Yotam walk into one of his delis or restaurants and take away half the food on display or the salad about to be served "because it's not smiling." The smiliest dish I'd seen that week was shakshuka—a North African breakfast from *Plenty*, cooked and served in little cast-iron skillets. It wasn't fancy: a couple of eggs poached in a spicy saffron, onion, tomato, and bell-pepper sauce, flecked with fresh herbs and dappled with drops of yogurt. But it was irresistible. I could taste it before I raised my fork.

Bar and Chang arrived at the apartment toward nine. Allen and I set the table. Ottolenghi put the mutabbaq in the oven, turned the plov back on, and chopped some parsley, coriander, and dill, for sprinkling. A few minutes later, we sat down and ate serious Jerusalem food served in the proper English dinner order. The plov was delicious, if you didn't count the undercooked rice and the pinkish chicken near the bone. Ottolenghi, who is known to be very precise at work— "He's always asking, 'How much of that? A teaspoon? A half teaspoon?'" Allen says—tends to get lost in thought or conversation when he cooks at home. He had doubled the number of chicken thighs in his recipe and added some extra rice, but not the extra water with which to cover and cook it all. ("The big secret at Yotam's house is that the food is much better when Karl cooks it," Meitlis, who stays in their spare bedroom when he comes to London, says.) It didn't matter. We chewed the rice, avoided the pink, and asked for seconds.

The pastry was a sweet success. We ate it slowly and talked till midnight. Ottolenghi was leaving for Israel in a few weeks, to be with his parents on the twentieth anniversary of his brother's death. He has been flying to Israel two or three times a year since he left for Amsterdam. He says that "the sense of a network there, the security in that, is what gives me the cohesion that I don't have here." He calls it "the feeling that, when I'm at my parents' house, anything wrong or difficult can be fixed." The Ottolenghis have both retired. His father gardens; his mother volunteers with the women of Checkpoint Watch, documenting the trauma of border crossings for Palestinians. Once a year they spend a week in England with Ottolenghi and Allen. His father has become a fan. Three years ago, at Yotam's fortieth birthday party (three days and thirty guests in a rented Dorset mansion), Professor Ottolenghi stood up, raised his glass, and said, "My wish for Yotam today is that he keep not listening to my advice."

In 2014, Yotam Ottolenghi published *Plenty More*, a companion to his transformative vegetarian cookbook *Plenty*, and a year later, the cookbook *NOPI*, written with NOPI's head chef, Ramael Scully. Today Ottolenghi is "back where I started, with pastry," finishing a luscious book called, appropriately, *Sweets*. He and his husband, Karl, now have two sons.

POST-MODENA

~♔~

The words "Italy" and "new gastronomy" were an oxymoron when Massimo Bottura opened the Osteria Francescana in Modena, in 1995, and started creating the dishes that would turn him into a luminary of the culinary avantgarde. Take Black on Black, his tribute, by way of squid ink, katsuobushi, and a black cod, to Thelonius Monk. Or Camouflage, his nod to Picasso, with a civet of wild hare "hiding" in custard under a blanket of powdered herbs and spices. Today, dishes like those have earned him three Michelin stars, raised Francescana to third place on San Pellegrino's famous list of the best restaurants in the world, and put Italy on the map for the kind of travelers who prefer to eat their spaghetti and meatballs at home.

Bottura gets emotional thinking about food. His friends know this because he thinks out loud. Very loud. It happens when he starts to imagine a recipe—inspired, perhaps, by the arrival of a new Big Green Egg cooker or a wheel of Parmesan that he's been aging for fifty months, but just as often by, say, a Robert Longo painting or some vintage Lou Reed

vinyl or a line he suddenly remembers from Kerouac or
Céline. He describes the process as a kind of synesthesia,
where the worlds he loves start coming together in his head,
and he has no choice but to call someone with the news.
It could be a childhood friend a couple of blocks away in
Modena or another chef thousands of miles from Italy, depending on who, in his words, "has to hear this." People
listen. They hear the beginning of a loud, breathless, unstop-
pable recitation, and know that, as one friend put it, "It's
Massimo, cross-pollinating again." Bottura calls it, "Tasting my
creativity."

The first time I heard Bottura "thinking," I wondered if
he was angry—or, worse, bored. I was wrong. I got used to
Bottura's shouts. I began to think of them as bardic. I would
wait for him to jump up from the breakfast table—"the best
place to catch him focused," his American wife, Lara Gilmore, maintains—grab his cell phone, disappear into the
library, where he keeps a gleaming 1970s Transcriptors hy-
draulic turntable, a pair of MartinLogan speakers, and his
vast collection of CDs, tapes, and records, and, with the
music blasting, begin to shout. I would watch him brake his
motorcycle in the middle of a busy Modena street, dig for
his phone, and, to the accompaniment of honking horns,
begin to shout. I learned a lot about food, listening to Bottura
think, though I would happily have skipped the night he
punched a number into his phone and yelled, "*Senti questa!*"—
"Listen to this!"—while driving a Mercedes at perilous speed
down the autostrada to Reggio Emilia and, at the same time,
leaning low into the windshield to take pictures of the moon
rising under the arch of a Santiago Calatrava bridge. That
was unsettling, given that I had hoped to get to Modena
alive that night and sample the Eel Swimming Up the Po

River on Bottura's Sensations tasting menu, and even to beg a chef 's reprise of Black on Black, which had been "retired," like the number of a star pitcher.

Bottura thinks of his dishes as metaphors. They tell stories. His eel—cooked sous vide, lacquered with a saba sauce, and served with creamy polenta and a raw wild-apple jelly— refers to the flight of the Estense dukes to Modena in 1598, after Clement VIII seized their capital at Ferrara and claimed its eel marshes and fisheries for the Church. Camouflage— with its custard of foie gras, dark chocolate, and espresso foam—comes from a conversation between Picasso and Gertrude Stein, as a camouflaged truck rolled past them on Boulevard Raspail, in 1914. (Picasso, who had never seen camouflage before, cried, "Yes, it is we who made it, that is cubism.") And the short story that inspired Black on Black is about a French chef who turns out the lights when a group of irritable gourmets sit down to dinner, telling them, Eat with your palates, not your eyes. Bottura thought of that story late one night in his library, listening to Monk in the dark. He decided to create a recipe that would honor Monk, but he couldn't turn out the lights at Francescana. So he filleted the cod; seared its skin in dehydrated sea urchin and an ash of burned herbs; flipped it over to nestle in a layer of slivered root vegetables and ginger (for "spaghetti"); and poached it in a dried-tuna broth, blackened with the squid ink. At Francescana, it came to the table as a beautiful deep black circle in a bowl. The "lights" went on when you picked up your knife and fork and cut into the cod's bright white flesh. "Black and white," Bottura says. "Piano keys."

Bottura is one of a small far-flung brotherhood of exceptionally gifted and inventive chefs who have deconstructed, distilled, concentrated, and with uncommon respect, reconstructed the flavors of their own traditional cuisines. They are in constant touch. They text, they tweet, they call. They travel across the planet to share their ideas and secrets and techniques—the thermal immersion circulators, micro-vaporizers, precision smokers, and freeze dryers. They convene in August for the MAD weekend—the Noma chef René Redzepi's annual gathering of the tribe in Copenhagen. They fish and hunt and forage and cook together at wilderness outings like Cook It Raw, gastronomy's extreme sport (which Redzepi once, possibly to his regret, described as Boy Scout camp). They meet at the food writer and impresario Andrea Petrini's Gelinaz! (don't ask) cook-offs and riff on the history of one dish. This year the destination was Ghent and the dish was a classic nineteenth-century meat-and-vegetable timbale; Bottura sent his brother Paolo, who is a car dealer, to be "Massimo Bottura" and present his version, along with a video of the two men trading clothes at the airport—to make the point that no chef can claim to own a recipe, even one he has invented. They recount their most catastrophic gastronomic adventures to enraptured foodies at places like the New York Public Library, where Bottura was last "in conversation" with two of the American brothers, Daniel Patterson of the San Francisco restaurant Coi and David Chang of Momofuku.

He told a story about trying to cook seventy reindeer tongues sous vide, in a bath of ashes and olive oil, on the floor of a small hotel bedroom somewhere in the forests of Lapland, with the thermal circulators set so low that he had to spend twenty-four hours on the floor with them, waiting for the molecular miracle that would transform those thick, rubbery lumps into tempting morsels. This fall, in an exhibit at the Palais des Beaux-Arts, in Paris, you can see the "black meteorite" sculpture of carbon ashes, ground coffee, flour, and egg whites in which he had cooked a veal tongue—an image that came to him while thinking (out loud) about the artist Lucio Fontana's mid-century series *Concetto Spaziale*.

Bottura was born in Modena and grew up in a big house not far from the restaurant he owns now. Modena is a small city in Emilia-Romagna, half an hour northwest of Bologna in the Po River Valley, which is to say in the country's bread-basket, a source of agricultural wealth that is the envy of all Italy. The Po and its web of tributaries—Modena sits between two—account for a food tradition that includes the country's only authentic Parmesan (Parmigiano-Reggiano), its best prosciutto and culatello, its richest sausages (try pheasant stuffed with cotechino), its darkest Vignola cherries, and its finest balsamic vinegars, some of which were already on Modena's tables when Cicero, writing the Philippics, described the colony by its Latin name, as *Mutina firmissima et splendidissima*. Modena is steeped in praise, history, and satisfaction. Bottura says that when he opened Francescana the local borghesi—few of whom actually thought to eat there—were instantly suspicious, convinced that no one could cook better than the way they had always cooked, meaning exactly the way their mothers and grandmothers, and all the mothers before them, had. This of course could be said of anywhere in Italy, a country so resistant to culinary experiment that grown men will refuse to eat their wives' cooking and go "home" for lunch instead.

So it's probably more shocking than surprising that at first, Modena—home to a twelfth-century university and cathedral, to Italy's West Point, to the Ferrari founder and the Maserati factory, to a concert hall, an opera house, seven theaters, three good museums, and a foundation with one of the best photography collections anywhere—was immune to the lure of gastronomic refreshment. The problem was pride as much as provinciality. "When you taste a Bottura dish, the flavors you thought you knew become deeper, wider, longer," his friend Massimo Bergami, the dean of the Alma business school, at the University of Bologna, says. "He's building on the genuine identity of Italian cuisine. But to most Italians, identity has to do with borders, with saying, Go no farther. Our towns were walled once, and the ones with the most 'identity' within their walls have often preserved it obstinately, defensively, in a very static way." It seems that, while Spain was ready for a Ferran Adrià, Denmark for a René Redzepi, and Brazil for an Alex Atala, Modena was not quite ready for a Massimo Bottura, who said, "I want to donate my dreams to people" in the same breath as he talked about the tortellini his mother, Luisa, made.

Luisa Bottura cooked all day. She didn't have to. Her own mother had helped found and run a very successful fuel company, dealing first in wood and then in coal, and when Luisa married Alfio Bottura, who came from a rich landowning family, he took over her family's business, switched to diesel fuel, and made another fortune. But she could usually be found in the kitchen, where with the help of her mother and her maid, she cooked for a daughter and four sons, their hungry friends, a brother-in-law and a sister-in-law who had moved in, and anyone her husband wanted to bring home for lunch or dinner except his mistress—"he had two 'wives'" was the local term.

Bottura was the youngest son by six years. He says that his brothers would come home from school, find him watching the women cook, and chase him around the kitchen with whatever makeshift weapons were at hand. He took to hiding under the kitchen table, where, being five or six and always hungry, he "discovered my palate" by devouring the bits of tortellini dough that fell to the floor from the women's rolling pins. It was instantly addictive, he says, like the taste of his wife's cookie batter dropped from a wooden spoon. "That kitchen, under the table, was my safety place," he told me. "I remember the yellow of the pasta on a warm day, with the sun streaming through the window. I could see it through the slats. 'A perfect color,' I thought. 'Good for tagliatelle, too.'"

In 1988, after a trip to Southeast Asia—"my first exotic vacation," Bottura calls it—ended with a bout of food poisoning in Chiang Mai, he thought about how soothing a bowl of his mother's "birthday tortellini" would be, and began to work on a dish that he called the Tortellini Are Walking on the Broth. Two layers of broth, thickened with a seaweed agar "to create the movement of water, and six tortellini bobbing between them, in a layer of warm broth, crossing the Red Sea, going home." His wife, Lara, describes it as "Max's ultimate provocation of a town where no one would say, 'I'm better than la mamma.'" Eventually he made his compromesso storico with Modena. He called that dish Noah's Ark, because every family's tortellini tradition was in it. Bottura says, "My thought was you don't let tradition bind you. You let it set you free. The broth of Noah's Ark is the broth of many mothers. I put all their traditions together in one pot—duck, pigeon, guinea fowl, chicken, veal, beef, pork, eel, and frog's legs, with some kombu seaweed from Japan, for a wise cultural contamination—and make the broth. When all those flavors are concentrated, the meat comes off the bones, the bones are roasted, and each handkerchief of tortellini is filled with one of those broth meats." I asked his mother, who is eighty-nine, what she thought. "Massimo's cooking is fantastic," she said. "But I cook better."

Bottura began to cook for his friends when he was still in high school. They were a notorious crew—"six of us, plus twenty worshipers," one of them told me, laughing—known as either the bad boys or the golden youth of Modena, depending on who was talking. They were all good-looking. They threw the wildest parties. They were into every Italian teenage preoccupation—music, motorcycles, cars, soccer, girls, and clothes. (Bottura's taste once ran to Gigli, Gaultier, and Moschino; now he's happy in jeans, T-shirts, and a comfortable pair of New Balance.) "There were the serious, political kids, and there was us," Massimo Morandi, a Modena businessman who is one of Bottura's oldest friends, says. "Most of us came to school by public bus. Okay, I had a car—a Rabbit—but Max had his choice of cars. One day it was his father's gray Mercedes, the next his brother Andrea's green Porsche, the next his brother Paolo's black Saab. Cars like that, parked outside the school next to the teachers' little Fiats, created a lot of envy. But Max wasn't showing off; he was just being crazy."

Bottura was also irrepressibly hospitable, like his mother. Whenever he and his friends were through partying for the night, they trooped to Luisa Bottura's door for pasta. They called it the after party. "It was never a problem," she said. "My door was always open. I loved to watch them eat." It wasn't long before Max took over the three-in-the-morning shift in Luisa's kitchen. "The atmosphere around Max was pure *Animal House*," his friend Giorgio de Mitri, who owns the Modena arts-communications company Sartoria, says. "But when the playing stopped it was aglio, olio, e peperoncino, and there was Massimo at the stove. He was very good at cooking fast."

There is some debate in Modena as to when Bottura became the serious cook he is now. His mother says, "In my kitchen." Morandi says on a camping trip, in the late seventies: thirty kids, a couple of tents, and on the last night, "a celebration, with Max cooking a spaghetti carbonara so perfect that we all clapped." But Paolo Bottura knows that it happened when his best auto electrician left his dealership to open a restaurant. Paolo wanted the electrician back, wooed him, and two years later, told Max that there might be a restaurant for sale. It was a truck stop, really, in a village near Modena called Campazzo di Nonantola, but Max was at loose ends. He had finished high school with amazing ease, considering that he rarely studied. He had put in his obligatory year with the Italian army stationed at home in Modena—and won so many titles for his base's soccer team that no one stopped him when he took to driving in and out of the base without permission, honking at the gates and calling, "Open up. It's me, number one."

He went to law school to appease his father, who wanted a lawyer in the family business. "I liked it, but it wasn't the right place," he says. "I didn't feel that I was living my own life." He was also working afternoons for his father. That ended when the two men fought over a commission that his father refused to pay, saying, "You sold too low." Bottura told me, "I started screaming and never went back. I pictured myself waking up every morning, foggy, fighting with my father over one cent per liter of diesel gas. I had no money. But I bought that falling-apart trattoria. I thought, 'Why not?' I was already cooking for all my friends. I wanted to show that I could do it."

Marco Bizzarri, who shared a desk with Bottura in high school and is now the president and CEO of Bottega Veneta, says, "I was doing my military service, and I remember calling Max's mother, asking for him, and Luisa saying, 'He's opened a restaurant.' I couldn't believe it. I was the blue-collar bad boy; my parents worked in a tile factory. But I had gone through life with Massimo. We had aced our French tests together, with Max reading from the book we were supposed to know and me mouthing the words and trying not to laugh. I knew Max could be anything he wanted. He was like a child, someone always growing, and you never knew what was coming next. But I never expected Campazzo. The truckers were still eating there, they were yelling at him, 'What is this? We're paying more but eating less!' "

It was 1986. Bottura was twenty-three and trying to transform a roadside trattoria where, by all accounts, the chipped glasses were as old as the trucks outside, and everything else was brown and muddy yellow except the hideous gold-painted metal food trolley that he wheeled around, pretending not to see his friends. Most of the bad boys were on their way to respectable lives, but their nights were reserved for the Trattoria del Campazzo, the consensus being that, wherever Max was, there would be a party later. His worst problem was the "entertainment"—an accordionist with a singing wife who came with the place and whom Bottura was either too timid or too kind to fire, until after six months of forbearance, his friends gave him an ultimatum: us or them. Meanwhile, Campazzo was looking prettier. Bottura's girlfriend at the time was studying interior design. She hung curtains and replaced the old tablecloths with creamy linens. Her mother filled in nights, washing dishes, and Luisa Bottura came every day with her maid to make the pasta, while Massimo got busy at the stove and started riffing on their old Modena recipes. "Economically, it was terrible," he says. "But the food got better."

A few months after Campazzo opened, a woman from the village knocked on the door, asking for the new owner. Her name was Lidia Cristoni. She had been cooking in Modena for thirty-five years, many of them at what was then its best restaurant, but she was losing her sight and could no longer negotiate the city's streets. Bottura installed her in his kitchen that morning, and two days later saw to it that she had an operation on her eyes. She had planned to stay for a year or two, and stayed for seven. "She was my second mother-mentor," Bottura says. "A master pasta-maker. She could handle a hundred and sixty eggs a day." I asked Lidia about Campazzo one day last summer, when Bottura and I visited her at the clinic where she had just had heart surgery and was already complaining about the food. "Massimo had a fantastic will," she said while Bottura dug into the lunch she had refused to finish. "But he was so nervous about the restaurant. He was grinding his teeth, he wasn't sleeping, he wasn't eating—he was down to sixty kilos. I gave him salamis, I told him, 'Mangia! Mangia!' or I'll leave. One day the health people showed up to say that we couldn't use any eggs at all because of salmonella. Max didn't know what to do, but I did. I told the inspector that I had twenty fresh eggs from my own hens. He said, 'Give me ten,' and left."

The truckers left, too, once Bottura had replaced the electrician's menu with wild-arugula salads, soft-boiled egg yolks on oysters splashed with vinegar, and wine that actually came in bottles. The crowd got younger. "It was like having a big family dinner every night," Lidia said. "But once the service ended, it was a bordello, because Max kept a little apartment above the restaurant, and everyone went upstairs. One New Year's Eve, we were a hundred and fifteen people. Max suddenly disappeared. Everyone was asking, 'Where's Max?' I covered for him. He was at my mother's house. He had walked over with a big dish of her favorite panna cotta— the kind with a base of caramel and fruit. She was ninety-two and still making tortellini, but she couldn't do panna cotta anymore. He was the one who thought of her, alone on New Year's Eve."

Giorgio de Mitri once described Bottura to me as "like a sponge, because he has that rare ability to absorb influence and at the same time to stay absolutely himself, absolutely original." With Lidia, the influence was traditional Modena cuisine. Next came the basics of French cuisine, adapted to Emilia-Romagna's bounty, and Bottura's teacher was a French chef named Georges Cogny, who had married a woman from Piacenza and eventually moved his pots and pans to Farini, a peaceful village in the Apennines, where he opened a restaurant called Locanda Cantoniera. Bottura ate there a few months after he bought Campazzo, tasted Cogny's demi-soufflé of chocolate, and asked if he could watch him cook. For the next two years, he spent every Sunday and Monday, when Campazzo was closed, driving two hours into the mountains to learn.

"I was starting to feel like a real chef," he told me toward the end of a sweltering day in late July. We were in Farini, at a chefs' ceremony in memory of Cogny, who died there in 2006. "That was the gift Georges gave me. I remember the day it happened. He was doing oysters, wrapped in pancetta and sautéed, and asked me to taste them. 'Too salty,' I said.

He wanted to know what I would do. I told him, 'Crunchy pancetta, but keep the oysters raw.' He said, 'Massimo, your palate is going to take you far.' "

In 1989, a year after his lessons with Cogny ended, Bottura opened the Harley Club—named in honor of his new purple Springer—for the after parties that had quickly become much too big for an apartment above a trattoria. The club was next to his motorcycle mechanic's shop in Modena, a few blocks from the city's historic center. The neighbors complained, but it was otherwise a wild success. The best DJs and rock groups in Emilia-Romagna heard the buzz about this improbably cool place in fusty Modena and booked their nights. On Thursdays, well-known comedians came to hone their stand-up routines. Bottura himself was on a killing schedule, cooking lunch and dinner at Campazzo and then, as soon as the last dinner guest was gone, heading to the Harley to cook again. He says he had never been so happy.

Bottura met Lara Gilmore in New York, in the spring of 1993, on the day they both started working the two-to-midnight shift at Caffè di Nonna, a hitherto uninspired Italian restaurant in SoHo, with Gilbert behind the bar, dispensing wine and cappuccino, and Bottura in the kitchen, cooking. Bottura had fallen in love with America, despite (or possibly because of) an "amazingly weird" trip in 1991 to Arkansas, where he and a friend from home encountered a biker by the name of Ed at a Domino's Pizza, endured a session at Ed's favorite tattoo parlor (Bottura chose a winged buffalo head, which by now looks like a bunny with serrated ears), drank like "Harley men" (beer and Jack Daniel's), and were stiffed on an order of custom bikes (made from parts of a 1968 white-and-yellow Harley classic), which were nowhere in evidence six months later when they flew from Italy to Ed's mechanic in Daytona Beach to claim them. The experience did not discourage Bottura—not, at any rate, enough to keep him from moving to New York for six months to "taste its food, look at its art, listen to its music, and reignite my passion." He was turning thirty-one, and had decided to close the club, put Campazzo on the market, and use the money to open a different kind of restaurant. He was "looking for energy and inspiration to tell me what that restaurant would be." His one problem in New York was coffee. "I was desperate for good coffee" is how he describes the odyssey that took him from the middle reaches of Columbus Avenue, where he had rented a one-room walk-up, to SoHo, where, on his search for the perfect espresso, he noticed an illy coffee sign in the window of a restaurant at Grand and Mercer, walked in, ordered a double, and the next morning had a job.

Gilmore was twenty-four and living with a drummer in a sublet on the Lower East Side. Her parents lived in Bedford, in Westchester, where her father, Kenneth Gilmore, had just retired as the editor in chief of *Reader's Digest*. She had gone to Andover, studied art and theater at Hampshire College, with a year off, painting at the New York Studio School—after which she had interned at the Kitchen and then at Aperture, the photography-book publisher. When she met Bottura, she was at the Actors Studio and auditioning for parts. "Lara was my dream of America," Bottura says. She was smart, beautiful—with dark eyes and light-brown hair—and to his surprise, knew Italian, having spent summers studying art in Florence. Bottura, in his New York incarnation, was sporting a goatee, a pair of round blue John Lennon glasses, and a Kangol hat. Gilmore thought he looked "very cool," and a few months later invited him to a Wooster Group play. "I didn't understand a thing happening on that stage," he told me. "I slept through most of it. But Lara took over my education. She opened the world of the avant-garde to me." His Modena girlfriend, who had been living with him in New York, left him. Gilmore and her drummer parted. The party had moved to Bedford.

"They would arrive at my house late Saturday night, after the Nonna closed," Lara's mother, Janet Gilmore, told me. "My husband and I would wake up Sunday mornings and find all these wonderful young people sprawled out on the sofas, the chairs, the floors, the beds. In the summer, we always rented a big family house on Block Island. Later, when Max came, he took over the kitchen there. If we were out of wine, he would marinate the fish he'd caught in white tea. If there was nothing for lunch, he'd improvise and make everybody's children pizza. He was so full of energy, like an active volcano, flowing ideas."

Late that summer, Bottura flew home to sell Campazzo and start looking for the right place in Modena for a new restaurant. Gilmore surprised him there on his birthday, moved in with his old girlfriend—they had become friends—and the two women opened an American vintage-clothing store. "Max was happy," Gilmore says, "but I was thinking, Isn't it time we had a conversation?" Two weeks later, the French chef Alain Ducasse, who was in Modena tasting balsamic vinegars, sat down to lunch at Campazzo. When the service ended, he walked into the kitchen and invited Bottura to cook with him at the Hôtel de Paris in Monte Carlo. Bottura went, and Ducasse became his new mentor, the one with the exemplary kitchen battery and the scrupulous mise en place. Gilmore visited once. She and Max had their conversation. "I asked him what to expect," she told me. "He said something appalling like 'Gee, I don't know, there are so many beautiful women out there I haven't met.'" She left without saying another word.

Bottura couldn't believe she was gone. He left Monaco to find her. Two weeks later, he tracked her down in Bedford. They flew back to Modena together, and in October of 1994 Bottura rented a small building on a quiet cobblestoned street that had once been an inn named Osteria Francescana, after San Francesco, the neighborhood's thirteenth-century parish church. He restored it, opened in March, and in July, he and Gilmore married. The groom cooked dinner for two hundred guests. The bride did the flowers and the tables. Bottura was thrown into the swimming pool (the bad boys again). "And I had my revenge for that awful Ducasse moment," Gilmore said when she showed me a picture in which she digs into the wedding cake with both hands, scoops out a large chunk, and rubs it into her husband's face. "It felt great."

For the next three years, Gilmore and Bottura led fairly separate lives, with Lara at di Mitri's company, Sartoria, putting out an arts magazine called CUBE, and Max at the restaurant, cooking. "The first year, we were full," Bottura says. "Everyone I knew came, especially my friends who had helped paint it—they ate free." The second year, we were empty. I was ready to close." Bottura's father was not forthcoming, and in any event, Bottura wouldn't have asked for help. (By the time his father died, he had sold his business and transferred nearly all his property to his mistress; Bottura didn't receive a cent.) It was the Gilmores who saved Francescana. "Well, we believed in Max," Janet Gilmore told me. "We saw that he had a vision. It was a very modest sum we advanced, and we knew it wouldn't be used for a Ferrari."

Francescana survived. Bottura began to experiment more. "I was making 'foam' with a blender," he says. "It was more foamy than it was foam, but it was different. I thought my cuisine was very interesting." It must have been, because Francescana was getting a reputation abroad. It wasn't at the cutting edge of molecular gastronomy—Bottura didn't have money for that kind of equipment anyway—but he was creating small miracles of taste with the equipment he had. In 1999, Ferran Adrià came to Modena. He tasted Bottura's food—with the result that Bottura spent the next summer in Spain, working at elBulli. Gilmore, who at the time was pregnant with their second child, says, "Max didn't bring the fireworks back from Spain, just one siphon"—the secret of which turned out to be nothing more alchemical than two small cartridges—"but what he did bring back was a new way of thinking about Italian ingredients, at every station of the kitchen."

Bottura says the experience changed his life. "Right away, I realized that it wasn't just about technique. Before, I had made my foam in a blender, and the only difference now, with the siphon, was that I could make foam airier and better. What changed me was the message of freedom that Ferran gave me, the freedom to feel my own fire, to look inside myself and make my thoughts edible. There were three of us interning with him that summer. René Redzepi was there from Copenhagen—that's how we met—and there was this older hairy guy from Rome, who had a bar near the Trevi Fountain. René and I were moving from one station to another, doing cold savory, doing pastry with Ferran's brother, Albert, learning so much, and trading reflections on how to eat. But the guy from Rome, all he wanted to learn was how to make Parmesan ice cream. Ferran was pissed. He put him to work, hard labor: sixteen hours a day with his hands in ice water cleaning sardines, or peeling pine nuts. Late one night the three of us were standing looking at the sea. It was one o'clock, and we had been working nonstop since eight forty-five in the morning. We were so tired that we were almost asleep on our feet. The next morning, the Roman came in, strangely happy. He said, 'Guys, I'm back to Rome. Fuck you!' An hour later, he was gone."

Adrià was Bottura's last mentor, and Bottura thanked him in a new recipe for pasta e fagioli. The dish is layered. The bottom layer is a crème royale of foie gras, cooked with pork rind, in honor of Ducasse. The next three layers are for his grandmother, his mother, and Lidia; he calls them "compressed tradition." Lidia's layer is radicchio and pancetta; Luisa's is a cream of borlotti beans; and la nonna's, "where the pasta should be," is Parmesan rind cooked with more beans and sliced to a chewy crunch. The top layer is for Adrià, an air of rosemary so delicate and light that it's almost invisible; you know it's there by the burst of flavor on your tongue. When I asked Bottura how he did that, he said, "Water is truth"—distilled and vaporized.

I ate at Francescana three times (four, if you count the night I was waiting for Bottura—reading a book and having a glass of wine in one of its three small dining rooms—and a feast materialized at my table). The first time Bottura served me Sensations (thirteen dishes that take you on a trip through Italy, from the Alps to the boot and across the Strait of Messina to Sicily), along with a couple of dishes from his Classics tasting menu (recipes so popular that he can't retire them), which he thought I should try. Three hours later, I got up feeling as light as if I'd eaten no more than a simple pasta and a plain green salad—the reason, as Bottura put it, being that "my mediums are holy water, a little olive oil, and *basta!*" His crèmes royales have no cream. The foam in his Memory of a Mortadella Sandwich (which is not a sandwich) is whipped with distilled mortadella "water," concentrated in a Rotavapor. The cotechino in his ravioli loses its fat in the process of being steamed and chilled.

I learned some interesting things from Bottura. I learned that he made risotto broth the way his grandmother had made it, with Parmesan crusts, simmered in water until their flavor leached. The night I came home to Umbria, where I was spending the summer, I sliced the crust from some Parmesan in the fridge, tossed it into a pot of water, and served my husband the best risotto Milanese either of us had ever eaten. A week later, I made Bottura's home version of a splendid tagliatelle ragù that had appeared the night I was waiting for him at Francescana (its meat softened, as I'd suspected, in the restaurant's thermal circulator). I didn't have a circulator. I didn't even have any veal cheeks or veal tongue or beef tail or marrow, nor could I possibly have hoped to find them at my country co-op.

I was comforted by the fact that Bottura had said to relax, to use whatever was in the house, because the important thing was "no tomato" and the secret was not to grind the meat: wait until the ragù is cooked, and then do what the grandmothers did—chop it or tear it apart. Taking him at his word, I defrosted a couple of veal scallopini and a chunk of beef fillet, dusted them with a little flour, browned them in olive oil, and cooked them in leftover wine for the minute it took the liquid to evaporate; crisped some bits of fresh sausage and pancetta in a hot pan; made the soffrito—

onion, carrot, and celery stalk—and for marrow, chopped and browned a handful of lardo; put everything in a big pot with rosemary and bay leaves from the garden and left my ragù to simmer in beef broth for two hours, over heat so low that the flame on my burner kept going out. I ignored the homemade-tagliatelle part, opened a box of fettuccine, and while the pasta cooked, tore the meat with my fingers. Bottura was right. It made all the difference.

Bottura and Gilmore work together now. She is his house skeptic, his sounding board and critic, his editor, and often his ghostwriter, the one who translates those loud, bardic bursts of creativity into something focused and coherent, strips the stories he tells so well of any traces of what could be called the local operatic style, and shapes them for publication. He never neglects to say how much of the magic surrounding Francescana is hers. "She introduced me to a deep conceptual world, she gave me a critical point of view, a way of seeing," he says. "She told me, 'We are contemporary people. We don't have to cook in a nostalgic way.'"

Gilmore is rarely at the restaurant. If you see her there, it's usually in the afternoon, arranging fresh flowers, or at a table with friends, eating—never at the door, greeting customers, or notepad in hand, taking orders like the traditional Italian chef's wife. When we met, last summer, she was polishing Bottura's eponymous third book, which has the working title *Never Trust a Skinny Italian Chef*. The book, which comes out next year, is one of new gastronomy's art-of-the-chef tomes—photography, autobiography, history, food philosophy, and, usually reluctantly, recipes—that rarely make it from the coffee table to anybody's kitchen, the photographs being too beautiful to subject to stains and oil splotches, and the recipes too complex for anyone without, as in Bottura's case, a hanging eel skinner and deboner or the right syringe for injecting aged balsamic vinegar into a bar of almond-and-hazelnut-lacquered foie gras on a Popsicle stick. Gilmore was organizing its chapters, which have names like "Working-Class Heroes" (Bottura's tribute to the foods of Italy's traditional peasant larders) and "Image and Likeness" (for the transformative effect of art, music, literature, and travel on his cooking). She was also choosing the photographs of plated food from a stack that had just arrived from the Milan artist Carlo Benvenuto, whose picture *White Tablecloth and Glasses* was one of the first pieces that Bottura bought for what is now an impressive collection of contemporary art, much of it American, and is the first thing you see when you walk into Francescana. (Benvenuto describes himself as "the guy Max calls in the middle of the night, throws out some clue as to what he's thinking, and asks how an artist would interpret that, what kind of food would an artist eat, walking around with that thought.")

Gilmore enjoyed the work. The hard part was transcribing the recipes that Bottura dictated, on his feet and thinking rapidly out loud, without much patience for specifics. They were trying to adapt a few of his recipes for home kitchens, and the closest they came to arguing while I was with them involved a simple kitchen utensil. "Beat everything together," Bottura said toward the end of one recipe. "Beat with what?" Gilmore asked him. "Just say 'Beat,'" Bottura told her. "But with what? A spoon? A whisk? A mixer?" She needed to know that. "Will you just say 'Beat'!" Bottura shouted and left the room. A few minutes later, he was back, looking contrite. "A whisk," he whispered. Gilmore opened her laptop and wrote it down, trying not to smile.

Today most of Modena wants to eat at Francescana. The problem is getting a reservation. Bottura has brought the world there, and the world books tables in advance. He is now the city's most famous citizen, like Pavarotti before him. The mayor loves him. Strangers hail him on the street. The cook at his local pizzeria named a pizza for him. Bottura, for his part, has become the very visible face of Emilia-Romagna's foods. He blends and sells a line of aged balsamic vinegars. He appears at nearly every event having to do with agriculture, from the culatello celebration we went to at a villa near Parma (complete with haystack seats and a pen of sleek black piglets) to meetings at the two agriculture schools that he has persuaded the government to revive by adding cooking courses, "to give young farmers a sense of belonging to the community, a sense of the connection between what they do and what the rest of us eat." He works with dairy farmers to renew their herds of the area's vanishing Bianca Modenese cows, and with chicken farmers to switch their production to its heritage Romagnola hens. He makes videos about old eel fishermen on the Po who have lost their livelihood to riverine neglect, and, because of his fame, and the charm of the stories he tells (they're like Italian folktales), he has shamed the regional politicos into allocating large grants to restore fishing to the river.

Last year, when a hundred-mile swath of the province was devastated by weeks of earthquakes and more than three hundred thousand huge wheels of Parmesan were damaged, he offered his services to the Parmesan consortium, invented a recipe for risotto cacio e pepe, made with Parmigiano-Reggiano instead of Pecorino, and dispatched it to cyberspace. The recipe went viral. Thousands of people bought cheese and cooked it. Six months later, nearly a million kilos of Parmesan had been sold, with one euro per kilo of the proceeds going to earthquake victims.

It's hard to keep up with Bottura. Giuseppe Palmieri, his estimable sommelier of thirteen years, says, "Max met me one night (he was having dinner at the restaurant where I worked), called from his car on the way home, and invited me to follow him. I'm still running. I love him, and if you work with Max, to love him is essential." Bottura hires like that—fast, on instinct. His three head chefs, who take turns traveling with him, have been at Francescana since 2005: Yoji Tokuyoshi knocked at the door, "starving," on the last day of a two-week visa from Japan, was given a place to stay and a six-course feast that began with a leek-and-truffle tart and ended with a "hot-cold" zuppa inglese, and started working the next day; Davide di Fabio had just begun sending out applications when his phone rang and a voice said, "Hi, I'm Massimo. Come to my kitchen"; Taka Kondo arrived as a customer, ate lunch, and before he knew it, was at the stove, making sauces.

Bottura's staff worries that, at fifty-one, he has been racing through maturity the way he races through Modena on his new Ducati. Enrico Vignoli, who studied engineering and now manages Bottura's office (and his micro-vaporizer), says, "Max's frenetic energy is a curse. If he stops, he dies." His daughter, Alexa, who is seventeen, reads Greek and Latin, and seems to have inherited his palate—he calls her "the queen of passatelli"—says, "My dad is always challenging me. Do better. Do better. It's like he challenges the guys in the kitchen. It's stressful, but it stretches you. He stretches himself most of all." Bottura has had some sobering wake-up calls. His brother Andrea died of cancer at forty, and not long ago he lost Kenneth Gilmore, whom he calls "my other father," to Parkinson's disease. His son, Charlie, who is thirteen, was born with a rare genetic syndrome and requires special care. What drives Bottura today includes a strong desire to secure the future for his family.

Next January, and with trepidation, he is opening a traditional Italian restaurant, in Istanbul, for Oscar Farinetti's Eataly chain, and is sending Yoji Tokuyoshi to run it for him. He describes the project as "introducing Italy to Turkey with a reflection on my past—on osso buco with risotto, on veal with a little sage, a little lemon." He has been sifting through offers to endorse everything from refrigerators to shoes. Back in July, I drove with him to Milan for a photo shoot for Lavazza coffee, at the Ambrosiana Library. When I left at eleven to take a walk, he was arguing with a woman from the company who had just informed him that his shoot was going to include a model. When I came back, half an hour later, he was smiling over a big pot for the photographer, with three Leonardo codices behind them. And there was the model—dressed, from her bondage stilettos and sexy black sheath to her chaste white collar and owl-rimmed glasses, as a Helmut Newton librarian about to engage in some seriously painful discipline—mincing back and forth with a stack of books for him to drop into the pot to simmer. Bottura suggested calling the shoot "Cook the Books," but he was overruled.

Toward the end of my last week in Modena, I asked Bottura about his worst moment as a chef. He answered right away: spring 2009. He had his second Michelin star and had just jumped to thirteenth place on the "world's best restaurants" list. People were flocking to eat at Francescana—not to mention cook there. And a lot of Italian chefs were jealous, or jealous enough to pick up the phone when Canale 5—Silvio Berlusconi's version of Fox News—called with invitations to appear on its nightly show *Striscia la Notizia* ("The News Slithers"), where they accused him of poisoning Italy with his "chemical" cuisine. "Eight million people heard this," he told me. "Alexa came home from school crying—saying, 'Daddy, is it true you're poisoning people?' I said, 'Alexa, no way! They're talking about natural things, things like soy lecithin and agar, things you find in every kitchen—even Nonna Luisa's.'"

The truth is that everything that happens when you cook is chemistry. Anyone who has watched a steak char, or the broth in a risotto bubble away, or the sugar in a couple of drops of water turn to caramel, knows this. But in much of Italy words like "chemical" still mean magic, science is heresy, and if you add postmodern or molecular to that virtual pasta pot, they become political—codes for something foreign, dangerous, and worse (Berlusconi's favorite), Communist. They marked Bottura as a culinary terrorist, serving chemical weapons disguised as a new kind of Italian food to innocent Catholic people. Bottura is thin-skinned; I have heard him quote, detail by detail, a bad review in a restaurant guide from 2002. But *Striscia* was arguably much worse. "They had sent people to eat at Francescana who filmed my plates with hidden cameras," he said. "After *Striscia*, we had health inspectors there all day. Twice. I called my guys at the restaurant together, and I said, 'If you believe in what we're doing, stay. If you want to leave, you're free to go.' All of my guys stayed."

Bottura wasn't alone. The other important poisoners were Adrià and the British chef Heston Blumenthal. The difference was that the people where they lived laughed. People in Italy stoked a debate about "authenticity" and "the health of Italy" that went on for months, and of course was nightly television fodder. It probably didn't help that the well-known art critic and historian Achille Bonito Oliva, speaking in Bottura's defense, called him "the sixth artist of the transavanguardia." (The rest were painters like Francesco Clemente and Sandro Chia.) But Bottura was thrilled. He likes to repeat those words. The irony for him lay in his obvious devotion to Italy and its food—and to the demonstrable fact that whatever "chemistry" he had introduced and whatever tastes he had incorporated from abroad, Italy was vivid in every dish he served at Francescana.

Italians have made a myth of all those mothers and grandmothers happy in the kitchen. They have lived (profitably) with the country's revolutions in design—in fashion, in furniture, in everything from cars to espresso makers—but "the way we have always cooked" remains their last defense against modernity. Four years ago, Bottura, having reinvented the grandmothers, added a selection called Traditions to his tasting menus. "I did it for the locals," he told me. "It was an homage to the food they liked, a way to show that it could be improved, that it was okay to improve it."

Massimo Bottura's cookbook, *Never Trust a Skinny Italian Chef*, came out in 2014, and two years later his Osteria Francescana in Modena was voted the best restaurant in the world. Since then he has opened two permanent soup kitchens—first the Refettorio Ambrosiano at the

Milan Expo and then at the Olympic Village in Rio, using volunteer chefs to create healthy hot meals for the poor, using tons of food waste that would otherwise have rotted or been thrown away. The next refettorio will be in Queens.

PART III

Books, Essays, and Adventures

THE QUEST

❧

I read cookbooks. I am addicted to them. I keep a pile on the floor of my study in New York, knowing that if I manage to write a couple of decent pages I can treat myself to a $4.50 Chinese lunch special in the company of Richard Olney or Jasper White or Ruth Rogers and Rose Gray, thinking of all the succulent things I would cook for dinner if I didn't have to go back to work in the afternoon. I keep another pile on my bedside table, knowing that if I wake in the middle of the night I can pick one up and drift off into a soothing dream of Joël Robuchon's mashed potatoes or Claudia Roden's pumpkin dumplings or Marcella Hazan's red-and-green polenta torta, with a layer of onions, pine nuts, and ground pork between the spinach and the tomato. In my kitchen dreams, there are no crises. My books preclude them. The leg of lamb is never withering in the oven, waiting for a late guest. The chicken pot pie never collapses under the tug of its own crust. And I have sous-chefs—I think of them as husbands— standing quietly behind me, ready to shuck the oysters, stir the cornmeal, pit the olives, pound the pesto, grind the achiote, whisk the sabayon, or at a nod, fly to my side, like angels, bearing sieves and spoons and spatulas, Thai fish pastes and fresh banana leaves and rare Indonesian spices and thick French pots so well calibrated that the butter browns without turning into cinders. My own husband, who is an anthropologist, finds my passion for cookbooks peculiar, something on the order of my addiction to thrillers and crossword puzzles. When we were first married, he would leave a copy of the *Tractatus* on my pillow, hoping that Wittgenstein would cure me. But Wittgenstein, of course, kept me up worrying about reality. My cookbooks are more like the lipsticks I used to buy as a tenth grader in a Quaker school where not even hair ribbons or colored shoelaces were permitted. They promise to transform me.

Some fifteen hundred cookbooks are published in America each year, and Americans buy them by the millions—no one knows exactly how many. Barbara Haber, who was the curator of the Schlesinger Library on the History of Women in America at Harvard for thirty years—and in the process invented the history of women and food—once told me that the sales figures for cookbooks are one of the real mysteries of the publishing business, perhaps because small presses with a cookbook or two in their catalogues don't always report those figures separately. But one thing seems clear: the only people who can touch us, when it comes to writing and buying cookbooks, are the British, and they are only just beginning to catch up. Until a few years ago, not even the French were much interested in cookbooks. The great professional chefs inherited the old French classics, but a Parisian bride, say, could expect to find one good copy of Escoffier, from a godmother or an aunt, among the wedding presents (brides in the South got *La Cuisinière Provençale*, known in

France as "that yellow book" because of its shiny yellow cover). And for her kitchen, that amounted to the canon. Italians rarely admitted to buying cookbooks or, for that matter, to consulting the classics that were their—and their mothers' and grandmothers'—wedding presents. Those books had names like *Il Talismano della Felicità* or *La Scienza in Cucina e l'Arte di Mangiar Bene*, which was written in the 1890s, and includes, in its section on dolci, a recipe for a Roman pudding said to be as "seignorial" in its pleasures as the puddings from Turin or Florence. (I think of those books as Italian versions of the Christian-housewife marriage manuals that used to advise women to greet their husband at the door at night wearing a black lace teddy and carrying a shaker of cold martinis.)

But Americans have been buying cookbooks since the eighteenth century, and by now it seems as if half the people who ever read one eventually write their own. There are more new cookbooks in my local Barnes & Noble than there are new biographies or novels. There are 17,000 cookbooks listed on Amazon.com; 16,000 cookbooks in Barbara Haber's archives; and at least 10,000 in the splendid collection at the New York Academy of Medicine. More to the point, there are 12,000 titles (not counting the used books) in stock right now at my favorite bookstore—the small scholarly warren on the upper reaches of Lexington Avenue called Kitchen Arts & Letters. It has to be said that Kitchen Arts's cookbooks go back to a facsimile of a Mesopotamian cookbook in cuneiform on clay, and that Nach Waxman, who owns the store, is more likely to be reading up on the sixteenth-century Hindu shastra called the *Supa Shastra*, which "treats of the arts of cookery and the properties of food," than settling into an armchair with the new Batali. In fact, his perennial bestseller isn't even a cookbook; it is a book called *On Food and Cooking*, by Harold McGee, which involves a lot of biology and chemistry, and not a single recipe.

Every man I know who cooks seriously owns McGee, but I am less interested in how things work than in how they taste and whether they taste perfect. And never mind the theories that would have me the victim of some late-capitalist delusion that it's possible—indeed, my American birthright—to put a purchase on perfection, or even of some embarrassing religion of self-improvement. It is my theory that American women started reading cookbooks because they had left their mothers behind in Europe and never "received" the wisdom that is said to be passed spontaneously from generation to generation, like the gift of prophecy, in the family kitchen. My mother could not cook. She had no interest in cooking, making her about as helpful for my culinary purposes as a mother I would have had to cross the Atlantic to ask, say, if it was all right to substitute Port for Madeira in the sauce for ham on a bed of spinach. Nor could my grandmother cook. I set up housekeeping without benefit of one of those frayed looseleaf notebooks or little black file boxes filled with cards that grandmothers supposedly gave to mothers and mothers copied for their daughters. What's more, I had married a graduate student—which is to say that we had no money for the Cordon Bleu. I learned to cook from cookbooks.

I bought my first cookbook during a year and a half of fieldwork in Morocco, mainly because I needed a recipe for ras el hanout, the spice mixture I use in couscous, that wasn't like my friends' recipes—laced with hashish. (This was the late sixties.) My next cookbooks were the two volumes of *Mastering the Art of French Cooking*, written by Julia Child,

Simone Beck, and (for the first volume) Louisette Bertholle, but quickly known to the world of would-be sixties and seventies cooks as Julia. And the first important dinner I made from them was beef Wellington. This took me two and a half days, owing, among other things, to the fact that my kitchen was so small then that I had to scrub the hall floor in order to roll out the dough for the pain brioché after each rising. (There were two.) I made the beef Wellington for my husband in an effort to dazzle, or perhaps to convince him that despite all evidence to the contrary, I was a doting, domestic sort of person, a woman who squeezed oranges in the morning and wrote discreetly in the afternoon while the foie gras softened and the dough rose. (About twenty years later, he said, "I was just wondering, why don't we have beef Wellington anymore?")

It wasn't long before I persuaded my mother that I could not survive without the *Larousse Gastronomique* for Christmas, and talked my aunt Beatrice—who was just learning to cook herself and fed us chicken with rosemary and crème fraîche every Sunday—into handing over her new *Gourmet* cookbooks, two massive volumes in grainy brown bindings that turned out to be as grave and useless as a *Britannica* yearbook. I don't remember ever opening the *Larousse*, but I did make a sweet-potato-and-walnut casserole from one of those old *Gourmet*s and never consulted them again. My addiction to cookbooks properly began a few years later, when I made a pilgrimage to Vienne to eat at Fernand Point's restaurant, La Pyramide. Point was the greatest French chef of his generation, and his widow had kept the restaurant open in tribute to what he had always referred to, modestly, as "ma gastronomie." He had written one cookbook, and that of course became the title. The book, which I bought that night, was short, gracious, and taught me two extremely important things about cooking. The first was how much I didn't know—nap your lobster with a sauce à l'américaine, it said, but what was a sauce à l'américaine, and how did you make it, and was it really American? (Or was it Breton?) The second was not to be frightened of what I didn't know, because if making a sauce à l'américaine was so simple that, from the point of view of Fernand Point, it didn't even merit a recipe, then surely I could make one. Not exactly. It took me seven years and, of course, a cookbook. The book was *The Saucier's Apprentice*, the author was Raymond Sokolov, and the recipes were so satisfyingly complex that even Simone Beck, a notorious French snob when it came to Americans cooking, had been forced to admit, "This would be a useful book even in France." I made the sauce in two days of hard labor, preceded by a day of collecting veal and chicken bones from half a dozen butchers and calling neighbors who might be willing to drop by and kill an angry lobster with a chopping knife. But it was a sauce worthy of Fernand Point, and I had been determined to produce one. By now I own more than a hundred cookbooks, and I am determined one day to turn a few plump oysters and some tapioca poached in cream, buried in sabayon, and topped with caviar into a dish worthy of Thomas Keller, whose *French Laundry Cookbook* actually tells you how to do this if you happen to have six hands.

I feel a certain affinity for Thomas Keller, despite the fact that he is the best chef in America (his "oysters and pearls" and his parsnip soup are hands down the best things I have ever eaten) and has real sous-chefs, and I am merely one of the two best cooks—my friend Juliet Taylor is the other—on the fourth floor of a Central Park West apartment house. We share a weakness for lobster rolls, Reuben sandwiches, hamburger joints, and Fernand Point. "So genuine, so generous, so hospitable" is the way Keller describes *Ma Gastronomie*, which he first read at the age of twenty, working for a classical French chef at a Narragansett beach club whose members, if my childhood memories serve, usually sat down to dinner three sheets to the wind and unlikely to taste the difference between a homemade demiglace and a can of College Inn. I met Keller in May at his New York restaurant, Per Se, toward the beginning of what I am reluctant to call research. I wanted to talk to cooks who read cookbooks all the time, and to cooks who hated cookbooks, or claimed to. I had already discovered that a couple I know in Los Angeles read cookbooks aloud to each other in bed, as part of what could be called their amatory ritual; and that another couple, in Berlin, nearly divorced over an argument about which cookbooks to pack for a year in Cambridge; and that a friend in New York got headaches just by looking at the teaspoon measurements for thyme and garlic in a coq au vin. I had learned that some of my friends cooked only from recipes they had clipped from magazines and newspapers, and wouldn't touch cookbooks, and that others cooked only from hardcover books and wouldn't even touch a paperback, let alone a page torn from the Wednesday food supplement of the *Times*. Now I wanted to know if the people who cooked for a living and whose food I loved read cookbooks. Keller reads them as well as writes them. He had just bought three new cookbooks on the day we talked, and he keeps the classics in his restaurant kitchens, "for sous-chefs looking for inspiration." Not many of the great chefs admit to buying three cookbooks on their way to work, especially other chefs' cookbooks.

Keller began cooking mainly because his mother—who ran restaurants but whose culinary genes started and stopped at "spaghetti and onions tossed with cottage cheese"—handed him an apron when her cook got sick. (A few days later, I was pleased to learn that the mother of Judith Jones, the Knopf editor who had brought me Julia Child, Marcella Hazan, Madhur Jaffrey, and Irene Kuo, was no better at the stove than mine or Keller's; she owned one copy of *Fannie Farmer*, and had a bluestocking's horror of garlic.) Keller had never really read a cookbook before he drove to Narragansett, hoping to find a job that would float him through a season of America's Cup partying in Newport. He met his mentor, Roland Henin, on Narragansett Beach, and he says that what he admired most about Henin then was less his stock reductions than the fact that "he was six foot four, French, in his thirties, and had a great-looking girlfriend and his own jeep."

Jacques Lameloise, the Burgundian chef, tells a French provincial version of the same story. He started cooking only because his older brother, who was expected to take over the family restaurant and its three Michelin stars, got smart and went off to college and was soon running a business of seven hundred people. Jacques, however, hated school. What he liked was hanging around Chagny and playing soccer, and so, faute de mieux, the family consigned him to its famous kitchen. "At first I cooked like I played foot," he told me when I stopped at Lameloise, in June, to pick up his cookbook and treat myself to his poitrine de pigeonneau rôtie à l'émiettée de truffes, parmentier de béatilles—something I wouldn't dream of attempting myself, though of course I have the recipe. "There was no sacred flame. It was simply a matter of learning that if you're going to cook, it's better to love

cooking and to cook well. This idea of genius is overblown."
Lameloise rarely admits to reading cookbooks. Why would
I do that? was the look he gave me when I asked. "What I
adore is simple things," he said. "For lunch at home, I will
make a lobster salad, then frog's legs, sautéed the way my
father made them, then a côte de boeuf, then a crème caramel. Simple!"

When I saw Frank Stitt, the Birmingham restaurateur
who wrote the wonderful cookbook *Southern Table*, he told
me that his recipe for squab—my favorite, with grits and a
bourbon red-eye gravy—was "inspired" by eating at local
diners where tired truckers would stop for a wake-up meal
drenched in ham fat and coffee dregs. "It's the playful take-
offs I do best," he said when I told him how much I loved
that recipe, if not those last few minutes at the stove,
known in the trade as "the assembly," when everything is
supposed to come together. Stitt's first good cookbook
was Richard Olney's *Simple French Food*, and he bought it
while he was studying philosophy at Berkeley and volun-
teering in Alice Waters's kitchen at Chez Panisse. A few
days later, he bought his second Olney, and after that it
seemed quite reasonable to call his parents in Birmingham
to say he was quitting school in the second semester of his
senior year to cook. Eventually he went to Provence to work
with Olney, who was famously misogynistic and fired Stitt
after his girlfriend "started dropping in with a suitcase."
Today Stitt reads food histories and old cookbooks. *Charles-
ton Receipts*. The old Delmonico's cookbook. Compilations
of New Orleans recipes from the nineteenth century. Not
that he keeps them at his restaurants, though he will sometimes cut out a picture from one of Alain Ducasse's
cookbooks—"things like how to cut a lemon"—and show it

to his staff. "Remember, most of my staff have never eaten in a great restaurant," he told me. "So I'm more like a coach to them, or a team leader. I go to the market, see the food, and I click in. The dish comes to me, like a thought to an idiot savant, and I show them how to make it. I am totally unlike, say, Ferran Adrià at elBulli"—Adrià being the Spanish chef with the gadget that turns everything to foam, and whose own cookbook, which comes with a CD, will set you back $350, plus the price of a laptop for the kitchen.

I divide my cookbooks into two categories: the ones I'm not worried about getting dirty—about spilling sauce or spattering fat on the best pages—and the ones like Keller's, which I tend to think of as coffee-table books, not only because of their size and their gloss and their four-color illustrations but because they seem to have replaced art books as the status offerings you find casually stacked in front of the couch in Manhattan living rooms. I don't keep cookbooks in the living room, but I treat them cautiously, like a new silk shirt that hangs in the closet for a month before I give in, risk the inevitable spot, and actually put it on. It took me at least a month, more like two, to move Keller onto my kitchen counter, ready for its first splotch and for the careless company of the books I think of as my workhorse cookbooks—homely, tattered affairs with awkward drawings of hands folding ravioli and boning capons.

In Paris this summer, I visited the French-cookbook historians Mary and Philip Hyman, who were hard at work on an *Oxford Companion to French Food*, and learned that there was nothing new about coffee-table cookbooks. The Hymans had shown me a few of the sixteenth-century workhorses from their collection—recipes lifted from the court classics and sold by street peddlers as soon as there were customers literate enough to read them—and those books were plain little things, like penny dreadfuls, no bigger than four or five inches, that could be carried home in a pocket or a small purse. Then they showed me the books they called the "here's what's happening at the table where you'll never be allowed to sit" cookbooks—the ones that probably never saw a kitchen and lived in the libraries of the new rich, gold-tooled and bound in Moroccan leather, alongside the Virgil and the Voltaire and the folders of Veronese prints and the first editions of Diderot's encyclopedia. There was Taillevent's *Le Viandier*, written in the fourteenth century for Charles V and considered by the French to be the first major cookbook in Europe since Apicius; and La Varenne's seventeenth-century *Le Cuisinier François*, which according to the Hymans marked the beginning of modern cooking; and Vincent La Chapelle's eighteenth-century *Le Cuisinier Moderne*, in five volumes, written with a certain amount of borrowing from other chefs and filled with engravings of spectacular serving dishes and foldouts of table settings for a hundred guests.

There wasn't a woman among the writing royal chefs, which may be why none of their books looked used. But by the nineteenth century, when many of those chefs had been reduced to opening restaurants or cooking family dinners in the kitchens of the bourgeoisie, some of them looked to the future and took to writing profitable, practical cookbooks—cookbooks for housewives—although their shame was such that they often published under women's names. Hence the irresistible Tabitha Tickletooth, an "Englishwoman" whose book was published under the title *The Dinner Question, or How to Dine Well and Economically.* ("Economically" was not a word likely to burnish the reputation of a male chef de cuisine, moonlighting from a precarious job at an English castle.) The women who actually did write cookbooks then were not important chefs. I like to think of those women as more like me: women who read cookbooks and learned to cook that way. The Americans among them often simply collected recipes from European books and translated them, adding a bit of cautionary down-home commentary. I own a tiny edition of Miss Leslie's *Domestic French Cookery*, which was published in Philadelphia in 1832 and stayed in print for the next quarter century, and which I cherish for its recipe for oyster stuffing and its maidenly shudder at the voluptuary French practice of fattening geese.

Authentic American cooking, in all its regional variety and ethnic influences, really came into its own when women's groups—book clubs, church groups, suffrage groups, daughters-of-this-or-that groups—started putting together "community cookbooks." Community cookbooks are a purely American phenomenon. They began to appear during the Civil War, written by housewives, North and South, who contributed their best and hitherto secret recipes, published them locally on a shoestring, and sold them to raise money for the hometown troops. And they outlasted the war by at least a century, because for one thing, everyone covets a recipe so good that generations of your neighbor's family have refused to share it, and because for another, they carried the imprimatur of charity and were considered a respectable womanly pursuit—not likely to produce a bonneted Martha Stewart, abandoning hearth and husband for fame and fortune in the big city. (I like to think that Miss Leslie, whose name was Eliza Leslie, assumed her literary "Miss" in order to reassure her readers that she was not sitting at a desk, neglecting some man's hard-earned household.)

Community cookbooks still account for about half the American cookbooks published, though the ones you find in bookstores now are mainly regional or ethnic cookbooks, not charity books, and the women who put them together, and even the women who contribute recipes, usually want to make a few dollars for themselves. And why not? Charity aside, Mrs. Clarence W. Miles, who contributed "tomatoes brown" to the cookbook *Maryland's Way*—tomatoes brown are tomatoes stewed for hours in brown sugar, and they make a gooey treat—deserved to be collecting royalties.

It occurs to me now, sitting in a farmhouse in Umbria, surrounded by thirty new cookbooks recommended by my daughter—a screenwriter and fellow cookbook addict—and wondering when to start dinner, that there is a strong connection between women who write and women who cook and who love recipes. This is something anyone who has read *To the Lighthouse* knows. It is impossible to follow Mrs. Ramsay through her vegetable garden and into the kitchen for that long braising of the boeuf en daube and doubt that Virginia Woolf read cookbooks, though she was too crafty to say so. It is, however, possible to sit through twenty or thirty of Trollope's Sunday dinners and never know how the roast got to the table. Henry James never taught me how the Florentines made pasta, Proust never taught me how the cooks in Combray made madeleines, and I don't remember that Flaubert even mentioned what Emma Bovary made for the doctor on the maid's day off, let alone how she cooked it. I know how Hemingway grilled the fish he caught, but nothing about how he sauced them or what he did for dessert. I do, however, know what Rachel Samstat cooked in Nora Ephron's roman à clef *Heartburn*, because the novel is full of recipes, surely making it the only saga to emerge from Deep

Throat Washington whose revelations involve a stove. The list is long. Patrizia Chen's lovely Italian memoir *Rosemary and Bitter Oranges* sent me straight to the kitchen with recipes for Livornese fish soup and lemon tea cake. Even Frances Mayes—whose ubiquitous memoir *Under the Tuscan Sun* has two chapters of recipes—started cooking as a young poet, which may account for some of the poetic license in those recipes; I have yet to read a real Tuscan cookbook or enter a Tuscan kitchen where the olive oil was so often replaced by butter and heavy cream.

Maybe I am an anxious cook, like the woman who famously botched a recipe for "green onions" that she had taken so literally as to throw away all the white parts of her scallions. Not only do I keep buying cookbooks, I usually cook with three or four of them on my kitchen counter, open to different recipes for the same dish. But that is nothing compared with my psychoanalyst friend J. J. Dayle, who cooks from more than two hundred cookbooks, subscribes to (among other things) *Cook's Illustrated*, *Saveur*, and *The Rosengarten Report*, and stocks forty kinds of sea salt in his kitchen. J. J. Dayle is not his real name, but it's the name he is planning to use when he writes his cookbook, so that his patients won't associate their gentle shrink with the man who refers to a great therapy as "like a great dish—something you know, in the first five minutes, where it's going." J.J. once drove down the Mediterranean coast sampling the fish soup in every town, and he describes his own bouillabaisse by crying, "I am Samson Agonistes with my soups! God damn it, I have to wrestle them to the floor."

I was quite comforted by J.J.'s quest for the perfect fish soup. It reminded me of my quest for the perfect sauce à l'américaine. Usually I try to avoid quests. Like most cookbook addicts, I buy a book, read it, and if I'm lucky, find a couple of recipes that sound right, and forget the rest. I can always locate those recipes, because my books fall open to the pages I cook from most, and after ten or twenty years they even fall apart at those pages—which I find convenient. My old *Joy of Cooking* is split at the Bulgarian cucumber soup and again at the fruit preserves; my Craig Claiborne at the Yorkshire pudding; my *Silver Palate* at the salmon mousse; my "Julia" at the choucroute garnie; my Madhur Jaffrey at the shrimp curry with the best spices. This is something I wait for—the spine of my first River Café cookbook is just beginning to go, at the zucchini soup and at the penne alla carbonara—the way I wait for splotches. (My latest splotches are on the Circassian chicken in Roden's *Picnic* and on the boneless chicken breasts with lemon and capers in *Southern Table*.) But certain recipes elude me, and I go on quests. A few weeks ago, I almost went on a quest for calamari sauce. I had stopped at a small restaurant on the Lago di Garda called Nuovo Ponte, eaten a wonderfully inky pasta with calamari sauce, and asked the chef, Fiorenzo Andreoli, for the recipe. He wasn't at all surprised. He had once spent two years in San Francisco, working for an old friend with an Italian restaurant, and he said that the thing he remembered most—the one thing that always made him smile when he met an American—was how everyone in the kitchen besides himself and his friend "cooked with his nose in a cookbook." He told me that his calamari sauce "just came to me when I started cooking, because this is how calamari sauce is made on the Lago di Garda." A little aglio, a little olio, a little basilico, he said, when I asked if he couldn't be more precise.

I don't usually cook from books in Italy; my garden tells me what to eat and the butcher tells me what he's got, and I go from there. (Call it a vacation; to me, it's cold turkey.) But this summer I packed up my new cookbooks and sent them off—and was quite lucky to receive them, inasmuch as they disappeared for ten days and had to be dug out of the customs shed at the Milan airport, where they were held for commercial duty on the ground (roughly translated) that "no one person has that many cookbooks." I think it was also the exotic titles—*Lulu's Provençal Table, Couscous, Savoring the Spice Coast of India, The Key to Chinese Cooking, Hot Sour Salty Sweet*. Italians have no interest in foreign food, and as for their own food—a lot of my new books were Italian—it is considered an insult not only to your mother's kitchen but to your mother herself to suggest that anyone else's mother may have cooked better.

In the event, it was impossible to find any of the things I needed to savor the coast of India or make a proper couscous (for one thing, Umbrians do not eat turnips) or to unlock the door to Chinese cooking. In Italy, it is even impossible to sit down to a Provençal table. The one time I tried—I served braised rabbit on a bed of noodles to some Roman neighbors—they said, "Pasta is for before the meat," and scraped the noodles off their plates. (On their last visit, they arrived with a new black garbage pail as a house gift.) Italians today are arguably more broad-minded than they were in the fifteenth century, when a food-loving papal secretary named Bartolomeo Sacchi was thrown in jail by Pope Paul II as a "sectarian of Epicurus." (Under a nicer pope and using the pseudonym Platina, he produced the legendary cookbook *De Honesta Voluptate*.) But they do not willingly eat anybody else's food.

The quest I am on right now is for the perfect-au-feu—

which is to say, a pot-au-feu as good as the one I ate this Easter in New York at the house of my friend Susannna Lea. Susanna is an English vegetarian who never cooks, so it stands to reason that she did not have a great recipe for pot-au-feu at her fingertips, or indeed any interest at all in pot-au-feu. But she is also a Paris literary agent married to a French writer, and having moved to New York last fall, they wanted to serve something ur-French at Easter to their American friends. Susanna's pot-au-feu was in fact a kind of long-distance literary collaboration between three cookbooks she had bought for the occasion—Patricia Wells's *Bistro Cooking*, Anthony Bourdain's *Les Halles* Cookbook, and Guy Savoy's *Simple French Recipes for the Home Cook*—and one of her Paris clients, a novelist named Marc Levy whose first book, a romance involving a lonely architect and a young woman in a coma, sold so many millions of copies that he went out and bought a six-burner Gaggenau stove and grill and a couple of Gaggenau ovens and started "reflecting," as he told me himself a few months later, on reinventing pot-au-feu. His version takes at least two days, and he had walked Susanna through it by telephone, starting early on the morning of Good Friday and ending at noon on Sunday. It was very fussy. It involved not only hours of braising—not to mention steaming vegetables one by one over meat broth; poaching marrow bones wrapped in tinfoil; and making a vinaigrette with riced eggs and capers—but also a hunt for beef cheeks, which are not easy to come by if you live in New York, where the only people who sell them are wholesale butchers and you have to buy them in frozen blocks of thirty pounds. Susanna had to give up on beef cheeks, but even so, the work was worth it. I copied the recipe from the back of an old manuscript envelope by the phone on her kitchen counter. My quest began there.

I now own twenty-two recipes for pot-au-feu, if you count the Italian versions of bollito misto, and am halfway through the biography of a Paris film-world hostess whose own recipe was so renowned that the book is called *Le Pot-au-Feu de Mary Meerson.* What I am really doing is waiting for fall, because it is much too hot in Umbria to cook a pot-au-feu, and anyway, my butcher, who is hard put even to cut a chicken into four pieces, has never heard of anyone eating beef cheeks. He says it is "not Italian." (He means not within shouting distance of his own shop.) So I am concentrating on calamari, and if I succeed tonight I will not look at another cookbook until I am back in New York making "oysters and pearls." My husband has offered to do the cooking while I recover. He is (his word) an "instinctive" cook and claims that cookbooks are a waste of time. He goes to the fish store, picks what's fresh, and makes it in fifteen minutes. It may be that the best recipe I ever got came from M. Picot, the patron of Le Voltaire, my favorite Paris restaurant. I was there in June, and ordered a sole meunière that was so buttery and delicious that I asked M. Picot how he did it. He smiled wisely and said, "Madame, il faut choisir le poisson."

DOWN UNDER

NOVEMBER 2010

When I was a girl, lost in poetry, the only root on my mind was the mandrake root in John Donne—the one that made you pregnant. Roots were scary, the cautionary stuff of fairy tales and folklore. Consider the girl with the long gold hair whose parents promised her to a witch in exchange for a basket of roots that her mother craved. The roots turned out to be a kind of rampion—a radishy-tasting taproot—which Germans call Rapunzel and my summer neighbors in Umbria, who crave them, too, call *raponzolo*. And while no one can say for sure if the root was named for the girl or the girl for the root, most people would agree that there is something dangerous about a vegetable so alluring as to be worth its weight in daughters.

My family lived on a leafy, manicured street in Providence, Rhode Island—then a city of 200,000 people—but around the corner cows still grazed in a small pasture at Cole's Farm, the last farm left in what for three centuries had been a neighborhood of family farmsteads. Sometimes the cows broke fence and wandered across the street to nibble the grass under my mother's dogwoods, and if I led them home, I had the run of the Coles' kitchen garden, where I picked rhubarb in the spring and cadged tomatoes in September. But if their garden harbored root vegetables, waiting to be dug up and spend the winter in a root cellar, I never saw one.

Our own cellar was occupied by a freezer, a washing machine and a dryer, and a big, comfortable room with a couch, a dartboard, and a Ping-Pong table. Our vegetables arrived twice a week in the truck of a produce peddler known to the neighborhood as Louie—a man whose most exotic roots were carrots and potatoes. My mother's nightly admonitions to eat my vegetables referred almost entirely to Louie's iceberg lettuce and to the bowls of formerly crisp green things leached in the "boil, butter, and serve" style of New England kitchens of the 1950s. But she never said, "Eat your carrots." She never had to. I loved carrots long before I acknowledged that they might once have been gnarly things deep in the ground, and may even have shrieked with pain and deadly intentions, as mandrake roots were said to, when they were pulled from the darkness into God's fresh air. My father's outsize edition of the Judeo-Roman historian Flavius Josephus, which I used to consult for the illustrations, included the chilling advice that the only safe way to procure a mandrake was to tie your dog to it, walk away, and let the dog do the pulling, and suffer the consequences for you.

Childhood habits of mind can be hard to break. I cooked happily with all manner of root vegetables—carrots, potatoes, and also parsnips, rutabagas, turnips, and sweet potatoes—for more than thirty years before I thought of them as a family or even put the words "root" and "vegetable" together. This changed five years ago, when I flew to Stuttgart on assignment and stopped at the Staatsgalerie, where my friends Renata Stih and Frieder Schnock, conceptual artists from Berlin, had installed two round potato patches, ringed by gilded metal acanthus leaves, on the museum's front lawn. The patches referred to a lean winter early in the nineteenth century, when an art-loving local king named Wilhelm I of Württemberg petitioned the city to buy a choice collection of Northern Renaissance paintings (van der Weydens and Memlings among them), and was rebuffed by a politician who stood up in the city's parliament and cried, "Who needs art? We need potatoes!" The collection went to Munich instead. But in Stuttgart, nearly two centuries later, Württembergers were enjoying a feast of art and potatoes—an occasion commemorated, inside the museum, by photographs of potatoes that, according to Stih and Schnock, resembled the heads of many of their favorite artists. (I have two hanging in my front hall: a smooth, perky potato called *Dorothea Tanning* and a wizened spud called *Jerg Ratgeb*, for the turn-of-the-sixteenth-century German painter.)

Walking up to the museum, past the patches, I came upon two gardeners on their knees, and was reminded of a family of rooting boar that my husband and I had seen a few nights earlier, driving along an old post road through the forest between Berlin and Wannsee. It occurred to me then, in what Homer Simpson would describe as a "d'oh" moment, that the only difference between the Stuttgart gardeners and the Berlin boar, as rooting descriptions go, was that the gardeners' prehensile thumbs and small shovels put them at one remove from a snout and allowed them the use of the more delicate word "dig."

A few months later, I flew home to New York and made a slow braise of root vegetables and lamb shanks. The recipe came from Jasper White's *Cooking from New England,* a book that by the end of the nineties had transformed New England's kitchens. And it was full of delectable things: garlic, shallots, tomatoes, rosemary, oranges and lemons, and a medley of serious root vegetables, braised in olive oil and simmered in white wine and a veal stock reduced to a demiglace. I had made it for years, with a little cheating on the vegetables. That day I didn't cheat. I followed White's recipe to the letter and, for the first time, went eye to eye with a celery root, which I cubed to simmer along with the parsnips and the rutabagas—root vegetables that appear in my New York greengrocer's bins so improbably shiny and appealing as to belie their origins.

There is no way to disguise the origins of a celery root, or really even to think of it as a vegetable. It is a hideous-looking creature, and it takes work. You need a sharp knife and a strong arm and the composure to hack away at a warty and unyielding surface, made doubly unpleasant by writhing extrusions and matted, fibrous hair. The process left me bloody, but I got through it by reminding myself that the root leaping off my chopping board and onto the floor with every whack of my sharpest knife was the source of all the silky céleri rémoulade I ordered for lunch whenever I worked in Paris. The celeriac that emerged from my parings, much reduced in size and menace, was just as silky and just as good to eat. I cook with it all the time now. I can toss off the chestnut, apple, and celery-root soup in Daniel Boulud's *Café Boulud Cookbook* (if I buy the chestnuts cooked, peeled, and in a can) and have even produced a credible rémoulade; the moans and howls and alarming ouches that still punctuate my encounters with a chopping board and celeriac are usually sufficient to drive my husband from his study to finish the chopping for me. He is quiet, quick, and focused, chopping, but my cubes are neater.

Botanists distinguish root vegetables morphologically. There are true roots: taproots (celeriac is one, carrots are another) and storage roots (sweet potatoes). There are modified stem roots: corms (Chinese water chestnuts, say, or taro); rhizomes (arrowroot, ginger); tubers (as in yams and potatoes); and finally, slipping just under the botanical wire, bulbs (from garlics to onions, and everything in between). Forget those categories. For kitchen purposes, a root vegetable is any vegetable where all or most of the part you eat grows underground—or as the food writer and historian Anne Mendelson describes them, "a bunch of people who happen to be named Smith." But my old distinction between kind roots and cruel roots was not so fantastical, after all, although the difference has nothing to do with the way roots look but, as it turns out, with the amount of oxalic acid or hydrogen cyanide—prussic acid—they produce. (Rapunzel, despite the folklore, are quite benign. Mandrake roots, which, as Vladimir tells Estragon in *Waiting for Godot*, sprout from the ejaculations of hanged men, can kill you.) A plant of any kind can be toxic: try eating a rhubarb leaf and see what happens. There are, as the food scholar Frederick J. Simoons memorably put it in a book title, "plants of life" and "plants of death." I would add that they are often the same plant.

The manioc root—otherwise known as yuca or cassava— is one of the most important food staples and sources of carbohydrates in the world, and if you happen to be a Quechua, farming in the western lowlands of Peru, your manioc is sweet and harmless. But if you are an Amerindian in the tropical lowlands of the Amazon Basin, the root is bitter, and you have to soak or boil it for hours to extract its deadly

juices and make it safe to eat. Years ago, in Brazil, I bought a
six-foot-high basket called a tipiti—a long woven tube, really,
with a loop for a pole at each end. It was a lovely, mysterious,
and as it turns out, essential object, having been used by the
Canela Indians, a small rain-forest tribe isolated for centuries in the basin, for squeezing the cyanide out of shredded
manioc before pounding it into flour. And given that I am addicted to moqueca de camarão—a rich shrimp stew, traditionally cooked with urucum berries, chili, onions, lime
juice, coconut milk, and palm oil, dusted with toasted manioc flour, and served on rice—which I ate for the first time
that year at a restaurant in Ipanema, I keep my tipiti in the
living room as a memento mori of all the Canela who must
have died looking for ways to make their manioc roots safe
and tasty. I have never used the basket. Today you can buy
manioc flour, not to mention the tiny pearls of manioc starch
called tapioca, at any Brazilian grocery in New York.

But imagine New York in the mid-eighties, when I brought
my tipiti home. The only manioc you could find north of the
ethnic-food emporium called Kalustyan's in Murray Hill was
instant tapioca-pudding mix. And practically the only kinds
of potato besides "boiling" or "baking" on sale south of Fairway, on the Upper West Side, were in the bins of Dean &
DeLuca, a new grocery store in SoHo, where the man who
chose the market produce was an aspiring sculptor from the
Midwest named Lee Grimsbo, whose father happened to be
a horticulturist and potato researcher at the University of
Minnesota's North Central Experiment Station. Grimsbo
left Dean & DeLuca after seven years, but many New Yorkers still refer to "the Grimsbo years" as the city's root-
vegetable awakening. He began by raiding the produce stock

room at Fairway. Soon he had two assistants and was driving up to the Hunts Point wholesale market, in the South Bronx—the distribution center for most of the farm produce entering the city. "Seven circles of hell," he called it when I caught him at his apartment, about to leave for the art-supply store where he works now—a short, brisk walk from the best root-vegetable stand at the Greenmarket in Union Square. He found daikon radishes at Hunts Point, and Japanese turnips—"little snowy white things that look like radishes but taste like turnips"—and salsify and its cousin the long black-skinned white-fleshed root called scorzonera. He even discovered white carrots. His explanation: "Something's in them, but it's not beta-carotene." He started adding those carrots to the potatoes he used when he made vichyssoise for supper—which was fairly often, because by then he was also flying to San Francisco for Dean & DeLuca and coming home with five or six varieties of gourmet potatoes that most native New Yorkers had never even heard of. His best trip, he told me, was to the sprawling wholesale food market in Rungis, outside Paris, which had replaced the central market called Les Halles by the 1970s but still served coffee with cognac when the farmers arrived in their trucks at three or four in the morning. Rungis was a treasure trove of root vegetables. "I almost wept," Grimsbo says, talking about that visit. "It was heaven. Root heaven."

Late last spring, I asked Nach Waxman to give me a capsule history of root vegetables. Waxman is the anthropologist turned food scholar and bibliophile who owns the bookstore Kitchen Arts & Letters in New York. He carries the contents of twelve thousand volumes in his head—they run from facsimiles of ancient cuneiform recipe tablets to the

latest vegetarian offerings from the London chef Yotam
Ottolenghi—and the first thing he told me about root vegetables was that in twenty-seven years in the business, he has
come across "maybe half a dozen root-vegetable cookbooks,
at most." It saddened him, he said, to see a food that we eat
all the time so conspicuously unacknowledged.

Waxman is a lover of roots. He collects root-beer labels
and root-beer lore from the nineteenth century, when root
beer was the hot new patent medicine—a miracle elixir with
just enough alcohol in it to convince you that your dyspep-
sia or quinsy or "female complaint" was gone—and it was
brewed, as Waxman put it, in its purveyors' "caldrons, the
ingredients secret beyond belief." The labels said things like
"sassafras plus," and the recipe that Waxman cherishes most,
from *The Picayune's Creole Cook Book*, which was published
in 1901, calls for a half pint of root-beer extract to "ten gallons
of lukewarm filtered Mississippi River water." He told me
that by the middle of the 1890s root beer was such a huge
business that in one year alone, the Philadelphia pharmacist
Charles Hires sold enough of his own extract to produce
sixteen million gallons of elixir—a figure that translated to
about four glasses of Hires Root Beer for every man, woman,
and child in the United States.

Waxman's favorite root vegetable is horseradish. He grows
his own, in shallow pots in his living room on the Upper
West Side. He nourishes the roots with rinse water from the
dinner dishes and then, come spring, trims them and sets
them, with their leaves intact, in the middle of his family's
Seder platter—a bit of commemorative decoration he describes as "a little patch of sod with greens on top." Meanwhile, he grates and pickles the best horseradishes he can find
at the Korean markets on Upper Broadway, and produces the

bitter Passover herb known in Hebrew as maror—after which, he says, it's good for a year of roast beef and bloody marys. "I'm utterly persuaded that the real history of root vegetables is that there's no 'history,'" he told me. "I mean, they're simply part of the history of who we are. Primates dug for them. The hominids—chimps—even made tools to get them out. So it followed that when our brothers and sisters, out hunting and gathering, saw what the other animals were doing, they did it, too. They knew that the roots were there and they valued them. Aside from the fact that their great-great-great-ancestors ate them, they saw that root vegetables had a lot of advantages."

The obvious advantage is that we might not have survived without them. For millennia, root vegetables were the most dependable source of nourishment that most people on the planet had. For one thing, they kept better than any other plant form. For another, you could take what you needed and leave the rest underground. "Storage in situ," Waxman called it. "Plus, you could keep the competition away by not telling anybody where they were." The result was that thousands of years before anyone had even heard of a carbohydrate, people knew that they needed root vegetables. And for equally obvious reasons, those people were extremely wary of roots that were not their own—a fact of culinary history that I used to think of as early man's "beware of Greeks" syndrome. Then I discovered that it was modern man's syndrome, too, because the wariness persisted well into the sixteenth century, when newly discovered root vegetables filled the hold of every ship returning to Europe from the Americas.

By then the problem was less digestive than theological— born in large part of the coincidental arrival in Northern Europe of the potato and the Reformation. Anne Mendelson told me that to Europe's newly minted Protestant peasants, and to their cousins settling in North America, "God-fearing vegetables were seed vegetables, plants that 'looked up' to heaven, like wheat and barley—the kind of plants that were cultivated by Christians like them, by the sweat of their brows." She said that not only were potatoes regarded "with puzzlement and suspicion"—too many people having sampled "the wrong ends," as she describes the potato's poisonous leaves and berries—they were also known to Protestants as "the lazy root" (in the Massachusetts Bay Colony, it was the devil's root), because all you had to do to grow them was dig some holes, put in the pieces of spuds with eyes, cover them up, wait for five or six months, and dig them out and eat them. Potatoes, in short, were something Catholics did, and there was some truth in that, since the Spaniards had taken to root vegetables with huge enthusiasm. So, for that matter, had the Anglican upper classes. In 1610, the gentlemen farmers who wrote "A True Declaration of the Estate of the Colonie in Virginia" were happily eating potatoes—along with the parsnips, carrots, cucumbers, and turnips that they had brought from home—and praising them as food "which our gardens yeelded with little art and labour." (There is no evidence as to whether they burned in hell for that one phrase.) Still, as late as 1845, when the Great Potato Famine hit Ireland, preachers all over England and America were warning their impressionably evangelical flocks that the Irish had brought suffering upon themselves with slothful and ungodly agriculture.

A few of those preachers may still be around. Late last summer, when I was working my way through a plate of Ibérico charcuterie topped with sliced black radishes—taproots—at a small Paris restaurant called Le Basilic, a vegetarian from Norway at the next table, who had been eyeing my plate with a certain horrified interest (I'd assumed that it was the ham), announced that she never touched radishes. We started talking, and I asked what root vegetables she ate at home. She replied, "I don't eat things that hide in the ground. I eat only things that grow in the light, toward God." "Not even potatoes?" I asked her. "Especially not potatoes!" she said.

I have always had problems with potatoes, though admittedly this has nothing to do with God. I love potatoes when other people cook them, but my own repertoire is limited (unless you count sweet potatoes, an entirely different root family and, more to the point, nearly impossible to ruin). True, I can bake a potato, fill it with butter and sour cream, and plate it next to a rare, juicy porterhouse steak. And I am particularly fond of making rösti—a foolproof Swiss potato pancake whose ratio of butter to grated potatoes rivals Joël Robuchon's famously fattening purée de pommes de terre (a quarter pound of butter to each pound of potatoes). But for years the sight of a plain potato—so humble, unpromising, and eager for attention—filled me with kitchen jitters. I had mastered a lamb en croûte, a cloud of raspberry angel-food cake, and a seafood risotto of such mysteriously delicate flavor (the secret is fresh fennel) that even Italians asked for the recipe, long before I attempted the layers of the milky, cheesy, but hardly complicated casserole called gratin dauphinois. And even then it took years more for me to produce one in which the potatoes were neither rubbery nor mush.

That happened at last one summer after I discovered that my erstwhile Italian gardener had been planting huge potato crops in a field hidden behind my kitchen garden and selling them at a produce stand the minute I left for New York each fall. I demanded my potatoes and went to work under the tutelage of my friend Caroline Moorehead, an inspired potato cook who happened to be staying in our guest room at the time, working on a book. Caroline could slice the potatoes, chop the garlic, grate the Gruyère, and produce a gratin dauphinois in less time than it took me to open my Julia Child to "vegetables." Watching her, I got the recipe under control, and we even turned it more or less "Italian," with the addition of Parmesan and pancetta. But I have yet to attempt it for a dinner party. When I have friends for dinner and a sack of new potatoes in the kitchen, I take the smallest ones I can find, boil them in their skins until they're just tender, add them to a pot with olive oil and garlic—a lot of both—crush them slightly with a pair of forks, toss them for a minute over a low flame, add some parsley, and that's that. (Crushing is the essential part; it adds an illusion of creativity.) Better still, I turn off the voice of thrift in my head— my aunt Beatrice intoning "Waste not, want not" as she dried used paper towels in her oven on Sutton Place—and ignore my potatoes entirely. When that happens, I make a purée of turnips or carrots, with a sprinkle of cardamom, fresh savory or chervil, and an unhealthy amount of cream. Or the parsnip-and-walnut fritters in Jane Grigson's exemplary cookbook *Good Things*. I never have problems with roots like those.

The Romans loved roots; Apicius cooked a mash of parsnips, red wine, cumin, and rue. The Babylonians loved roots, too; Nebuchadnezzar is said to have grown carrots in his Hanging Gardens—that is, if you believe that there were hanging gardens in Babylon. In those days, most carrots were a skinny deep-purple forked wild root. (The others came from a faded mutant strain.) They stayed purple for a couple of thousand years, even though nobody really liked their carrots purple—perhaps because the color bled into soups and sauces, turning everything else in them purple, too. I gleaned this bit of culinary history from a conference paper called "The Carrot Purple," which the Washington food writer Joel Denker presented a few years back at an Oxford Symposium on vegetables. It wasn't the only paper on roots. There was one on a tuberous root from the Dutch Caribbean called a pomtajer (which tastes a little like taro, a little like potato, and is sweet enough to have been used in Holland in a clafoutis), and even one on potatoes in Ireland, which contained the surprising news that before the potato arrived, the Irish were eating more butter than anybody else in Europe, and close to the largest amount of meat and cheese. But Denker's paper got the most attention, because so few people had suspected that, botanically speaking, orange carrots were brand-new carrots—a seventeenth-century Dutch invention and a product of the same entrepreneurial enthusiasm and scattershot genetic engineering that produced the tulip bubble.

Denker, who at the time was also pursuing the history of horchata (a drink that Spaniards make from a root they call "earth almonds"), told me that food scholars were still debating whether orange carrots were a shrewd tribute to the House of Orange or the result of an equally shrewd assessment that a bright, sunny color like orange would make more people want to eat them. Everybody did. Today, some three hundred and fifty years later, purple "heritage" carrots are just starting to appear in the more expensive groceries of New York. New Yorkers, of course, eat root vegetables because they like them. Sandy Oliver, who writes books about American foodways, told me that living on an island in Maine, as she does, means eating roots, whether you like them or not. She said that the Europeans who first settled there had had to get up so early and work so hard—clearing woods, building stone walls, plowing fields, and raising livestock, not to mention children—that they needed the calories. Oliver put it this way: "Now, what vegetables were going to be truly satisfying to those folks, with their urgent, exhausted life? I'll tell you, it wasn't lettuce!"

Like most year-round Maine islanders, Oliver has fashioned a root cellar of her own. "You're not going to eat vegetables like that in the summer," she says. "You're going to make them last as long as you can, because in winter, if you eat any vegetables at all, it will have to be the root vegetables." She and her husband, who comes from a Cape Breton family and is no stranger to the culinary privations of North Atlantic winters (his mother cooked turnips every night from October to April), store onions, potatoes, beets, carrots, rutabagas, and turnips in their cellar, and she gave me instructions, should I ever happen to have a root cellar in Manhattan. "It's not a very beautiful arrangement," she said. "We use big white five-gallon plastic buckets. I heave them into the cellar and make cardboard tops so the air can circulate, and hang them up on a nail from the beams to mouseproof them. But our cellar is an ideal storage space—first of all, because it's a stone-walled cellar with a cool dirt floor, and second, because we don't have central heating."

I have neither of those advantages in New York, but my apartment building does have an unused roof, and I have heard that many similar buildings, not to mention corporations, are going fashionably green with rooftop vegetable gardens. Can root cellars be far behind? The board of my building has already made a foray into root status by

planting—depending on which doorman you ask—either potatoes or sweet potatoes around the trunks of twenty topi-
ary boxwoods that sit in an alley of stone urns on the way to
the front door. (Back in September I was told that this year,
when the potatoes were dug, every apartment would get
one.) Oliver goes "grocery shopping" in her cellar, the way I
go past those potted potatoes to my neighborhood farmers'
market. The only roots she doesn't cellar are the fresh spring
parsnips in her garden. She digs them up in April, and the
day they are out of the ground they go into a traditional parsnip stew—a "yummy ceremonial dish," she calls it—that you
make like chowder, but with parsnips instead of fish. She gave
me the recipe, more or less, which is to say, in the "some of
this, some of that, and a sprinkle of something else, if you
have it" style that I first encountered reading the great
English food writer Elizabeth David. I made Oliver's chowder
this fall, feeling my way through her bracingly vague instructions: "You cut up some bacon, sauté it, add some onion, some
parsnips, a few potatoes, and some water, followed by milk
and cream."

    The turnip is one of my favorite root vegetables. I braise
turnips in broth and ras el hanout whenever I make a couscous, for their smooth texture and curiously tangy sweetness.
I glaze them whenever I roast a duck. If I come across a lonely
turnip, in the vegetable bin of my fridge, I figure that it is
waiting there just for me and I slice it and eat it raw. But at
the top of my list are parsnips and sweet potatoes—never,
I've learned, to be confused with the ubiquitous and lowly
yams that appear at my corner store marked "sweet potatoes"
around Thanksgiving. Yams (orange-fleshed doppelgängers
from an entirely different root family) are native to West
Africa and Asia, sweet potatoes to South America. More to

the point, yams are usually a lot sweeter than the native American sweet potatoes that a proper Thanksgiving casserole or pudding calls for. For years, I had no idea.

In New York, September is the time when the sweet potatoes I buy are really sweet potatoes, and the fall parsnips are young and fresh. In Oxford, they are still at their best in November—which is where and when I first sampled my friend Patricia Williams's "chicken-with-both," as I have come to call the most satisfying comfort food I've eaten since warm rice pudding with maple syrup. It was a raw, drizzly day. I had been out since early morning, interviewing Anglican clerics on the subject of women bishops, and by the time I got back to Patricia's house, where I was staying that week, I would have settled for a sandwich or, this being England, a cold pasty. Instead, I was greeted by a medley of the most captivating smells, and naturally I wanted to know what was in the pot. "Oh, just a chicken and things," she said. "A simple one-pot dinner."

I asked her what things. The list was so long that I gave up listening and made her promise to e-mail the recipe, leaving nothing out, as soon as I got home. But peering into the pot, I could see at once that we shared an excellent culinary principle: only the foods you like and more than you need of the ones you like best—in Patricia's case (as in mine), sweet potatoes and parsnips, plus a good deal of cumin, coriander, garam masala, and turmeric—and it doesn't matter at all if the result is a little India, a little Morocco, a little South America, and a little England. There were chunks of oranges, carrots, red onions, and garlic in her pot, too, submerged and simmering slowly in chicken stock and white wine with the sweet potatoes and parsnips, the spices, and of course the chicken, a plump local bird that sat in the middle of them all, breast up, nearly submerged, and draped with rashers of streaky bacon. It was a memorable meal—made more so when Patricia sent the recipe and I read a disclaimer that, like Sandy Oliver's instructions for parsnip chowder, put her squarely in the Elizabeth David tradition of whatever works. "I know this is not a helpful thing to say," she wrote, "but I do vary the amounts and ingredients of this according to how I am feeling . . . this is *roughly* what I do."

This fall I cooked it for friends. I hadn't intended to. I had ordered a rabbit, which I was planning to stew in a parsley-root, carrot, and spiced Marsala sauce—a Berlin-doctored recipe from the kitchen of Renata Stih's Croatian grand-mother. Parsley root was the last vegetable on my list of "new" root vegetables to tackle, but it turned out that no green-grocer in my neighborhood sold parsley roots or had even heard of parsley roots—nor, in fact, had I until Renata cooked her grandmother's stew for me a few years earlier, in Ger-many. (All I can really tell you about parsley roots is that they are white, shaped like parsnips, taste a little like celeriac, and are reportedly easy to peel.) Then my butcher called to say that his rabbit supplier's truck had broken down.

It was noon by then, so I thought fast and—given the bas-ket of Yukon Golds that had sat accusingly on my kitchen counter since my last trip to the farmers' market—ordered a chicken to roast and serve with rösti. I also decided, by way of a symbolically local-produce gesture, to claim my allot-ted potato from my building's potted patches and add it to the potatoes I was about to grate. But when I asked the door-man if I could dig one up, he told me that I would have to wait for the "distribution." What's more, he said, the super had it from the gardener that the potatoes this year were in fact sweet potatoes, which have similar pale-green leaves.

The thought of sweet potatoes, potted or not, sent me off on some serious root shopping, and I started the peeling and chopping for a chicken-with-both. My spice shelf was somewhat depleted, but I heeded Patricia's second disclaimer: "I put in something like a tablespoon of each if I am using a big pot and a lot of liquid. But I also sometimes use a mixture or some or all of them, depending." The truth is, you can never miss with a pot full of root vegetables. And never mind that last week, when my building's potatoes were finally dug, they turned out to be neither true sweet potatoes nor even—as a Norwegian might put it—Irish potatoes, but a twisty sweetish cultivar called a Margarita. The leaves were the same, but bigger. "Ornamental," the gardener said.

THE FOOD AT OUR FEET

✁

NOVEMBER 2011

I spent the summer foraging, like an early hominid with clothes. It didn't matter that the first thing I learned about that daunting pastime of hunter-gatherers and visionary chefs was that nature's bounty is a thorny gift. Thorny, or if you prefer, spiny, prickly, buggy, sticky, slimy, muddy, and occasionally so toxic that one of the books I consulted for my summer forays carried a disclaimer absolving the publisher of responsibility should I happen to end up in the hospital or, worse, in the ground, moldering next to the *Amanita phalloides* that I'd mistaken for a porcini. I was not deterred. I had foraged as a child, although it has to be said that children don't think "forage" when they are out stripping raspberry bushes and blackberry brambles; they think about getting away before the ogre whose land they're plundering catches them and turns them into toads. I could even claim to have foraged as an adult, if you count a mild interest in plucking berries from the caper bushes that cling to the walls of Todi, the old hill town near the farmhouse in Umbria where my husband and I go in the summertime to write. Caper berries are like blackberries; they amount to forage only in that they are not *your* berries.

I wasn't the first throwback on the block. The pursuit of wild food has become so fashionable a subject in the past few years that one eater.com blogger called this the era of the "I Foraged with René Redzepi Piece." Redzepi is the chef of Noma in Copenhagen (otherwise known as the best restaurant in the world). More to the point, he is the acknowledged master scavenger of the Nordic coast. I'll admit it. I wanted to forage with Redzepi, too.

JUNE

I began working my way toward Denmark as soon as I arrived in Italy. I unpacked a carton of books with titles like *Nature's Garden* and *The Wild Table*. I bought new mud boots—six euros at my local hardware store—and enlisted a mentor in the person of John Paterson, an exuberant Cumbria-to-Umbria transplant of forty-seven, who looked at my boots and said, "What's wrong with sneakers?" Paterson is a countryman, or as he says, "not a reader." He is the kind of spontaneous forager who carries knives and old shopping bags and plastic buckets in the trunk of his car. (I carry epinephrine and bug repellent.) Being lanky and very tall, he can also leap over scraggly brush, which I, being small, cannot. Cumbrians are passionate about foraging—perhaps because, like their Scottish neighbors, they have learned to plumb the surface of a northern landscape not normally known for its largesse. What's more, they share their enthusiasm and their secret places, something the old farmers in my neighborhood, most of them crafty foragers, rarely do.

The peasants of Southern Europe do not easily admit to foraging—at least not to strangers. For centuries, foraged food was a sign of poverty, and they called it "famine food" or "animal food." The exception was truffles and porcini, which today command enough money for a good forager to be able to wait in line at the supermarket, buying stale food with the bourgeoisie. Some of my neighbors have truffle hounds penned in front of their chicken coops, ostensibly keeping foxes at bay. But they never ask to truffle in the woods by my pond when I'm around and, by local etiquette, they would have to offer some of the precious tubers they unearth to me. They wait until September, when I'm back in New York, and keep all my truffles for themselves.

Paterson got his start foraging—"Well, not actually foraging, more like scrumping"—as a schoolboy, combing the farms near his uncle's Cockermouth sawmill for the giant rutabagas, or swedes, as the English call them, that children in Northern Europe carve into jack-o'-lanterns at Halloween. He worked in his first kitchen at the age of twelve ("I washed the plates," he says. "I was too shy to wait on tables") and twenty-five years later arrived in Umbria, a chef. Today he has a Romanian wife, two children, and a thriving restaurant of his own—the Antica Osteria della Valle—in Todi, where people used to reserve their accolades for the meals that Grandmother made and, until they tasted his, had already driven away two "foreign" chefs, a Neapolitan and a Sicilian. In early June, I was finishing a plate of Paterson's excellent tagliarini with porcini when he emerged from the kitchen, pulled up a chair, and started talking about the mushrooms he had discovered foraging as a boy in a patch of woods near a bridge over the River Cocker. "All those beautiful mushrooms!" he kept saying. He told me about

green, orange, and red parrot mushrooms and parasol mushrooms and big cèpes called penny buns and bright, polka-
dotted fly agarics "so huge they could fill a room" and
mushrooms "like white fennels that grow from the shape of
saucers into gilled cups." He ate judiciously but admired
them all. In Italy, he started foraging for porcini to cook at
home. At the Osteria, where he has to use farmed porcini,
he roasts the mushrooms in pigeon juice, fills them with
spinach, and wraps them in pancetta. He said that foraging
had inspired his "bacon-and-eggs philosophy of little things
that work together."

A week later, we set out for some of his favorite foraging
spots. We stopped at the best roadside for gathering the tiny
leaves of wild mint known in Italy as mentuccia ("Fantastic
with lamb") and passed the supermarket at the edge of town,
where only the day before he'd been cutting wild asparagus
from a jumble of weeds and bushes behind the parking lot
("Great in risotto, but it looks like I took it all"). Then we
headed for the country. We tried the field where he usually
gets his wild fennel ("The flowers are lovely with ham and
pork") and found so much of that delicious weed that the
fronds, rippling across the field in a warm breeze, looked like
nature's copy of Christo's *Running Fence*. I was hoping to find
strioli, too. Strioli is a spicy wild herb that looks like long
leaves of tarragon. It grows in fields and pastures in late spring
and early summer and makes a delicious spaghetti sauce—
you take a few big handfuls of the herb, toss it into a sauté
pan with olive oil, garlic, and peperoncini, and in a minute
it's ready. But there was none in sight, so we turned onto a
quiet road that wound through fields of alfalfa and wheat and
soon-to-be-blooming sunflowers, and parked next to a shut-
tered and, by all evidence, long-abandoned farmhouse that

I had passed so often over the years that I thought of it as *my* house and dreamed of rescuing it.

Foraging places are like houses. Some speak to you, others you ignore. I wasn't surprised that the land around that tumbledown house spoke to Paterson. He jumped out of the car, peered over a thicket of roadside bush and sloe trees, and disappeared down a steep, very wet slope before I had even unbuckled my seat belt—after which he emerged, upright and waving, in an overgrown copse enclosed by a circle of trees. Cleared, the copse would have provided a shady garden for a farmer's family. To a forager, it was perfect: a natural rain trap, sheltered against the harsh sun, and virtually hidden from the road. Everywhere we turned, there were plants to gather. Even the wild asparagus, which usually hides from the sun in a profusion of other plants' leaves and stalks, was so plentiful that you couldn't miss it. We filled a shopping bag.

Wild asparagus has a tart, ravishing taste—what foragers call a wilderness taste—and a season so short as to be practically nonexistent. It's as different from farmed asparagus as a morel is from the boxed mushrooms at your corner store. I was ready to head back and start planning my risotto, but Paterson had spotted a patch of leafy scrub and pulled me toward it. He called it crespina. I had never heard of crespina, nor, after months of searching, have I found it in any Italian dictionary. It's the local word for spiny sow thistle—a peppery wild vegetable whose leaves taste a little like spinach and a lot like sorrel and, as I soon discovered, come with a spiky center rib sharp enough to etch a fine line down the palm of your hand if you've never handled them before. (I regard the small scar that I got that day as a forager's mark of initiation.) We added a respectable bunch of leaves to the shopping bag, and carried the overflow up to the car in our arms. An hour later, we were separating and trimming the morning's spoils in the tiny restaurant kitchen where, six days a week, Paterson cooks alone for fifty people ("Where would I put a sous-chef?" he asked, stepping on my foot) and comparing recipes for wild-asparagus risotto. Here is his "most beautiful way" to make it: Snap off the fibrous ends of the asparagus spears and crush them with the blade of a knife. Simmer them in water or a mild stock until the stock takes flavor. Strain the stock. Pour a cupful of white wine into rice that's been turned for a minute or two in hot olive oil and some minced onion. As soon as the wine boils down, start ladling in the stock. Keep ladling and stirring until the rice is practically al dente and the last ladle of stock is in the pan. Now fold in the asparagus heads. In no time, all you will need to do is grate the Parmesan and serve.

I made Paterson's risotto for dinner that night, along with a roast chicken and the crespina leaves, sautéed for a minute, like baby spinach, in olive oil and a sprinkling of red pepper flakes; the spines wilted into a tasty crunch. The next night, I chopped my fronds of wild fennel and used them to stuff a pork roast. When I called Paterson to say how good everything was, he told me, "Free food! There's nothing like it. It always tastes better."

JULY

I went to Oxford to give a talk and got to forage in Pinsley Wood, an ancient forest near a village called Church Hanborough. You can find the original wood in the Domesday Book—the "unalterable" tax survey of English and Welsh

landholdings compiled for William the Conqueror in 1086—
and indeed, the only altered thing about that venerable preserve is that now it's a lot smaller and everyone can enjoy it. In
spring, when the ground is covered with bluebells, foragers
complain about having to contend with lovers, nestled in
sheets of sweet-smelling flowers, watching the clouds go by.
By July, the bluebells are gone and there are no distractions.

My friends Paul Levy and Elisabeth Luard—writers, foragers, and distinguished foodies (a word that, for better or
for worse, Levy is said to have coined)—walked me through
Pinsley Wood, armed with bags and baskets. Our plan was
to make a big lunch with everything edible we found. Levy,
a polymath whose books range from a biography of G. E.
Moore during his Cambridge Apostle years to a whirlwind
sampler of culinary erudition called *Out to Lunch*, has been
the food and wine editor of *The Observer*, an arts correspondent of *The Wall Street Journal*, and for the past eight years, the
co-chair of the Oxford Symposium on Food & Cookery. Luard, who began foraging as a botanical illustrator and traveler
and whose many cookbooks include the estimable *European
Peasant Cookery*—a virtual travelogue of foraged and home-
grown food—is the symposium's executive director.

My husband and I were staying with Levy and his wife
(and self-described "arts wallah"), Penelope Marcus, at their
Oxfordshire farmhouse, a rambling place, almost as old as
Pinsley Wood, with a kitchen garden so vast and various in
its offerings that I was tempted to ditch my mud boots, which
had turned out to be plastic-coated cardboard (six euros do
not a Welly make), and do my foraging there, in flip-flops,
with a pair of gardening shears and a glass of iced tea waiting on the kitchen table. In fact, we began our foraging at
the Levys' barn wall, in a small overgrown patch of wild

plants where fresh stinging nettles were sprouting like weeds (which is what they are) among the blackberry brambles and the dandelion greens and the malva, a purple flower often used in melokhia, the delectable Egyptian soup that I once ate in London but alas have never been able to replicate. We were going to use the nettles for an English broad-bean-and-vegetable soup that afternoon.

We drove to the wood in Luard's old Mazda—past a village allotment with wild oats growing outside the fence and, inside, what looked to be a bumper crop of opium poppies—and listened to Luard and Levy talk about forest plants. Don't bother with "dead nettles"—stingless flowering perennials that had no relation to *our* nettles and, to Luard's mind, were not worth eating. Don't overdo the elderberry unless you need a laxative. Beware of plants with pretty berries or pretty names, and especially of plants with both—which in the Hanboroughs means to remember that the flowering plant called lords-and-ladies, with its juicy scarlet berries and sultry folded hood, was more accurately known to generations of poisoners as the deadly Arum "kill your neighbor." "A stinky plant," Levy said. I wrote it all down.

Levy considers himself a "basic local forager," which is to say that he doesn't drive three or four hours to the sea for his samphire and sea aster; he buys them at Waitrose. He loves wild garlic, and knows that sheets of bluebells in Pinsley Wood mean that wild garlic is growing near them. He "scrabbles" for the food he likes at home. "I can identify Jack-by-the-hedge for salad," he told me. "And I can do sloes, brambles, elderberries. Anyone who lives in the countryside here can. Elisabeth is the more advanced forager, but I do know a little about truffles and wild mushrooms. Three of us once identified more than twenty mushroom species near here in Blenheim Park, and I'm quite good at chanterelles and porcini." Levy thinks of Pinsley Wood as his neighborhood mushroom habitat. It has an old canopy of oak and ash, but it also has birch trees (chanterelles grow in their shade), and most of the interior is beech (porcini and truffles). Summer truffles are pretty much what you find in England. They are black outside and pale grayish brown inside, and you have to dig twice as many as you think you'll need to match anything like the deep flavor of France's black winter truffles in a sauce périgueux.

Levy and my husband, who had been planning to spend a quiet day at the Ashmolean Museum but was shamed out of it, immediately started following a network of burrowed tunnels—a "sett"—that led them into the wood near clusters of beech trees with small circular swells of dark moist earth beneath them. Swells like those are a sign of truffles, pushing up the ground. Setts mean that badgers probably got to the truffles first. A good truffle dog, like a hungry badger, can sniff its way to a truffle by following the scent of the spores left in its own feces from as long as a year before. The difference between a truffle dog and a badger—or for that matter, the boar that trample my sage and rosemary bushes in their rush to my pond to root and drink—is that your dog doesn't go truffling without you, and when it digs a truffle, as many Italian truffle dogs are trained to do, it mouths it gently and gives it to you intact. Or relatively intact. A few weeks later, when Paterson and I went truffling with an obliging local carabiniere named Bruno Craba and his two truffle terrier mutts, one of the dogs surrendered so helplessly to the intoxicating smell of semen that the tubers emit—known to foodies as the truffle umami—that she swallowed half a truffle the size of a tennis ball before presenting the rest of it to her master.

Being without benefit of a truffle dog, let alone a small spade or even a soup spoon for loosening the soil, Luard and I abandoned the men, who by then were up to their wrists in dirt, hoping to find a truffle that the badgers had missed. They didn't. With lunch on our minds, we went in search of more accessible food. "Pea plants—plants of the Leguminosae family—are mostly what you get here," Luard told me. You have to look for seed-bearing pods and single flowers with four "free" petals (which *The New Oxford Book of Food Plants* describes as "a large upper standard, 2 lateral wings, and a boat-shaped keel"). I left the identifying to her. Luard, who has foraged in twenty countries, has been called a walking encyclopedia of wild food. She was.

While we gathered pea plants, I learned that British countrywomen thicken their jellies with rose hips, crabapples, and the red fruit clusters of rowan bushes, which people in Wales, where Luard lives, plant by their doors to keep witches away. (There's a recipe for "hedgerow jelly" in her new book, *A Cook's Year in a Welsh Farmhouse*.) Passing what looked to be the remains of a wild ground orchid, I was instructed in the virtues of "saloop," a drink made from the powder of crushed orchid roots which for centuries was the pick-me-up of London's chimney sweeps—"the Ovaltine and Horlicks of its time, with more protein than a fillet de boeuf," Luard said. (You can read about saloop in Charles Lamb, who hated it.) We walked past silverweed plants ("edible but not tasty") and meadowsweet ("the underscent of vanilla in the flowers makes a nice tea") and the leaf shoots of young wild carrots ("skinny as can be means good in soup") and teasel ("not for eating; for combing wool") and butterwort, which, like fig-tree sap in Italy, is a vegetable rennet, "good for making cheese." Along the way, I discovered that farm children in southern Spain, where Luard lived with her family in the seventies, ate wild-fennel fronds and "sucked on the lemony stalks" of wood sorrel on their way to school, by way of a second breakfast. "Children are a huge source of information about wild food," she told me. "In Spain, I would ask the village women to tell me what they foraged and how they cooked it, and they wouldn't answer—they were embarrassed by foraging, like your Italian neighbors—but their children knew. My children would walk to school with them, eating the leaves and berries that their friends plucked from the roadside verges. They learned from their friends, and I learned from them. I've lived in a lot of places, and I've discovered that a basic knowledge of food runs all the way through Europe. The people I lived with cooked, of necessity, what they grew, and the wild food they added—the changing taste of leaves and nuts, for instance—was what gave interest to those few things. It taught me that when you grow enough to eat, you begin to make it taste good. That's not a frippery, it's a need."

Luard, as senior forager, was in charge of lunch. Levy was in charge of fetching claret from the cellar and coaxing heat from an unpredictable Aga. Marcus was in charge of setting the garden table, while my husband, who had volunteered for the washing up, wandered around, keeping up the conversation. And I was stationed at the sink, sorting and cleaning a good deal of Pinsley Wood. It was an unfortunate assignment, since I tend to daydream at kitchen sinks, and the better the dream, the slower my pace. Sorting our forage took me half an hour. Cleaning it took twice as long, given the number of bugs clinging to every leaf and flower, not to mention Luard's instructions, among them separating the yarrow leaves we'd collected from any lingering trace of petals, and scraping the hairy calyxes from the bottom of borage flowers. We sat down to lunch at four-thirty. The soup was a vegetarian feast of flageolets with (among other good, wild things) nettles, yarrow leaves, and dandelions, and the salad a spicy mix of wild sorrel, dandelions, onion flowers, and borage flowers. But my favorite dish was the scrambled eggs that Luard made with an unseemly amount of farm butter and double cream and a mountain of fresh sorrel. The sorrel for that came from the Levys' kitchen garden, a few feet from the back door.

AUGUST

I wasn't really ready for René Redzepi. I had tried to prepare. I downloaded the stories that appeared last spring, when a jury of chefs and food writers, convened by the British magazine *Restaurant*, named Noma the world's best restaurant for the second year. I studied the photographs in Redzepi's cookbook, memorized the names in his glossary of plants and seaweeds, and even tried to improvise on some of his simpler recipes with my local produce—impossible in a part of Italy where the collective culinary imagination is so literally "local" that broccoli is considered a foreign food and oregano is dismissed as "something the Tuscans eat." But I flew to Denmark anyway, planning to make a trial foraging run in western Zealand with my Danish friend (and fellow journalist) Merete Baird, who spends her summers in a farmhouse overlooking Nexelo Bay—a trove of wilderness food—and likes to eat at Lammefjordens Spisehus, a restaurant run by one of Redzepi's disciples. My foraging trial ended before it began, in a freezing downpour, and as for the restaurant, the storm had left me so hungry that at dinner that night, I passed up the young chef's lovely deconstructed tomato-and-wild-herb soup and his leafy Noma-inspired offerings and ordered two fat Danish sausages and a bowl of warm potato salad.

I met Redzepi at Noma early the following afternoon. He arrived on an old bike, chained it outside the restaurant— a converted warehouse on a quay where trading ships once unloaded fish and skins from Iceland, Greenland, and the Faroe Islands—and tried to ignore the tourists who were milling about, their cameras ready, hoping for a shot of arguably the most famous Dane since Hamlet. In fact, most of them barely glanced at the small young man with floppy brown hair, in jeans, battered sneakers, and an untucked wrinkled shirt, locking up his bike. Redzepi is thirty-three, with a wife and two small children, but he can look like a student who slept in his clothes and is now running late for an exam. The most flamboyant thing about him may be the short beard he frequently grows—and just as frequently sheds. It is hard to imagine him in a white toque or a bloody apron or, à la Mario Batali, in baggy Bermudas and orange crocs. When I left for my hotel that day, one of the tourists stopped me: "That kid you were with earlier? His bike's still here."

Redzepi opened Noma in 2003, at the age of twenty-five, backed by the gastronomical entrepreneur of a successful catering service and bakery chain (whose bread he doesn't serve) and a "new Danish" furniture designer (whose advice he routinely rejects). He was nine years out of culinary school, during which time he had apprenticed at one of Copenhagen's best restaurants, endured a long *stage* in the unhappy kitchen of a testy three-star Montpelier chef, and made molecular magic in Catalonia with Ferran Adrià. "I ate a meal at elBulli," as he tells the story, "and as soon as I finished I went up to Adrià and asked for a job. He said, 'Write me a letter.' So I did. A few weeks later, I found a job offer, complete with contract, in the mail." He stayed at elBulli for a season, and in the course of it, landed his next job—at Thomas Keller's French Laundry in Napa Valley, where he was much taken with the emphasis on local food. He was back in Copenhagen, cooking "Scandinavian French" at the restaurant Kong Hans Kælder, when the call came asking if he'd like a restaurant of his own.

"We had the idea: let's use local products here," he told me the next morning. We were at a diner, making a caffeine stop on the way to a beach at Dragør—a town on the Øresund strait, about twenty minutes from the outskirts of Copenhagen—where he likes to forage. "But I was very unhappy at first. Why? Because we were taking recipes from other cultures, serving essentially the same 'Scandinavian French' food, and just because you're using local produce to make that food doesn't mean you're making a food of your own culture. I started asking myself, 'What is a region? What is the sum of the people we are, the culture we are? What does it taste like? What does it look like on a plate? It was a very complex thing for us—the idea of finding a new flavor that was 'ours.' "

Five years later, having raised the money for a research foundation called the Nordic Food Lab, he hired an American chef named Lars Williams—who arrived with a degree in English literature, a passion for food chemistry, and fifteen lines of the first book of *Paradise Lost* tattooed on his right arm—to preside over a test kitchen on a houseboat across the quay from Noma and begin to "release the umami of Nordic cuisine." At the moment, they were looking for some in a liquid concentrate of dried peas, which I had sampled on the houseboat the day before. (It was quite good, with the rich bite of a soy concentrate and, at the same time, a kind of pea-plant sweetness.) And they planned to look for more in a brew of buckwheat and fatty fish, starting with herring or mackerel. They were also "looking into" Nordic insects, Redzepi said. (On a trip to Australia last year, he had eaten white larvae that he swore tasted "exactly like fresh almonds.") "The question for us is how to keep that free-sprouting spirit here," he told me. "In gastronomical terms, we're not at the finish line, but we know what it could be."

A Nordic cuisine, for Redzepi, begins with harvesting the vast resources of a particular north—running west from Finland through Scandinavia and across the North Atlantic to the Faroes, Iceland, and Greenland—and using them to evoke and, in the end, reimagine and refine a common culture of rye grains, fish, fermentation, salt, and smoke, inherited from farmers and fishermen with hardscrabble lives and a dour Protestant certainty that those lives wouldn't be getting easier. Redzepi's mother, who worked as a cleaner in Copenhagen and loves to eat at Noma, comes from that Protestant Danish stock. But the cook in the family was his father, a mosque-going Muslim from Macedonia who drove a taxi. "When I was growing up, we'd leave the city for long periods in the summer and stay in the village where my father was born," Redzepi told me. "It was a two-car village, and cooking for him was kill the chicken, milk the cow. When he eats at Noma, he says, 'Well, it's not exactly up my alley.' His alley is homey stews, homey peasant flavors, and lots of beans." When I told Redzepi about a blog I'd read, calling him a Nordic supremacist, he laughed and said, "Look at my family. My father's a Muslim immigrant. My wife, Nadine, is Jewish. She was born in Portugal and has family in France and England. She studied languages. If the supremacists took over, we'd be out of here."

Redzepi remembers foraging for berries as a boy in Macedonia. He loves berries. Gooseberries, blueberries, blackberries, lingonberries—any berries in season, at hand, and edible. He carries a bowl of berries around Noma's kitchens, popping them into his mouth while he checks a prep station or talks to a chef or even stands at the front stove, finishing a sauce. He also loves mushrooms. There are some two hundred edible varieties in Denmark's woods, and he is working his way through them all. But at the moment, the food he cherishes is cabbage—from the big pale cabbages that he slices and steams at home, in a knob of butter and a half inch of his wife's leftover tea, to the tiny, vividly green-leaved wild cabbages that sit in pots, basking in ultraviolet light, on a steel counter in the middle of one of Noma's upstairs kitchens, waiting for the day they're ready to be wrapped with their stems around a sliver of pike perch and served to customers on a beautiful stoneware plate, between a green verbena sauce and a butter-and-fish-bone foam. One of the first things he told me, the day we met, was that for him the great surprise of foraging in Nordic Europe was to see cabbages sprouting from rotting seaweed on the beach, and to realize how much food value the sea, the sand, and the nutrients released in the rotting process could produce.

It's an experience that he wants the people on his staff to share before they so much as plate a salad or get near a stove. Seventy people work at Noma. They come from as many as

sixteen countries—English is their lingua franca—and it's safe
to say that every one of them has made a foraging trip to the
sea or the woods (or both) with Redzepi. "There's a new guy
from the Bronx working here," he told me when he was introducing the kitchen staff. "I want to take him to the forest.
I want to see the first time he gets down on his knees and
tastes something. The transformation begins there."

The beach near Dragør was bleak, but it was bursting
with plants I had never dreamed of eating, and I was ready
for transformation. "Foraging is treasure hunting," Redzepi
said; you'll find the treasure if you believe it's there. It's also
homework. When he began foraging in Denmark, he stayed
up nights reading. He bought botany books and field guides—
the most useful being an old Swedish army survival book
that had taught soldiers how to live for a year in the wilderness on the food they found. At first he foraged with the army
manual in his pocket. Then he began consulting other foragers. Now he forages with his iPhone. "I know a great professional forager in Sweden," he told me. "If I see something
I can't identify, I call her up, point my iPhone, send her a
picture of what I'm seeing, and ask her what it is. At the beginning, I had a little problem with beach thistles—my
throat started to close from those weird flowers—but that
was the worst time. I got connected to the sea and soil, and
now they're an integral part of me. I experience the world
through food."

We started out in a thicket of rose-hip bushes at the edge
of the beach, where wild grass was just beginning to give way
to sand and seaweed. The berries looked like tiny cherry tomatoes, and there were so many of them that after a few
minutes we left Redzepi's "scavenger sous-chef," who had
driven us out that morning—Redzepi hates driving—with

the job of locating a couple of large garbage bags and filling them. (I ate some of the berries that night at dinner, in a warm salad of lovage, zucchini, wild herbs, and an egg fried at the table in a hot skillet.) Redzepi pickles his rose-hip flowers in apple vinegar and preserves the berries as a thick purée, for winter dishes. The picking season is short in Denmark, and he has to start gathering in mid-spring in order to dry, smoke, pickle, or otherwise preserve—and in the process, concentrate the flavor of—a lot of the vegetables and fruits that his customers will be eating in December. He told me about beach dandelions with nippy little bouquets of flowers and tiny roots that taste "like a mix of fresh hazelnuts and roasted almonds," and about the vanilla taste of wild parsnip flowers, and about pink beach-pea flowers that taste like mushrooms. By the time we got to the water, we were sampling most of what we found. We ate a handful of short beach grass that tasted like oysters, and a cluster of spicy lilac beach-mustard flowers that made the mustard in jars seem tame. We snacked on enormous leaves of sea lettuce that came floating by. They tasted to me like mild, salty cabbage that had just been scooped out of a pot-au-feu. Redzepi serves a lot of sea lettuce at Noma. He breaks it down in a saporoso of white-wine vinegar (to make it "easier to eat," he says, and also to bring out its "ocean flavor") and wraps it around cod roe or oysters, or folds it into a poached-egg-and-radish stew.

The weather in Denmark begins to turn in August. It was too late in the summer for sea goosefoot, or for the bladder wrack that bobs near the shore like bloated peas and, according to Redzepi, is just as sweet. The scurvy grass we discovered was too old to eat. But the beach horseradish that day was perfect. It had the "big hint of wasabi taste" that Redzepi likes so much that he serves the leaves folded over sea urchin. By late morning, with the wind cutting through our sweaters, we were still roaming the beach and tasting. "It's amazing, all these foods in the sand," Redzepi said. "One of my most important moments foraging—important in the history of Noma—was on a windblown beach like this one. I saw this blade of grass, this chive-looking thing, growing out of some rotting seaweed. I put it in my mouth. It had a nice snap, with the saltiness of samphire. And a familiar taste. A taste from somewhere else. I thought, 'Wait a minute, it's cilantro!' This isn't Mexico, it's Denmark, and I've found cilantro in the sand." That night, his customers ate beach cilantro, which turned out to be sea arrow grass. "We put it in everything that was savory." There are never fewer than five or six foraged foods on Noma's menu, and usually many more. By now Redzepi depends on professional foragers to supply most of them, but he and his staff still provide the rest. Earlier this year they gathered 220 pounds of wild roses for pickling, and 150 pounds of wild ramps. By November, there were 3,300 pounds of foraged fruits and vegetables stored at Noma, ready for winter. Redzepi told me that 90 percent of everything he serves is farmed, fished, raised, or foraged within sixty miles of the restaurant, and while most chefs with serious reputations to maintain will occasionally cheat on "local," even the Jacobins of the sustainable-food world acknowledge that Redzepi never does. Early this fall, a food critic from *The Guardian* noted that the millionaires flying their private jets to eat at restaurants like Noma leave a carbon footprint far more damaging than the one Redzepi is trying to erase at home. Redzepi thinks about that, too, but not much. He says that the point of Noma isn't to feed the rich—that in his best possible world, Noma would be free, because "there is nothing worse than charging people for conviviality." The point is to demonstrate how good cooking with regional food anywhere in the world can be. His mission is to spread the word.

On an average Saturday night, Noma's waiting list runs to a thousand people. The restaurant seats forty-four, and Redzepi has no real desire to expand. His partners keep asking, "When will the money begin to flow?" He ignores them. For now, at least, whatever profit Noma makes (last year, 3 percent) goes right back into the business of sourcing and preparing the kinds of food that people who *do* get reservations come to the restaurant to eat. Most of the cultivated crops he uses (including his favorite carrots, which are left in the ground for a year after they mature, and develop a dense texture and an almost meaty taste) are grown for him on a polycultural farm, an hour away in northwest Zealand, that he helped transform. His butter and milk (including the buttermilk with which he turns a warm seaweed-oil vegetable salad dressing into an instantly addictive sauce) come from a nearby Zealand biodynamic farm. Everything else he serves is "Nordic" by anyone's definition. His sea urchin comes from a transplanted Scot who dives for it off the Norwegian coast. The buckwheat in Noma's bread comes from a small island off the coast of Sweden; I downed a loaf of it, watching Redzepi cook lunch. The red seaweed I ate that night at dinner—in a mysteriously satisfying dish involving dried scallops, toasted grains, watercress purée, beechnuts, mussel juice, and squid ink—came from a forager in Iceland. The langoustine that was served on a black rock (next to three tiny but eminently edible "rocks" made from an emulsion of oysters and kelp, dusted with crisped rye and seaweed crumbs) came from a fisherman in the

Faroe Islands. Even Redzepi's wine list, which used to be largely French, now includes wines from a vineyard that Noma owns on Lilleø, a small island off Denmark's North Sea coast. I tried an unfiltered moss-colored white from the vineyard. It looked murky in the glass, but I wish I had ordered more.

Redzepi was fifteen and finishing the ninth grade when his homeroom teacher pronounced him "ineligible" for secondary school and said that he would be streamed out of the academic system and into trade school and an apprenticeship. He chose a culinary school only because a classmate named Michael Skotbo was going there. Their first assignment was to find a recipe, cook it, and make it look appetizing on a plate. "You were supposed to dig into your memories of food, of taste, and my most vivid was from Macedonia," Redzepi told me. "It was my father's barnyard chicken—the drippings over the rice, the spices, the cashew sauce. I think that my first adult moment was cooking that spicy chicken. My second was when we found a wonderful cup and put the rice in it—with the chicken, sliced, next to it on the plate. I had an idea. I said to Michael, 'No, don't put the sauce on the meat. Put the sauce *between* the chicken and the rice. We came in second in flavor and first in presentation." I asked him who won first in flavor. "A butcher," he said. "He made ham salad. It was terrific."

The boy who couldn't get into high school now speaks four or five languages, publishes in *The Guardian* and *The New York Times*, speaks at Yale, and last year disarmed an audience of literati at the New York Public Library with a philosophical riff on the beauty of aged-in-the-ground carrots, not to mention a biochemical acumen that many scientists and most other chefs would envy. To call Redzepi an autodidact is beside the point. His friends say he was born bored. "Wherever I go, I read, I look, I taste, I discover, I learn," he told me. "I'm cooking with mosses now. They were a whole new discovery for me. I tasted them for the first time foraging in Iceland. Some mosses are hideous, but those were so lush and green I had to try them. I took some back to Reykjavík, where a guy I'd met ground it for me and put it into cookies. Then I went to Greenland. For years, in Greenland, it looked like the reindeer were eating snow. Now we know they were eating moss. We call it reindeer moss. The moss on trees and bushes has a mushroomy taste—we deep-fry it, like potato chips—but the ones growing from the ground, up near caves, they have the taste and texture of noodles."

I ate reindeer moss at Noma, deep-fried, spiced with cèpes, and deliciously crisp. It was the third of twenty-three appetizers and tasting dishes I ate that night, the first being a hay parfait—a long infusion of cream and toasted hay, into which yarrow, nasturtium, chamomile jelly, egg, and sorrel and chamomile juice were then blended. The second arrived in a flowerpot, filled with malted, roasted rye crumbs and holding shoots of raw wild vegetables, a tiny poached mousse of snail nestling in a flower, and a flatbread "branch" that was spiced with powdered oak shoots, birch, and juniper. I wish I could describe the taste of those eloquent, complex combinations, but the truth is that, like most of the dishes I tried at Noma, they tasted like everything in them and, at the same time, like nothing I had ever eaten. Four hours later, I had filled a notebook with the names of wild foods. Redzepi collected me at my table, and we sat for a while outside, on a bench near the houseboat, looking at the water and talking. I didn't tell him that I'd passed on the little live shrimp, wriggling alone on a bed of crushed ice in a Mason jar, that had been presented to me between the rose-hip berries and the caramelized sweetbreads, plated with chanterelles and a grilled salad purée composed of spinach, wild herbs (pre-wilted in butter and herb tea), Swiss chard, celery, ground elder, Spanish chervil, chickweed, and goosefoot, and served with a morel-and-juniper-wood broth. I told him that it was the best meal I had ever eaten, and it was.

SEPTEMBER

I came home to New York, checked my mail, and discovered that I had missed the Vassar Club's "foraging tour" of Central Park. It was quite a relief. I ordered a steak from Citarella (by phone, for delivery), walked to the Friday greenmarket on Ninety-Seventh Street for corn and toma-toes, and was home in fifteen minutes. I spun some salad from my corner store, unpacked my suitcase, plugged in my laptop, uncorked the wine, and cooked dinner. It seemed too easy. Surveying my kitchen, I wondered where I would put a Thermomix or a foam siphon with backup cartridges or a Pacojet or a vacuum-pack machine or even a No. 40 ice-cream scoop—all of which I would need just to produce the carrot sorbet and buttermilk-foam dessert that I'd been eyeing in Redzepi's cookbook. Where would Redzepi put them in his own kitchen? Then I remembered the sliced cabbage, steamed with a knob of butter in a half inch of leftover tea.

Noma isn't about home cooking or even foraging. The res-taurant is a showcase, a virtuoso reminder that only a small fraction of the planet's bounty gets to anyone's dinner table, and that most of it is just as good as what does get there—even better, if it's cooked with patience, imagination, and a little hot-cold chemistry. It seems to me now that if you take John Paterson's enthusiasm for little wild things that work together and Elisabeth Luard's conviction that those things express the timeless "taste-good" ingenuity of peasant cooking, the message is not so different from Redzepi's. Most of us eat only what we know. It's time to put on our boots (or our sneakers) and look around.

John Paterson is now the head chef/patron of a new restaurant in Todi, the Cantina del Mercataccio, where he commands a state-of-the-art kitchen and serves a clientele that arrives from all over Europe to eat his food.

Paul Levy is reviewing music, art, and theater in England while working on two new food books, including a long-awaited riposte to culinary political correctness called *Why We Don't Eat Worms*.

René Redzepi has since published a three-volume "work in progress"—one volume of Noma recipes, one of his journals, and one of the snapshots he has taken over the Noma years. Early this year (2017), he closed Noma, and by fall will be reopening what he calls "an urban farm," complete with biosphere, research lab, and seasonally staggered restaurant in the middle of Copenhagen.

A FORK OF ONE'S OWN

MARCH 2013

Your kitchen may not be the mirror of your soul, but it can produce a pretty accurate image of where you've landed on the timeline of domesticity. Take a tour through it. You'll find not only the food you eat (and don't), and the objects with which you preserve, prepare, cook, and serve it, but very likely, tucked away in the back of the highest cupboard, the abandoned paraphernalia of your mother's or grandmother's kitchen life. And if you think seriously about this, you will eventually start asking questions about what went on in other people's kitchens during the twenty thousand years since one smart *Homo sapiens* picked up a rock and ground a handful of wild barley into something he could eat—the most obvious being which came first, the food that sits in your fridge today or the technology, from the rock to the thermal immersion circulator, that got it there and puts it on the table.

I have two kitchens. For most of the year, I cook in an Upper West Side apartment in Manhattan. It was designed in the 1890s and is probably best described as a landlord's misguided attempt to lure tenants with horizontal evocations of the upstairs-downstairs life. The "public" rooms, meant to be seen and admired, were large and well proportioned. The "private" rooms, out of sight off a long back hall, were for the most part awkward and cramped, and perhaps the lowliest room on this totem pole of domestic status was the kitchen, where your cook, emerging each morning through the door of a tiny bedroom—in my apartment, it opened between the icebox and the sink—was expected to spend her waking hours. At the time, no one except presumably the cook cared that the kitchen was hot and smelly, or that she had to climb onto a chair or a stepladder to fetch the plates, or crouch on the floor to reach into the cabinets where she kept her pots and pans. Nobody else went in. There was room for only one chair, perhaps to discourage the cook from sitting down with the cook next door for a conversation, and no room at all for a table where she could have a meal.

This was the kitchen where I unpacked my own pots and pans in the 1970s—a mirror of somebody else's moment in the saga of domestic life. There would be no company while I cooked, no friends sharing a glass of wine while they chopped the tomatoes for my pasta. Supper would mean the dining room, which remains so stately and demanding that I feel obliged to break out the family silver and the wedding china and lay the plates for a four-course dinner even when I'm eating alone with my husband. (Perhaps I should make a seating plan or put out place cards.) More to the point, there was no way to expand my kitchen to accommodate my own moment—not, at any rate, without paying a plumber to move a century's worth of corroding pipes. The cook's bedroom became the cubbyhole study where I shut the door and write.

I am consoled, however, by my other kitchen. It is the

"please come in" room of the Umbrian farmhouse where I work and cook in the summer—a much more satisfying image of the way I like to live. It was once occupied by cows. And while the house itself could be considered small—given the size of the peasant families that used to live together in four or five rooms above the animals—the *stalla* where I built my kitchen was enormous. The first things I bought for it, after the stove, the fridge, and the dishwasher went in, were an eleven-foot table, ten chairs, a pair of outsize armchairs, and an old stone Burgundian fireplace wide enough for a side of pork. The shelves for my pots and pans are low and open. The front door, which leads directly into the room, is also open. My friends are welcome to my wine, my knives, and my chopping boards.

I was at the table in that companionable kitchen, sniffing the basil and garlic I had just ground to a mash for pesto in a mortar and pestle, when I started leafing through a book called *Consider the Fork: A History of How We Cook and Eat*, by the British writer Bee Wilson, and came upon a chapter called "Grind." It was full of intriguing scholarship on the false starts and transformative successes without which there would have been no pesto on my table, but what intrigued me most was a paragraph on the subject of Wilson's mortar and pestle. It was black granite from Thailand, and much nicer to use, she said, than the white china variety, which set her teeth on edge "like chalk on a blackboard." I felt a wave of kitchen kinship, first because the mortar and pestle I'd been using was also stone, but also because she called hers "an entirely superfluous piece of technology," given the far easier ways of grinding and crushing available to her in a twenty-first-century Cambridge kitchen. She used it infrequently, she said, only when she had the time and the

urge for the "bit of kitchen aromatherapy" that pounding together a pesto brings. In fact she was terrified of getting it
down from the shelf where, presumably, she kept her only-
infrequently equipment. It was that heavy. She worried about
dropping it on her foot. I imagined it stored at the same
treacherous top-of-the-stepladder level where my paella pan,
my mother's biggest turkey platter, and my New York mortar and pestle, which is also stone and weighs nearly ten
pounds, have been gathering dust for years. In New York, I
share her terror. In Italy, where I can slide my mortar and
pestle across a counter, brace myself, and move it to the table,
the only thing that ever fell on my foot was a full bottle of
Barolo, and it was three in the morning, I had been working
late, and the fig tart in the oven was about to burn.

Bee Wilson describes herself as a food writer. That's half
the story. She is also a historian, with a Cambridge doctorate in early French utopian socialism, followed by a research
fellowship in the history of ideas, and she has carved out an
estimable place for herself in an energetically brainy family:
her father is the biographer A. N. Wilson; her mother is the
Oxford Shakespeare scholar Katherine Duncan-Jones; her
sister, Emily, is a University of Pennsylvania classicist; and
her husband, David Runciman, is a Cambridge political sci-
entist. Wilson, who is thirty-nine, took on the history of
food. She wrote a book about bees and honey, *The Hive*—
from which I learned, among other interesting things, that
Paleolithic man not only hunted for honeycombs but prized
them enough to paint them on his cave walls, along with the
elusive animals he hoped to catch, and that early Christians
regarded the flame of a beeswax candle as a symbol of divine
light—and then a book called *Swindled*, with the ominous

subtitle *The Dark History of Food Fraud, from Poisoned Candy to Counterfeit Coffee*. (It was.) Both were stylish exercises in what could be called painless pedagogy. They had the kind of narrative charm that could carry large chunks of scholarship; weave them together; sprinkle them with asides, experiences, suppositions, and strong opinions; and entertain you.

Wilson remains engaging, and nowhere as deeply or as smoothly as in *Consider the Fork*, where the information she has to juggle is at once gastronomic, cultural, economic, and scientific. She will begin a disquisition on, say, why the Polynesians, who had been making clay cooking pots for a thousand years, abandoned clay when they arrived at the Marquesas Islands from Tonga and Samoa, a hundred or so years into the Christian era, and went back to cooking on hot stones; she will lead you through the various explanations, the most recent (and "radical," she says) being that the yams, taro, breadfruit, and sweet potatoes that were their staples simply cooked better, or more efficiently, on hot stones than in pots; and then she will remind you that, short of ignorance, nostalgia, or necessity, there is always something mysterious about our choices and attachments, and do it with a homely story from her own kitchen—something recognizable.

"I used to have a large mug with all the American presidents on it," this one began. Wilson's husband had brought it home from a trip to Washington, and she had commandeered it for her morning tea, watching the presidents' faces fade year by year until she couldn't tell them apart, and loving it all the more for that, she said, because morning tea "didn't taste the same from any other mug." She never shared it. In fact, if she caught other people drinking from it she "felt they were walking on my grave." We've all had a mug like Wilson's. Mine broke—so, somewhat to her relief, did hers—and I am still searching for one that will make my morning coffee taste the same. Attachments like that—part habit, part fetishism, part association—are human for being inexplicable. It may be that the Polynesians, having just crossed two thousand miles of the Pacific in a fleet of outrigger canoes, were too exhausted to think about making cooking pots. Maybe they simply dug for roots near the beach where they had landed and, being quite hungry, heated the closest stones and ate their dinner. It would have tasted "better," like coffee or tea in the mug your husband gave you when you've dragged yourself out of bed and need some caffeine to start the day.

The technological leaps that interest Wilson—from spear and skewer to fork and knife, say, or from pounding stone and grinding mill to food processor—are, obviously, inextricable from the cultural leaps that moved *Homo sapiens* from cave to settlement, which is to say to agriculture and, with it, to concepts of wealth, property, and the kitchen. For millennia, a man's prosperity could be judged by who cooked his meals. If he was poor, his wife and daughters cooked, and the process was so arduous that—added to the burden of years of childbearing and child-rearing—those women barely saw daylight unless they were out gathering food to cook or drawing water for the cleaning up. If the man of the house was rich, a host of slaves or servants did the work. You could calculate how many servants were in his kitchen by the "refinement" of the food he served. "Refined," as Wilson notes, originally meant "processed," and gastronomically speaking still does. Think of the centuries of sorbets, fruit jellies, root purées, silky soups, and sauces that preceded the technology that gave us the super-refined flour and sugar that we now piously reject.

It took days, even weeks, and in all likelihood a hundred kitchen slaves to prepare the food for a proper Roman feast—that is, an orgy in every sense, given the tastes and textures and sights and smells that a rich man served up for his guests before the sex began. A few years ago, I heard the Oxford classicist Oswyn Murray deliver a witty conference lecture called "From the Greek Symposium to the Roman Orgy," in which he said that what really distinguished those entertainments from each other (besides a thousand years) was the presence of food and women at the latter. The symposia, of course, were orgies, too, and women did show up at some of them, at the end of the evening, to amuse the guests. But the ones that Murray described could be called Socratic. They were male, high-minded, and quite select. The wise men reclined, talked philosophy, and consumed a sickening amount of watered wine. The ephebes stood and poured, listening respectfully to the conversation until they were summoned to a couch. Rome, on the other hand, was not noted for Socratic party talk. A Roman orgy was a rave, and the fact that women not only served but were also guests, and that, once a couple of mad emperors took to throwing orgies, some of those guests were wives (summoned for what could be called command performances) suggests that, like wives today, they didn't think you could have a good party without providing dinner. Orgies became a potlatch of kitchen labor. You didn't see the kitchen; it was underground, or you might say, "downstairs." But you knew it was huge by the food you did see.

This winter I got out an "ancient Rome" recipe book—an old Christmas present that I'd never opened—and tried to approximate the work involved in mincing and seasoning the flesh of just one small bird, returning it to a simulacrum made entirely of pastry, and then pounding the appropriate herbs, vegetables, and spices to dust for a "refined" sauce. Notwithstanding a fair amount of cheating—I used frozen puff pastry—it took a day. (The crust broke.) I thought about how many cooks it would take to prepare a hundred birds for that one dish, and how many roaring fires and hand-turned spits to produce a hundred other dishes. A slave kitchen was an alarming place, where a whoosh of flame was likely to roast the cook along with the meat, and the heat and smoke were infernal. (In fact, most kitchens remained infernal until gas ranges and enclosed gas ovens evolved, by trial and error, in Europe in the nineteenth century.)

And Rome was a high point. The food technology of Northern Europe took centuries to catch up, though an argument could be made that the tribes of Germania that Tacitus found so barbarous owed their eventual triumph to the stamina that came from cooking outdoors in a cold climate and keeping their lungs intact. And when the technology did catch up (the strainers and colanders, the elaborately pronged spits), most of Europe was still eating like those old Romans—mainly with its hands.

The spoon is ancient, although, like the fork, the teaspoon and tablespoon we use today are not. Flatware began as fashion, in the 1600s, after centuries in which you came to your host's table with your own knife—by Wilson's account, a double-edged dagger—hanging from your belt. You carried it for protection, getting there, and again at dinner, for spear-

ing a chunk of meat from a passing platter—after which you
ripped it off your knife and, possibly bleeding from this awkward exercise, popped it into your mouth. Even women
carried their own knives out to dinner, and those, being
accoutrements to party clothes, hung from their waists in
silky sheaths that were as decorative as their dresses and often just as fragile.

The first revolution in cutlery was in fact revolutionary:
you left your dagger at the door and sat down to a table set
with flatware at every plate. It's said that the second began
in France, in 1637, at Cardinal Richelieu's table. As Wilson
tells the story, the cardinal became so agitated one night,
observing a dinner guest pick his teeth with the double-
edged knife still in use, that he ordered blunt knives for his
household. And thanks to his reputation as a social arbiter,
the fashion quickly spread. Sharp or blunt, table knives also
meant forks, if for no other reason than that once you stopped
impaling your meat (not to mention tearing it up with your
hands and teeth) and began cutting it on a plate, you needed
a fork to anchor it while you sliced. Blunt knives, of course,
were barely adequate for most meats. They were a symbol
of civility—a reminder that, at tables like Richelieu's, you
were expected to settle your arguments with piercing conversation, not by stabbing your antagonist. (This did not preclude stabbing him on the way home.) In time, place settings
became elaborate and involved a whole complement of
knives: blunt knives, fish knives, cheese knives, butter knives.
(And that was only the knives. An elegant French table setting soon included a different fork for nearly every course.)
The British, coming a century late to "ostentatiously blunt,"
as Wilson describes that Continental fad, took it up with a

defensive passion. It's still hard to order a steak or chops in a good London restaurant without having to ask the waiter to bring a steak knife, too.

This new cutlery transformed the way people ate. By the late eighteenth century in Europe, people were slicing their food into bite-size morsels and carrying them to their mouths with forks—those formerly weird things, Wilson calls them. And they hardly needed to chew such tiny pieces, which in most cases were already softened by pounding, overcooking, or long, gentle braisings. At the same time, the modern overbite began to appear prominently in upper-class Western European jaws. Do not confuse this with the seriously inconvenient condition known to the world as buck teeth (without which we would have no orthodontists, and no mortified adolescents with mouthfuls of rubber bands and wire braces). Wilson's modern overbite refers to "the way our top layer of incisors hangs over the bottom layer, like a lid on a box," as she nicely puts it, and is "the ideal human occlusion" for the way we now eat. Why this happened and how long it took to happen is open to some debate, but it's clear that *until* it happened, most humans had the bite of other primates—"where the top incisors clash against the bottom ones, like a guillotine blade."

Wilson's favorite theory comes from the American physical anthropologist Charles Loring Brace, a specialist in the evolution of hominid teeth. In 1977, Brace published an article that put the age of the Western overbite at no more than two hundred and fifty years—which is to say that flatware and, with it, a significant change in how we chewed were all it took for the edge-to-edge occlusion that we inherited from the Neanderthals to be replaced by the bite we now call normal. Brace was haunted by overbites. He had long assumed them to be an incremental and selective evolutionary change that began with agriculture and the consumption of grains. But the jaws he studied, on his way to building a database on the evolution of hominid teeth—apparently the biggest in the world—changed his mind. The transformation he'd seen in those eighteenth-century-gentlemen jaws was too abrupt and too radical to qualify as evolution, especially given the rapidity with which it then followed the spread of flatware into the middle classes, in the nineteenth century. In 1914, in the run-up to war with Germany, a stainless-steel alloy—developed to prevent corrosion in gun barrels—went on sale in Sheffield, England. Once stainless appeared on the country's dinner tables, the guillotine bite all but disappeared.

For Brace, the proof of his hypothesis as to the relation between jaws and cutlery came when, "on his eternal quest" for new teeth to study, he visited Shanghai's natural-history museum, examined the pickled jaw of a graduate student, dating from the Song dynasty (960 to 1279 A.D.), and discovered the same incisor overbite that by his reckoning had first appeared in Europe eight hundred to a thousand years later. More to the point, all the other Song "high-status individuals" whose jaws he then examined had overbites, too. The principle was the same, but the technological change in China obviously wasn't flatware. It was the tou—the wide, well-honed, flat-edged whacker of a knife that Chinese cooks used for everything from butchering to dicing and fine slicing—and the chopstick, which in the Song era came into common use.

The Song jaw is Wilson's ancient Asian reminder of the cultural and technological imperatives in the mixture of circumstances that in time produced our modern kitchen. The earliest surviving chopsticks were bronze, from late in the second millennium B.C., though for centuries only the rich used them, along with ivory, jade, lacquer, and even silver ones (a prophylactic court luxury: silver was believed to blacken on contact with any arsenic slipped into the emperor's food). The poor made do with wood and bamboo sticks. But in some ways, it was the legacy of their poverty that produced the Chinese overbite. Meat was the caviar in a Chinese peasant's diet, and what we now call Chinese cooking probably began as culinary experiments in making very little of it go a long way.

The trick was to cut small quantities of meat into paper-thin slices, season them with condiments, preserves, and spices, add whatever vegetables you could grow or barter, and keep adding until you arrived at a dish so tasty that you forgot how little meat was in it. Enter the all-purpose tou, the butchers and vendors who mastered that practical but scary implement, and the substantial savings in fuel that the quick stir-frying of tou-cut food provided. Apply all that new technology to an ancient lexicon of good manners that precluded not only the preparation but the cutting of food at Chinese tables, rich or poor, and you have no need for any tableware beyond your chopsticks, a couple of serving pieces, and a slippery porcelain spoon for soup. And if you have ever asked yourself why the Chinese eat the noodles in their soup with chopsticks, too—a Sisyphean labor that involves lifting a bowl to mouth level and slurping—think of Americans eating peas with a fork. Today the Chinese manufacture sixty-three billion pairs of disposable chopsticks a year—an industry and a habit inspired by Japanese Shinto taboos against sharing chopsticks or even washing and reusing them—and even that's not enough for nearly one and a half billion people. In 2010, a new American company called Georgia Chopsticks began exporting hundreds of millions of poplar and gum-tree chopsticks to China, Korea, and Japan. (A year and a half later, it went bankrupt.)

Americans are possibly the least tradition-bound of hominids, having in the main left their sentimental attachments behind in whatever unhappy place they or their families came from. Whether or not they arrived with overbites remains a matter of speculation. (Check out the thrust of the lower jaw in portraits of Washington and Jefferson; it's closer to Philip IV of Spain than to Brad Pitt.) But the enterprising spirit of the technology here, the trial-and-error search for the next best thing, has arguably done more for the modern kitchen than the competition in sterling that, as Wilson dutifully notes, produced the elaborate trefoil spoon of Restoration England, and the Victorian berry spoon, with its fancy holes, and for that matter, our own briefly ubiquitous silver spork.

It isn't surprising, given the superpower ambitions and imperatives of the last century, that many of the great technological kitchen leaps were the inadvertent results of research at the industries and agencies that helped us win the Second World War, not to mention our cold war/star wars with the Soviets. (One exception is the refrigerator; the application of thermodynamic research to refrigeration also took place in Europe with, among others, Albert Einstein, who patented his own fridge in 1930. Another is the gas oven; the first safe and successfully enclosed ovens came from Britain.) NASA scientists developed the technology for freeze-dried food—like ice, smoke, and salt, a milestone in the history of preservation. And we owe the microwave oven to Percy Spencer, the engineer who helped develop the Navy's radar system, and the Cuisinart to Carl Sontheimer, the engineer who invented a microwave direction finder for the Apollo moon mission. Sontheimer, it turned out, had a passion for the satiny poached purée of raw pike, cream, and pâté à choux known to the French as quenelles de brochet. ("A pain to make," Wilson says. "Soufflés are child's play by comparison.") In 1971, at a cookery show in France, he spotted a large, cumbersome metal drum with a rotary blade inside—a restaurant food processor called the Robot Coupe—and as Wilson puts it, "what he saw was quenelles." He set up shop in his garage, and two years later, his home-kitchen processor went on sale, named in homage to the art of French cuisine, but even then, as streamlined, versatile, and efficient as a room full of Noma prep chefs. Craig Claiborne, in the *Times*, called it an innovation comparable to "the printing press, cotton gin, steamboat, paper clips, Kleenex"—the greatest food invention since toothpicks. (Richelieu would have chosen toothpicks.)

Our kitchens were never the same. Nor were our cookbooks. The words "blitz everything" came to replace the pages of chop this, mince that, grind or fine-slice something else, sweat to soften, and force through a sieve, twice. The American housewife of postwar suburban fantasy, who had been expected to love her hours of kitchen labor as long as her fridge was the color of a lemon or an avocado and, as Wilson says, matched her cabinets, now had the time and curiosity to—guess what!—take up cooking well. By the turn of this century, her kitchen was filled with handy gadgets (Wilson is especially partial to the OXO peeler and the Microplane grater) and complicated culinary equipment, and the husband of *her* fantasies had long since moved the family to the city, where he could prowl the markets for heirloom tomatoes, humane steaks, Moroccan spices, and the best Thai fish sauce, or simply open his Julia Child and spend the weekend making cassoulet for a big, casual "supper party" around the kitchen table. For the time being, *pace* molecular gastronomy, all happy families were the same.

Everything in Bee Wilson's pithy book brings you back to the kitchen: her histories of weights and measures and pots and pans; her observations on the domestication of fire and ice (one is that a lot of the foods we now consider staples "principally came into being in order to give people something to put in their new fridges"); her homey riffs on small, exasperating "technologies" like egg timers, cake molds, tongs, and toasters. (The book came out in England last fall, the same week that Mrs. Hughes horrified Mr. Carson with one smoking, sputtering demonstration of a toasting machine, downstairs at Downton Abbey.) It's been said that the kitchen was invented when cooking moved indoors. This was a long process. The first kitchens were solitary structures, built far enough from your house to contain a sudden fire. Then they moved to a courtyard, or to a room across the courtyard from where your family lived, and eventually, like the big Roman-orgy kitchens, to the cellar. In any event, your food was at best tepid by the time it reached the table. It took millennia to bring kitchens safely to where they are now—at most, a pantry away from the dinner table.

Wilson's chronicle of the history of modern kitchens is socially astute and funny: a tour with stops at the small but "rational" 1920s Frankfurt Kitchen, with its Teutonic procession of fifteen aluminum drawers, moving you efficiently, if relentlessly, from task to task at counter height; and at the

American kitchen of the 1950s, with its pretty tiles and purring fridges; and earlier in the book, at the old-ways-are-the-best-ways kitchen of recent decades, filled with hanging salamis, butchering tools, laboriously polished copper, hand-turned spits, and homemade ricotta dripping its whey through cheesecloth on the windowsill. Wilson admires those "old-ways" kitchens and the tastes they produce, and has even taken courses in one, with the food historian and sixteenth-century-spit enthusiast Ivan Day, but given the choice of an old-ways life or the Cambridge archives, she seems to have made the wise decision. In fact, I have a list of questions, in the event that she considers the fork again. The most pressing is this: How do the Polynesians cook now?

Bee Wilson has since succeeded Paul Levy as chair of the Oxford Symposium on Food & Cookery and has also become a regular contributor to the *London Review of Books*. Her latest book, *First Bite: How We Learn to Eat*, came out in 2016.

GOOD GREENS

·⁒·

Three years ago, I retired the chili party that I used to give in Italy at the end of August. This was a shame, because I liked my party and thought that the chili made a nice reprieve from the ubiquitous barbecues of summer. Two of the twenty-four regulars at my party were vegetarians—one reluctantly, under a doctor's orders. A doable number, it seemed to me: for years, I put out a bowl of pasta al pesto just for them. Then, from one chili party to the next, everything changed. Seven formerly enthusiastic carnivores called to say they had stopped eating meat entirely and would like to join my vegetarians for the pesto. Worse, on the night of that final party, four of the remaining carnivores carried their plates to the kitchen table, ignoring the cubes of beef and pancetta, smoky and fragrant in their big red bean pot, and headed for my dwindling supply of pasta. "Stop!" I cried. "That's for the vegetarians!" Aggrieved, they replied, as in one voice, "But we're kind of vegetarian now." Some have yet to forgive me for scooping the pasta off their plates.

Until that summer, the only books I had read about food

proscriptions and taboos were Leviticus and Deuteronomy, those inadvertently comic masterpieces of the Old Testament, so addictive that I keep copies on my laptop. But since then I have collected a stack of vegetarian food histories with names like *Eat Not This Flesh* (by Frederick J. Simoons), *The Heretic's Feast* (Colin Spencer), and *The Bloodless Revolution* (Tristram Stuart), from which I've learned first, that people have been arguing about eating animals since the day they began eating or, more to the point, not eating them, and second, that the history of their arguments is a hermeneutical minefield. Take your pick. There is the ascetic argument, which can be religious (monks, holy men, and hermits, attached to the discipline of renunciation), or the philosophical one (as old as Pythagoras, whose belief in the transmigration of souls is said to have led generations of like-minded Greeks to follow a "Pythagorean diet"), or the mystical one (shamans, saints, and quantum physicists, searching for the ecstatic union or trippy oblivion produced by hunger hallucinations). Then there is the natural-man argument, which Rousseau, with a nod to Plutarch, used in making the claim that eating meat was an aberration, a sustained assault on the innocence and empathy of childhood, and produced "cruel and ferocious" people, like the English. (English vegetarians preferred "like the Tartars.") There is the caste, or "spiritual identity," argument, like the one advanced by Brahmans who renounced flesh in order to distinguish themselves, in matters of high-mindedness and noble breeding, from the hungry poor. There is the ethical, or animal-rights, argument, which holds that the pain and terror suffered by slaughter animals is morally indefensible. There is also the health argument (doctors and nutritionists, alarmed by the rise in illness and obesity in a high-fat

Big Mac world), and the carbon-footprint argument (environmentalists, equally alarmed by the amount of energy consumed, and ozone layer depleted, by the livestock industry that feeds that world).

Then there are the subsets of rejection. There are the orthodox Jains, who will eat the visible sprouts and leaves of root vegetables but not the roots themselves—which is to say, they will eat plants but not "kill" plants. There are the vegans, who will refuse not only animal flesh but anything that living animals produce, including honey (because it comes from bees), eggs, milk, and by extension, cheese. Some vegetarians will refuse fish but happily consume oysters, clams, and mussels—on the ground that those mollusks, having neither eyes nor a central nervous system, do not qualify as "real" animals, capable of feeling. The list goes on, because at the end of the day vegetarianism turns out to be a highly idiosyncratic spectrum. It runs from the strictest vegans to the "kind of vegetarian" vegetarians, who will eat fish and occasionally chicken, and even indulge themselves, once a year, in a Christmas rib roast, to the ladies who lettuce-leaf lunch and their stick-figure daughters, dreaming of a size 0 dress, who will ram their fingers down their throats in order to throw up whatever meat they are made to eat.

I'm not a vegetarian. I would describe myself as a cautious carnivore. The "cautious" dates from a trip to Texas in the mid-seventies, for a book that introduced me to the pitiable state of industrial feedlot cattle, crammed into pens to be fattened on quasi-chemical feed laced with antibiotics and hormones, to say nothing of the frantic baying of ranch yearlings driven through chutes to be branded and cut by cowhands, their testicles fed to the foreman's dogs. Not much later, I was in Europe watching the tubal force-feeding of

French ducks and geese, for foie gras. But the truth is that I worried much more about myself than about those animals. What drugs and diseases was I ingesting when I ate their meat? For that matter, what waste was I consuming with fish bred and raised in the dirty waters of industrial fish farms? Today I buy organic meat and chicken and milk and eggs, and the fishmonger at Citarella knows me as the woman who calls and says, "I don't want it if it's not wild." (You can't win this one, given the size of the dragnet fleets now depleting nearly every marine habitat on the planet.)

That said, I am unlikely ever to give up my applewood breakfast bacon, or the smoked salmon on my bagels, or the prosciutto that's always in my fridge. A week ago, I read about an Ibérico tasting in the *Financial Times*. It had reminded the writer of an episode of the British sitcom *The Royle Family*, in which the son invites a vegetarian girlfriend home for dinner and nobody knows what to feed her until his grandmother suggests, "Very thinly sliced ham." I'm with the grandmother, and should add that Spain's Ibérico pigs lead pampered and pristine lives in oak forests, feasting on tasty acorns.

Today, the best reason for people like me to love eating plants probably has less to do with vegetarians and their theories than with the great carnivore chefs and cookbook writers who started making vegetables delicious by approaching, say, a cauliflower with the same culinary imagination that they would otherwise apply to a Mexican short-ribs braise or an inside-out porchetta. It was about time this happened, given the dreary vegetarian cookbooks that had prevailed since the beginning of the nineteenth century, when a Lancashire housewife by the name of Martha Brotherton— her husband, Joseph, was the Nonconformist minister and animal rights crusader who helped found the Vegetarian Society of the United Kingdom—published what appears to have been the first one in the English language.

Mrs. Brotherton called her book *A New System of Vegetable Cookery*, and its particular evangelical mission was to banish all sinful pleasure from whatever legume was in your pot. Her culinary precepts, though not her book, outlasted her by more than a hundred and fifty years—as evidenced by the preachy vegetarian communes and collectives that began to proliferate in this country in the sixties and seventies, when a generation of postwar babies came of age. Those collectives were defiantly artisanal. Remember the breads and the carrot cakes that weighed nearly as much as the people eating them? The most enduring (and evolving) collective was the Moosewood Restaurant in Ithaca, New York—perhaps because for some years the healthfulness of the food was often camouflaged by blankets of sour cream, or seasoned with liberal splashes of soy sauce (with paprika running a close second), or even on occasion tossed in a somewhat unnerving combination of yogurt and mayonnaise. The original *Moosewood Cookbook*, assembled in 1977 by the Moosewood founder Mollie Katzen—who went on to become a consultant to Harvard's dining and "food literacy" initiatives—was exemplary in its "Eat it, it's good for you" style. The drawings were as folksy as the food, and, as if to drive home the point, the recipes were handwritten. Within a few years, it had sold a million copies.

In 1979, two years after Katzen's cookbook appeared, a young California chef named Deborah Madison left her job at Alice Waters's restaurant, Chez Panisse, in Berkeley, to open a vegetarian restaurant in San Francisco. She called it Greens, and you didn't need to be a vegetarian to want to eat there. Greens has been described as the first high-end vegetarian restaurant in the country. It was (and remains) minimalist rather than minimal, with glass walls looking out over San Francisco Bay to the Golden Gate Bridge and the soft hills of Marin County, and more to the point, with food that looked, and tasted, like something you had always dreamed of eating. "Farm driven" is how Madison described the menu. People kept asking for her recipes, and eight years later she and a Tassajara-trained cook named Edward Espé Brown, whom she'd met studying at the San Francisco Zen Center, put those recipes together as *The Greens Cookbook* and transformed the experience of a home-cooked vegetarian meal. The cookbook, like the restaurant, wasn't at all admonishing or self-righteous. Words like "healthy" were not in evidence. The operative words were "fresh" and "bright" and "flavor," and if you weren't a vegetarian there was nothing really to prevent you from sneaking some ham into Madison's recipe for herbed corn pudding, or adding a little beef or veal to her mushroom lasagna—the first lasagna I ever made— or a bit of pancetta to her winter-vegetable soup. If you were a decent cook, you knew at a glance that those deceptively simple recipes would stand up to some guilty tampering— and as often as not, you discovered that they didn't need it. For most of us, that was a revelation.

Madison's recipes are still deceptively simple. Her books— among them the encyclopedic *Vegetarian Cooking for Everyone*, from 1997—have none of the riotous potlatch spicing and herbal jumbling of Yotam Ottolenghi's *Plenty* or the sublime caloric decadence of Ruth Rogers's and the late Rose Gray's *River Café Cook Book Green*. But she is materfamilias to the dozens of other chefs who are rapidly turning vegetables into, as it were, the cash cow of the cookbook trade.

Depending on which polls you read, and whether it's herbivores or carnivores who have framed the questions and done the counting, somewhere between 5 and 19 percent of all Americans are now vegetarians or kind-of vegetarians, and between 2 and 9 percent are vegans. The market they represent, at a time when most book publishing is either in crisis or in Kindle, has been irresistible to writers hoping to strike pay dirt with a cookbook. At Kitchen Arts & Letters, the Lexington Avenue bookstore where I buy my food histories and cookbooks, the number of people shopping at its vegetarian and vegan shelves has just about doubled in the past ten years—and not only because of the rise in vegetarian conversions suggested by those polls but because of all the carnivores who have got interested in making whatever vegetables they do eat tastier.

Nach Waxman and Matt Sartwell, the patron gurus of Kitchen Arts & Letters, call this "the Ottolenghi effect," because it was Ottolenghi's strictly vegetarian *Plenty*, which came out in 2010, just a couple of years after his meaty, eponymous first cookbook appeared in England, that definitively took vegetables out of the good-for-you niche and into the "You're going to love this" sales stratosphere, and sent every envious meat-eating chef in search of what could be called a vegetarian feeding frenzy. Even Hugh Fearnley-Whittingstall—who had famously celebrated his passion for animal flesh (as in the lambs and chickens cosseted, killed with kindness, and cooked with "respect" on his River Cottage Farm) in a cookbook called *Meat*—entered the fray last year by writing a new book, *Veg*.

Vegetable Literacy is Deborah Madison's thirteenth book and her turf revenge. It turns the tables, though you probably won't know this until you read the recipes and discover, as I did, that while there is predictably no marrow or pancetta in Madison's cardoon risotto, there is permission to simmer it in a "light chicken stock," and even an acknowledgment that vegetable stock might "overwhelm" the flavor of that delicately bitter member of the sunflower family. I started cooking immediately, guiltless at last at my own stove, trying out soups in which the choice was water, vegetable stock, or chicken stock—especially the ones with chicken stock listed first. (Perhaps to mollify the purists, Madison's *The New Vegetarian Cooking for Everyone*, which came out this spring, remains unbendingly vegetarian; it's new mainly in that it now flags every vegan-friendly recipe with a big V and adds 200 recipes to the original 1,400, making it, at nearly seven hundred pages, the OED of vegetarian cuisine.)

The clue to Madison's heretical chicken stock is the word "vegetable" in her title. Before *Vegetable Literacy*, the meaning of "vegetable" in a cookbook's name was largely a function of its author's reputation and its audience's expectations— which is to say that the people who had rushed to the store to buy Alice Waters's third book, *Chez Panisse Vegetables*, were unlikely to be shocked that the vegetables in a stew called Beans Cooked in the Fireplace were meant to be sautéed, with bacon, in duck or goose fat, any more than the people who had bought Madison's ninth book, *Vegetable Soups*, were likely to be shocked by the absence of anything remotely resembling bacon, let alone goose fat, in her potage of mustard greens and black-eyed peas. The field is muddier now. Food writers new to the vegetarian canon tend to use "vegetarian" and "vegetable" interchangeably. (The shrewdest may have been Fearnley-Whittingstall, whose *Veg*, wittingly or not, let you end the word for yourself, according to how much "vegetarian" you hoped to find when you opened it in your kitchen; in fact, there isn't a trace of meat, fish, or fowl lurking among his plants.) Or they include the kind of conspicuously "carnivore" disclaimer that Simon Hopkinson, the chef responsible for *Roast Chicken* and *Second Helpings of Roast Chicken*, produced when he put a recipe for the broth of that estimable bird at the beginning of a book called *The Vegetarian Option* in 2009. (Not a vegetarian's vegetarian, the people who bought the book complained.) But *Vegetable Literacy* is first and foremost a book about vegetables, not about the kind of people who don't eat anything else—and, as Aristotle could have told anyone he found browsing the shelves of some Athenian Kitchen Arts & Letters, the fact that all vegetarians eat vegetables does not mean that all vegetable eaters are vegetarians.

The book is sly. Think of it as a pro-choice cookbook decorously wrapped in carrots and beans and lettuce leaves. Apart from the chicken broth, you won't find anything "animal" listed in Madison's recipes, but read what she has to say about some of those recipes, and you will detect the beginning of a stealth operation—a call to sit down at the dinner table together and put an end to the testy herbivore-carnivore divide. I should have guessed that Madison herself had crossed it, years earlier. And no doubt I would have if I'd looked more carefully at the author's bio on her jacket flap, and discovered that she had sat on the board of the Southwest Grassfed Livestock Alliance (a piece of information discreetly dropped onto the end of a list of worthy commitments, right after her place on the board of the Seed Savers Exchange), or if I'd found the old interview in which she confessed to being "not a strict vegetarian," and cheerfully added, "I eat everything, and eat whatever is served." But I didn't. A few weeks after I got the book, I took out a bowl of leftover wild rice that I'd served with a leg of lamb the night before. My first instinct was to chuck it, but, given that the book was right there, next to the fridge on the kitchen counter, I looked up wild rice in the index, turned to a recipe with the appetizing, if somewhat oxymoronic name Savory Wild Rice Crepe-Cakes, and glanced at the short passage with which Madison introduces all her recipes. "Try them with a dab of sour cream flecked with chives and smoked trout," it said. Trout? In a Deborah Madison cookbook? A license to poach on those sacrosanct vegetarian preserves? That was the moment I really started reading.

In no time, I was cooking Rio Zape Beans with Salt-Roasted Tomatoes, under the spell of this suggestion: "If you crave smoke with your beans, cook these with smoked pork shanks." For more "smokiness," I made my broth from the carcass of a smoked chicken, the way Madison allowed that she does whenever a neighbor with a smoker brings her one. I even doubled the amount of spices, as carefree in collaboration with a vegetarian recipe as I'd been when I bought *Greens* more than twenty-five years earlier—and rarely since. Soon I discovered bacon among the "good companions" that Madison suggests for collards; meats among the good companions for her potatoes; and—introducing a recipe for turnips in white miso butter—her paean to the fish soup, its clam broth sweetened by white miso, that she always eats during stopovers at the Atlanta airport. I bought the miso and made fish soup and, a couple of days later, her extremely delightful turnips.

Madison, of course, had never kept anyone from fiddling with a recipe before. She simply hadn't mentioned the possibility, perhaps for fear of offending any of her millions of constant readers for whom détente, let alone the thought of a pork shank sitting in Deborah Madison's bean pot, would amount to capitulation. But now she was out of the culinary closet, embracing difference. Her good companions for heritage and ancient wheats were braised and roasted meats, and if you didn't want meat with your farro, white bean, and cabbage soup, that was okay, too. The relief shows. *Vegetable Literacy* is a happy book—warm, chatty, and immensely informative without being at all didactic—and the odd thing is that Madison has never written so much or so well or so attentively about vegetables as she does now.

It had been easy to love *Greens*, maybe because the few vegetarians I knew back then were the kind-of ones, and the serious ones hadn't become so pious. And I had often cooked from *Vegetable Soups*, the book in which Madison, who by then had married and moved to the country outside Santa Fe, introduced me to a battery of Mexican herbs and interesting grain-and-vegetable combinations (as in masa dumplings and summer squash in a spicy tomato broth, which I have to admit my husband hates) that I probably wouldn't have found in any of the other cookbooks I owned twenty years ago. But my eyes had glazed over when I opened *Vegetarian Cooking for Everyone* for the first time. It weighed more than *The Raj Quartet* (a better read, but still bone-bruising if you happened to be reading in bed), which in itself discouraged browsing, one of the great pleasures of owning a good cookbook. Besides, there was no way anyone *could* browse through 1,400 (now sixteen hundred) recipes—not unless she was a vegetarian running out of things to make and willing to put in four years, trying a different recipe every night. *Vegetable Literacy*, by contrast, has 300 recipes and a lot more text. Read it as an introduction to your inner garden—a painless lesson in botany, sensibility, and appreciation that lets you celebrate the depth and beauty of plants in the context of whatever else you're making. The result may be that, like me, you will soon be serving Madison's corn and coconut-milk curry with a platter of grilled pork (a "good companion"), her sorrel, watercress, and yogurt sauce over a piece of salmon (another good companion), and little pieces of chicken (yet another) tossed with the tofu cubes in her soy and five-spice braise.

When I was reading *Vegetable Literacy* for the first time, the book that surprisingly came to mind was Fearnley-Whittingstall's *Meat*, which begins with a disquisition on good husbandry, takes you through the rituals of nurturing and feeding and slaughtering, and deposits you at your stove, cooking with an unexpected understanding of—and strong sense of connection with—the animals you are about to cook, the aromas that will fill your kitchen, and the flavors you will soon taste. *Vegetable Literacy* does the same for vegetables. "It started with a carrot that had gone on in its second year to make a beautiful lacy umbel of a flower" is how Madison begins, in her own garden. She noticed similar flowers blooming on herbs like parsley, anise, chervil, and cilantro, and quickly discovered that those herbs not only were related botanically to one another but shared the same culinary characteristics and correspondences as the big vegetables in their Umbelliferae family—the carrots, fennel, celery, parsnips, and celeriac—and would "flatter" those vegetables in a dish. She started experimenting. She curtailed the teaching and traveling she had been doing for years. She called this "committing to a garden"—tending to it, finding the richest organic soils for it, learning to plant and turn it in the company of fat worms, glossy beetles, "exotic wasps," and the occasional "creepy" desert millipede. She carried everything edible that it produced into her kitchen and tasted all the affinities she had reaped.

Madison describes her project as "cooking and gardening with twelve families from the edible plant kingdom." Each chapter of *Vegetable Literacy* is about one of those families. They are not necessarily small families (or even all the possible families), and in a few cases the consanguinity can be fatal. Think of a big extended Italian family with an uncle in the 'Ndràngheta, or an Arab one with a rogue nephew in Al-Qaeda, when you learn that the potatoes, peppers, eggplants, and tomatoes in Madison's garden are in the same family—botanically speaking, the Solanaceae—as the night-blooming datura, the base of my favorite perfume but stupefying if you stick your nose into a blossom and sniff, let alone sprinkle it onto your eggplant Parmesan. (And, by the way, beware of eating green potatoes; you won't die, but as Madison learned, dutifully sampling one for her Solanaceae chapter, you will never forget the cramps.) Madison sticks to the cousins you would want to eat for dinner, opening each chapter with a section on the properties of the family, and then, one by one, on each of those edible cousins, with a look at its history, advice on its varieties and cultivation, some kitchen wisdom as to what parts of it to use (or not to use), and of course, her thoughts on its good companions: the herbs and spices and other vegetables; the sauces and cheeses; and scattered judiciously among them, the fish and meats. By the time you get to the recipes for that plant, she has moved you seamlessly into a state of high anticipation and appreciation—which is to say, you have become a starving connoisseur. The recipes are perfect.

By now, there are ten or fifteen other new (to me) vegetarian cookbooks on my study floor. Most will soon be dispatched to Housing Works, and none have made me miss the garden I tend in Italy in the summer, the way that Deborah Madison just did. I miss the May peas and favas, the June garlics and onion shoots and basil, the July arugula and zucchini, the August melons, eggplants, and tomatoes, and the first pumpkins of September. Oddly, I no longer miss my chili party, or even regret those ten pricey pounds of beef abandoned in their red bean pot. I find that I'm not much in the mood for meat lately—well, maybe my breakfast bacon, or my monthly porterhouse fix, or one of Madison's good-companion roasts, braising in a pot of vegetables and herbs. But as often as not, I eat those vegetables first, and most of the meat goes in the fridge.

A few weeks ago, eight of my Italy friends turned up in New York at the same time, and I decided to get them together for a dinner party. I cooked one of my favorite recipes, a hot pot involving lentils, spicy Italian sausages, and prunes. Two of the friends were vegetarians—one had been at that final chili party—so I did what I usually do, and made a pasta al pesto just for them. This time my carnivores actually took the meat they were served, but when I got to the table I discovered that most had dipped into the pesto, too, and were eating it before I could take it back. Later that night, cleaning up in the kitchen, I asked my husband if everyone we knew could possibly be turning vegetarian. He found the question ridiculous. He said I should know by now that if you put people who lived in Italy anywhere near a bowl of pasta, they would take some, and it didn't matter if they were carnivores or herbivores, Americans or Italians. (He is an anthropologist and thinks like that.) I wonder. I pointed out that the sausages were the first "real" meat we had eaten all week, and that we'd already had vegetable soup one night (admittedly, with pancetta), and salad for dinner twice—and never mind if one of those salads had anchovies in it, and a little tuna. "That's kind of kind-of vegetarian," he said. "Different."

EAT, MEMORY

ꝏ

I love restaurants. I'm a serial eater-out, prowling New York for an uncommonly delicious dinner, at a bargain price, cooked by someone else. And never mind if the meal turns out to be disappointing. There is always the promise of the next meal, the next new place, and besides, the pleasures of eating privately in public tend to compensate for most culinary catastrophes that do not involve a cab to the emergency room after the latest hole-in-the-wall around the corner serves me last week's clams. My husband says that I never learn; if there's a new restaurant in our neighborhood, I try it.

Given that Paul Freedman's new book, *Ten Restaurants That Changed America*, is largely a history of eating out in this country, it's worth noting that the "restaurant," at least as food scholars define it, is historically quite recent. The word comes from the French *restaurer*, to restore, and was coined in the 1760s, after a nutritionally minded Frenchman known only as Boulanger (his first name has disappeared from the annals of gastronomy) decided to open a place in

Paris offering a choice of "restorative" meat broths, along with tables to sit at, wine to sip, and possibly a bit of cheese or fruit to end the meal. (BOULANGER SELLS RESTORATIVES FIT FOR THE GODS, the sign on his door said.)

People, of course, had been eating out for several millennia by the time the mysterious M. Boulanger boiled down the bones for his first soup. Cooking pots, set deep into stone counters, lined the main thoroughfares of ancient Rome. Street vendors in Southeast Asia hawked all the fixings you would need for an exceptionally tasty lunch or dinner, much as they do today. Inns served travelers from whatever provisions happened to be in the innkeeper's wife's kitchen; respectable women, forced by circumstances to travel alone, were expected to dine in their rooms (the beginning of room service); and couples could eat together downstairs in a room off the bar, which was reserved for men. What the French call maisons de rendezvous, not to mention the better brothels, served lunch and dinner to their guests—something I discovered toward the end of lunch one afternoon at an excellent restaurant near Tangier, when couple after couple (there were only couples) began to scamper upstairs with their bottle of amontillado before the cheese and the quince paste were even cleared. The great feasts of the aristocracy were cooked in the castle by a battery of chefs and consumed in vast dining rooms, where men and women could mingle freely. Status came with an invitation, not a reservation. The wealth that counted was measured in hectares, exclusivity was what you conferred on the friends (and more important, the enemies) you fed at your domain, and as likely as not, your menus were based on Cardinal Richelieu's famous dinner parties—fancy and, obviously, French.

The first commercial appropriation of seigneurial haute

cuisine was a Paris restaurant that opened in the late 1770s—
ten years before the storming of the Bastille and, appropriately, situated on the Rue de Richelieu. It was called La
Grande Taverne de Londres, perhaps to signal its neutrality
in the coming domestic head roll, a mile away on the Place
de la Concorde. Fifty years later—with new money already
flowing into New York by way of mining and stockyard bar-
ons, railhead property speculators, futures traders, and the
politicians whose pockets they lined—two entrepreneurial
brothers from Switzerland, Giovanni (soon to be John) and
Pietro (soon to be Peter) Del Monico, raised the money to
open the first important French restaurant in the United
States. It was at 2 South William Street, in the heart of the
financial district, and it came with 80,000 square feet of
seriously opulent dining space, including, in the Paris tradition, private rooms available upstairs for negotiating business
deals or, more frequently, the pleasant combination of adul-
tery and dinner. The brothers and their descendants—in
particular, a nephew by the name of Lorenzo, who turned out
to be a visionary restaurateur—followed the money steadily
and successfully uptown until at one point there were four
Delmonico's in the city, and in the third to open, a French
chef named Charles Ranhofer, who in short order became
the most celebrated chef in the United States. Together,
Lorenzo Delmonico and Charles Ranhofer generated a passion
in the public for their consummate if somewhat overwrought
French food, a passion that began to chip away at the social
wall between the city's established first families and its
new moneyed classes. If you were able to read a menu that
ran to more than a hundred dishes (one of the pleasures of *Ten
Restaurants* is its reproductions of dozens of menus), and

had the time to linger over fourteen courses, you could go to Delmonico's, and everyone who could did.

Delmonico's, fittingly, is the first of Freedman's ten restaurants. It lasted, in its various locations, for nearly a hundred years, during which time it established its style of haute cuisine as the gold standard in American dining and spawned generations of imitations in big cities across the country. It remained the standard until its name was sold by the family in the 1920s, and its lingering reputation was eventually surpassed by the sanctum sanctorum of Henri Soulé's Le Pavillon, another of Freedman's ten. Le Pavillon was a seriously snooty place that in fact began as a tourist restaurant in the French pavilion of the 1939 World's Fair in Queens, but by the 1950s it had morphed into an East Side gastronomic temple, where the possibility of dinner was conferred on a chosen few by its imperious patron, and nobody else could get a table. The fact that I ate there often (or at all) was entirely thanks to my friend and journalism's budding gourmand R. W. Apple, who at the time was a correspondent for the overnight shift at NBC News and testing the limits of an already famous expense account. I was a graduate student living down the hall and subsisting on Milton, Hawthorne, Faulkner, and tuna curry (as in a can of tuna, a can of cream of mushroom soup, and a tablespoon of curry powder).

Le Pavillon set the midcentury style for fine French dining in New York—much of it classic brasserie fare refined by its estimable chef, Pierre Franey, into an almost ambrosial simplicity. Meanwhile, the front of the house, ruled by Soulé's moody assessments of who mattered and who did not, kept customers in line through what Freedman calls the "intimidating ordeal of trial by snobbery," and replaced the dread of a curdled sauce with the dread of a table in Siberia (a fate visited on Harry Cohn, the CEO of Columbia Pictures, when he bought Le Pavillon's building, in the mid-fifties). It may be that Soulé himself shared the anxieties of a new urban postwar society eager to reconfigure old distinctions between different kinds of money and status. But, as chef after chef escaped his reign of terror and opened admirable French restaurants of their own—twelve in New York alone—that legacy was bound to pall.

Paul Freedman is a social historian—a medievalist by training, known in academic circles as the author of books such as *Out of the East: Spices and the Medieval Imagination*, a classic study of the spice trade as it affected taste and status in European culture in the Middle Ages; and now, among foodies, as the paterfamilias of the food-history program at Yale, where he teaches and where he has broken down another kind of exclusivity by inviting chefs, food scientists, and writers to teach and speak. He has spent the better part of the past ten years eating out, and it is clear from the first few pages of *Ten Restaurants* that those restaurants are not the whole story he has to tell, but simply what you could call transformative prototypes—platforms from which to open a discussion of the way America eats, the ethnic and racial and regional and class and immigrant realities that its kitchens represent, and the entrepreneurs with the passion or the wisdom or simply the ambition to embrace (and profit from) the simmering of the stockpot of social change.

A particularly illuminating example is the story of the Mandarin, the San Francisco restaurant presided over by Cecilia Chiang, an elegant and by all reports warmly hospitable woman who had grown up before the war in a fifty-three-room Peking palace, and who eventually made her way to California to serve what the *San Francisco Chronicle* columnist Herb Caen famously anointed as "the best Chinese food east of the Pacific." Established in 1960, it was one of the first upscale Chinese restaurants in America, as well as one of the first to offer authentically Chinese fare to the *yang guizi*—"white devils" is the common term—who ate there, as opposed to the bland Chinese-American dishes invented and served, at the time, almost anywhere beyond the precincts of the country's teeming Chinatowns. (In Providence, where I grew up, the Sunday-night takeout menu of our one neighborhood Chinese restaurant consisted entirely of a bag of cold, crispy noodles and a combination carton known as "chow mein-chop suey mixed.") Freedman's chapter on the Mandarin is a forty-page lesson in the history of Chinese immigration—from the indentured coolies who laid the tracks for the western end of the Transcontinental Railroad (many of whom were left to die when the work was finished) to the cooks of an ongoing Chinese diaspora who are introducing the wildly various tastes and peoples of "China" to the West. There are now more Chinese restaurants in the country—40,000, Freedman says—than there are McDonald'ses, Burger Kings, and KFCs combined. And yesterday's no-go Chinatowns have turned into thriving models of an ethnic-eatery tourist trade.

But in New York, the prize for selling the facts and fictions of ethnic bonhomie used to belong to the Italian restaurant Mamma Leone's—the extra *m* Americanizing the word "mama" being one example—which, as the story goes, "opened" in 1906, when Enrico Caruso invited a group of friends to shell out fifty cents a head for a down-home dinner in his friend Luisa Leone's living room. By the time Mamma Leone's closed, nearly a century later, it was the city's largest restaurant, with eleven dining rooms and 1,250 seats, not to mention more strolling accordionists than Manhattanites in sight. There were years when every tour bus entering the city was said to disgorge its passengers for an obligatory meal there, which made it an irresistible photo-op stop for sports celebrities, politicians, and college kids in New York for a weekend. Having once made that stop myself, I can report that the food, while leaden, introduced people who weren't Italian to the idea of Italian food at a time when the pasta most Americans dipped into was a can of precooked Franco-American spaghetti clinging to a thin coating of sugary tomato sauce.

Then there is Antoine's in New Orleans. It is one of the oldest restaurants in America—it dates from 1840—and continues to provide the kind of antebellum menu that Freedman describes and clarifies as Haute Creole cuisine, thus performing what for me is the invaluable service of defining the cultural and culinary differences between Creole and Cajun cooking. As spectacle, it makes upstarts like Mamma Leone's look like summer stock. I went once with my husband at the end of 1969, and sat with the other tourists in one of the fourteen high-kitsch dining rooms where all the king's men of Louisiana used to negotiate their deals, eating dishes so oversauced as to lose any particularity of flavor. (Freedman, who includes an appendix of recipes from each of his chosen restaurants, received, from Antoine's, one for a dish called Oysters Foch, which involves glopping Sauce Colbert—itself a combination of a complicated tomato sauce and a warm Hollandaise, whipped slowly over a double boiler—onto cornmeal-fried oysters perched on foie gras–laden toast.) I ordered the Oysters Rockefeller, a recipe from Antoine's turn-of-the-nineteenth-century kitchen and still promoted as a closely guarded secret, despite the dozens of versions available online today. The truth is that I remember nothing about those oysters or, in fact, about the rest of the meal, perhaps because later that night I conceived a beautiful daughter, somewhat hurriedly, in the middle of a hotel fire that we then managed to flee with two book manuscripts intact. How could a meal compete with that?

If you're looking for true Southern comfort in *Ten Restaurants*, you might want to forget about Antoine's and go straight to the chapter on Sylvia's, the enduring soul-food restaurant on Lenox Avenue, near the Apollo Theatre, which a waitress from South Carolina named Sylvia Pressley Woods and her husband, Herbert, bought for twenty thousand dollars in 1962, transforming a local luncheonette into a celebration of the African-American kitchen that had seen her through a hardscrabble Southern childhood. Woods's grandfather was hanged for a murder he did not commit; her father died of complications from German gas attacks suffered during the First World War. But her mother and grandmother, raising her on a farm with no elecriticity, no water, and only a mule for transportation, kept the culinary legacy of black America—what we now call Southern food—alive, warm, and sustaining on the kitchen table. (According to Freedman, "routine breakfasts" on the Pressley farm included "biscuits and syrup, grits, okra, tomatoes, and fried fish.") By the time Woods died five years ago, at the age of eighty-six, black communities North and South knew her as "the queen of soul food," a title that few who ever entered her restaurant would dispute. I ate at Sylvia's for the first time a few years after it opened in the early sixties, invited by a boyfriend at a time when Harlem was widely considered a no-go zone for white people of either sex. ("Don't tell your mother," my boyfriend, who was black, said when we got on the uptown train.) The menu was plain but irresistible, with fried chicken and smothered chops and candied sweet potatoes and, tucked among the greens and black-eyed peas, platters of macaroni and cheese. What you felt at the time was the hearth, the comfort of a woman in the kitchen—whether in fact or in spirit, or whether it was a Luisa Leone or a Sylvia Woods herself. Since then, Sylvia's has become a sprawling, landmark restaurant that can seat four hundred and fifty people. And yes, the tour buses stop there now.

New York, like Paris or London, still sets the style for the rest of its country, which may account for the fact that six of Freedman's top ten are or were once New York restaurants. Schrafft's, which began as a candy company in the 1890s, originated in New York and in its heyday, in the mid-fifties, maintained more than fifty locations in and around the city. In many ways, it was the prototype for the better national and regional chains that followed it, ensuring middle-class Americans affordable and dependable quality, along, alas, with the numbing conformity of most American tables— the difference being that Schrafft's was primarily a place for women to eat. The Schrafft's I knew best was at 61 Fifth Avenue, a few blocks north of my grandmother's Greenwich Village apartment, and I got to eat there as a child whenever I visited. It remains, in memory, one of my favorite places— an intensely and intentionally feminine restaurant where you took off your white gloves to lunch on tea sandwiches, iceberg salads, creamed chicken, or more exotically, chicken à la king, unencumbered by brothers or even waiters, or for that matter, by any noisy males demanding attention, and consequently so tidy and appealing in retrospect that, reading about it now, I had to remind myself that this was the

Eisenhower fifties, when women were not seated in most New York restaurants without a man to order for them, despite the fact that hundreds of thousands of working women in the city were thus consigned to eating their paper-bag sandwiches on park benches or at their desks. Schrafft's thrived under four generations of Shattucks, its founding family (most significantly, its women), and died, you could say, from feminism, in the late sixties. Freedman tells us that when women started demanding and at long last receiving equal rights as customers in the city's restaurants, the chain tried to attract men by installing stand-up bars and even advertising the perks of a cocktail hour. No one came.

Schrafft's was among the few restaurants in Freedman's ten to open with an explicit social purpose, and to succeed in serving it. Another, surprisingly, was Howard Johnson's, the brainchild of the testy and obsessively controlling entrepreneur from Quincy, Massachusetts, who gave it its name, its steep-roofed architecture, its orange and turquoise paint, and (for children) its thrillingly predictable menu—as in twenty-eight "personally created" ice-cream flavors, butter-grilled hot dogs, and deep-fried clams—and who in the process became the franchise food king of the American highway, providing millions of traveling families with a guarantee of the same fresh, tasty meals under any of its thousand orange roofs.

Johnson was not a populist. He began life with the burden of a family debt to pay and ended it a multimillionaire, with a yacht, three big houses, a penthouse on Sutton Place, a table at the Stork Club, and a taste for restaurants like Le Pavillon (although when it came to dessert, he much preferred HoJo's ice cream, and according to his fourth wife, always kept ten cartons in the freezer.) But he was also in many ways a pioneer. He controlled the franchises he dispensed, supplied everything from their napkins to their food, and retained the right to cancel their contracts at the slightest breach. He saw, before anyone else, that we were now a country of cars, a people on the road, and that nobody else had thought to feed us properly. Like Schrafft's, Howard Johnson's was part of my childhood. Whenever and wherever we drove, I waited to spot the iron pole with its hanging logo—Simple Simon the Pieman, and Simon's drooling dog—signaling the choice I would have to make between peppermint stick with hot fudge and marshmallow sauce in a sundae, or a double-scoop sugar cone with sprinkles. It was done in, Freedman says, by McDonald's. Not the same thing at all.

Meanwhile, in the more rarefied pockets of Manhattan, prominent people had already taken up "power lunching"—a term coined some years later by the *Esquire* editor Lee Eisenberg—in the sleek, modernist splendor of the Grill Room at the Four Seasons restaurant. There, at the penultimate eatery on Freedman's list, diners picked at simple seasonal American food, high-priced and superbly cooked, while surrounded by the seasonal flora selected by Philip Johnson, who designed the restaurant. Freedman rightly regards the Four Seasons, which opened in 1959, as an aesthetic and entrepreneurial triumph: a combination of the vision of the young Seagrams's heir Phyllis Lambert, who talked her father, Samuel Bronfman, into commissioning the most beautiful new building in New York for his headquarters; the partnership of the two men she chose to create it, Mies van der Rohe and Johnson, his on-site architect and designer; and the determination of the businessmen—Joe Baum from Restaurant Associates, being the first and most determined—who nurtured its restaurant until a real-estate speculator took over the building and, this year, forced it to move out. But Freedman also knows that "seasonal" does not necessarily mean "local" in a city like New York, and that, for its powerful clientele, the prospect of being seen by similarly powerful people, all of them negotiating lucrative, glamorous deals in hushed tones, was perhaps the truly satisfying part of lunching back to the wall at one of the Grill Room's coveted banquettes. What the Four Seasons did accomplish was the end of the three-hour, three-martini lunch, the kind followed by a nap at your desk. It is worth noting that by the time the restaurant closed this summer, the power brokers lunching at those banquettes were as toned and trim as a California surfer. They had daily sessions with their trainers, jogged in the park, played squash, and ate plenty of salad greens.

Which brings us to Alice Waters's Chez Panisse in Berkeley, the tenth restaurant on Freedman's list and by now the only one with a particular social mission to have succeeded not only in maintaining but in spreading it to, among other places, the California school system, the White House gardens, and the kitchen of the American Academy in Rome. I often ate there during a stint as a visiting professor at Berkeley, in the early 1990s, and by then it was already an institution, the unassuming, vine-draped shrine of a global culinary creed.

Chez Panisse opened in 1971, in a quirky, meandering house in Berkeley and, after a few rough years, was filtering not only the taste of France but the taste of Italy, Mexico, and Japan, to name just a few places, through an ur-locavore sensibility soon to be known as California cuisine. (The Momofuku-brand kitchen wizard, David Chang, is said to have called it "one fig on a plate" eating.) It was the first American restaurant to change the way I cooked at home, and given that the cookbooks produced there by Waters and her chefs were filled with dishes begging to be made "in season"—carrot soup with chervil, pasta with snow peas and salmon roe, pear ice cream with pear-caramel sauce—it nurtured my patience in Italy in the summer to wait for the surprises that a vegetable garden brings.

Reading Paul Freedman about America, stalking myself through the taste of meals at eight of his ten restaurants, each sampled for different reasons at different moments of my life, I began to draw the outlines of a world I shared with other people, people more or less like me, and to wonder what "like me" meant when it came to expectations of inclusion, of common flashpoints of reference, of understanding and participating in the coded language of what we eat and how it is prepared and who is sitting at all those tables around us in what we call a restaurant. I think that's what Freedman intended us to do.

I missed, of course, Delmonico's, which closed years before I was born, and to my regret, I also missed the Mandarin, in San Francisco, where I spent a couple of months in the late sixties, and perhaps because of this, rarely ventured out of Haight-Ashbury, where even the soy sauce came laced with Acapulco Gold. And I wish that Freedman had gone further afield in his travels, told the story of one exemplary Mexican restaurant in, say, Austin or Santa Fe; or of the first great steakhouse in Omaha or Chicago; or of one of the millennial beer-beard-and-baby places across the bridge in Brooklyn that have transformed (and democratized) eating out in this century. But for me, restaurants like Schrafft's and Howard Johnson's, with their wide demographic reach and the sense of community, however brief, that they created in the people who enjoyed them, balanced some of the privilege I had to acknowledge, the exceptional accidents and circumstances and associations of an East Coast life that accounted for my evenings at Le Pavillon, and my one power lunch at the Grill Room of the Four Seasons, where I consumed an unseemly amount of lobster salad, steak, and frites while suffering the stares and whispers of the mover-and-shaker regulars, trying desperately but unsuccessfully to place me.

I'm not sure how either of those restaurants changed America, although they certainly changed New York. In fact, it's hard to imagine that most Americans had actually ever heard of Le Pavillon or its overweening proprietor, even during his reign of terror among the city's moneyed classes. *Ten Restaurants* is a book as much about the contradictions and contrasts in this country as it is about its places to eat. It is designed to keep you up, thinking, and as I did this summer, returning to its rich and often troubling pages.

PART IV

Celebrating

PILGRIM'S PROGRESS

❧

Some stoves are made for Thanksgiving. My stove in New York is one of them. It has six burners and two ovens, which began to cooperate, more or less, in 2002, after five years of stealing each other's heat—with the result that the people who love sweet potatoes (my daughter, for one) and the people who can't manage Thanksgiving without mashed potatoes (my son-in-law) are finally happy, along with the ones who demand Brussels sprouts (my husband) and the ones (I won't mention them) who ask for string beans. I am the only person at my Thanksgiving dinner who insists on braised red cabbage, but then I am the cook with six burners and two ovens, and I always get it.

I bought my stove with Thanksgiving in my head. I imagined large birds, basted and browning nicely at 425 degrees in one oven, while apple and pear cakes rose, un-troubled, at 350 degrees in the other, and the stock for my bourbon gravy simmered on top, surrounded by pots and pans of everyone's favorite fixings. There was some discus-sion at home about the price of my new stove, but I didn't listen. By my logic, I was saving money, having dropped my long-standing campaign to replace the painted-plywood kitchen shelves with serious maple cabinets. The stove arrived in the fall of 1997 and broke down for the first time a month later, on Thanksgiving Day, leaving sixteen irritable people eating tuna sandwiches and cranberry sauce at two long laundry tables from the building's basement that I had squeezed diagonally, end to end, across my dining room, disguised under my mother's creamy Belgian linens, circa 1930. The emergency repairman appeared in February. With my stove functioning again, I had what would now be called a transformative thought: Thanksgiving but not Thanksgiving. No one would get to vote on the Brussels sprouts or veto the cabbage. No one could say "What? No turkey?" if my cornbread-and-pecan stuffing came spilling out of a couple of juicy capons instead of a turkey that was bound to be stiff by the time it was carved and on a platter. No one could possibly sniff if the sweet potatoes turned out to be butternut squash—so much lighter—cooked in crème fraîche and maple syrup, with a dab of chipotle sauce. No one would be disappointed if the pies and cakes transmogrified into an apple charlotte out of Julia Child, or even a plum pudding, spared that Christmas when the family voted bûche de Noël, albeit with a side of hard sauce.

The next morning, I got on the phone and reassembled my Thanksgiving table for the last Thursday (a traditional touch) in February, at eight o'clock (a civilized one). Everyone called it the best Thanksgiving dinner they had ever eaten, perhaps because the people gathered at my table that slushy February night included an English historian, an Italian judge, a German politician and his wife, and two French journalists. They were all fine sources in my writing life, but none were what I would call heavily invested in the menu offered up at the beginning of a brief Pilgrim-Indian rapprochement that, if it lasted at all, was mainly owing to the good manners of a party of Wampanoag braves, who, having diligently gorged on wild turkey for three days at the Pilgrims' harvest feast (by all accounts in early October 1621), burned off the calories deer-hunting in the Cape Cod woods—thus keeping the Plymouth colony in meat for the long winter. The capons were splendid, though not, as my family said, something you would have found lounging on a rock in seventeenth-century Massachusetts—which probably explains why, when I suggested capon again in November, I was voted down.

A few months ago, when my husband and I were driving to Paris from the farmhouse in Umbria where we spend the summer, we stopped in the village of Saint-Père-sous-Vézelay in Burgundy, for dinner at the restaurant L'Esperance, and over a drink at the bar afterward I mentioned those annual family votes to the owner and chef, Marc Meneau. He snorted at the word "turkey." He was bewildered, he said, by America's devotion to turkey. "*Un plat bas*," he called it. "*Pas du tout festival.*" He would have voted capon—a plump Bresse capon that had spent the last two months of its life reclining on cushions in a private cage and eating soft, "secret" food—but when I pressed him he allowed that if he were forced to serve a turkey he would stuff it with petit-suisse cheese and sautéed apples, simmer it sous vide for an hour, and then roast it, with little basting splashes of Perrier to brown the skin. I wrote it all down.

I am what you might call an *amateur* of Thanksgiving. My family prefers the phrase "regrettably hospitable," but I would add strategically hospitable, because Thanksgiving dinner has turned out to be the stealth weapon of my reporting life. Everybody knows something about Thanksgiving, though not necessarily what we eat or why we eat it. The word has entered the global lexicon; like Mickey Mouse, Elvis, and Obama, it opens doors. I discovered this as a young reporter attempting to interview a Berber woman in a tent encampment a few hundred miles into the western Sahara, where I was pursuing a misbegotten story about nomadic women's rights. Her name was Fatma, and she was squatting beside a charcoal brazier, cooking her family's dinner and answering my questions about sexual oppression with the terse forbearance of an earthling suddenly confronted with a chatty alien, when I thought to ask her what was in her pot. She said it was goat—or, rather, pointed to a goat tethered outside her tent—and, smiling for the first time, asked if Americans ate goat at "the big feast of the hunters and the Christians." We talked for an hour, through my increasingly bewildered (male) interpreter, during which time I learned that there was no word for "feminism" in her language, or for that matter, for "recipe." But she knew about the big feast. I stayed for the goat. It was very tasty.

By now I can say that most of the people whose lives I've invaded since then, notebook in hand, sooner or later asked me about the big feast, and if they didn't, I told them. (The exceptions tend to be politicians, who, being not much given to what I would call a fruitful exchange of thoughts, will talk about food only if it's their food and reflects highly on their status: Silvio Berlusconi, say, enthusing over the white truffles slathered on his pasta, or François Mitterrand, whose bird of choice was a two-ounce songbird, plumped for a month on figs and millet, drowned in Armagnac, and then roasted and eaten whole, beak optional, with your head draped in a linen napkin—the better to inhale the perfume of steaming brandy.) The subject of food, and kitchens and cooking, can lull even the most reluctant and suspicious people into conversation, and when I add Thanksgiving, where the food is not only plentiful but familial and friendly, to that conversation, they will shed any lingering doubts as to my good intentions and tell me what I came to hear. But it also means that at the end of the day, when my notebooks are full, I tend to be so overcome by the sense of friendship I have engineered— or so grateful, or perhaps so guilty—that I invite everyone to join my family for a Thanksgiving dinner. Anytime. Anywhere. Sometimes they come. Once our doorman buzzed on Thanksgiving morning to say that my "guests" had arrived from Italy. I opened the door to a rustic couple whom I had last set eyes on years earlier, while writing about a group of Communist peasants with a dairy cooperative (you turned in your cow and got back a stock certificate with her name and her snapshot on it). They had recently sold their farmhouse to a rich German, left the party, and, never having been on a plane before, decided to take me up on my invitation. They picked at the food. The next night I made spaghetti.

I inherited my Thanksgiving strategy from my mother. It is said that families produce a good cook, or a good gardener, only every second generation, but given that I am a good cook and my daughter a spectacular one, I have to assume that we are correcting a generational imbalance—making up for the fact that my mother, whose talents lay more in pruning rosebushes than in stirring pots, was a terrible cook, and my grandmother worse. My mother's one culinary achievement was a bland but passable Thanksgiving dinner. (Her stuffing was onions, celery, white bread crumbs, and a pinch of salt.) But it was memorable compared with what usually passed for culinary excitement in Providence, Rhode Island, in the Eisenhower fifties—a place where ordering frenched chops at the butcher was considered flashy or, as my mother put it, "something they do in New York." And part of what made it memorable was the collection of hungry foreign people—professors from Brown, musicians in town for a concert, war-refugee doctors my father had met on his hospital rounds—who sat in our dining room then, praising my mother's stuffing as something exotic and American, or, you could say, *authentically* bland. It was a beautiful room, a room for feasting—the result of years of assaults on estate sales and hapless dealers who, as she liked to say, arriving home with a twenty-five-dollar cache of Georgian silver or an eighteenth-century Connecticut corner cabinet, "didn't know what they had." After she died, I moved almost everything in her dining room to my apartment in New York, hoping to move the spirit, if not the stuffing, of those Thanksgivings with them. My husband is an anthropologist, and it took a while for all that mahogany and silver to settle in with the Sepik River ancestor masks and assorted Pacific totems in their new room, but once they did, I wrote "Thanksgiving" on a manila folder and started clipping recipes.

My stuffing began as a recipe from the *Times*, circa 1974: onions, green bell pepper, and celery hearts, sautéed in butter, mixed with cornbread and some crumbled toast, and bound by a cup of chicken broth and a few raw eggs, according to the yellowed page that is now disintegrating between my daughter's Indian-pudding recipe and one for parsnip-and-pear purée. (Thanksgiving that year was "Southern," the paper said, "plus a few trimmings of European inspiration"—which may or may not explain the red cabbage I started making then.) The stuffing has expanded over the years,

with my kitchen confidence, to accommodate sausage, orange juice, parsley, thyme, sage, and an extravagant amount
of toasted and chopped pecans. It is still expanding, but in
1976, when I got out my mother's stuffing spoon and served
my first Thanksgiving dinner at her table, I followed every
recipe I used down to the quarter teaspoon. Clearing out a
closet the other day, I discovered a box of snapshots from that
Thanksgiving, taken by my friend and, at the time, downstairs neighbor Jane O'Reilly, who had appeared at my door
at nine in the morning, bearing fresh coffee cake to fortify
us for a long day's cooking. One of those pictures is on my
desk now; I am basting what looks like a twenty-pounder,
balanced precariously on the open door of the oven that
preceded my new stove. There are children and dogs under-
foot, and grown-ups hovering with potholders and coffee
cups in their hands. We are all laughing. Thanksgiving looks
easy, and it probably was, back in those early feminist days
before the idea of the perfect meal invaded the heads of otherwise accomplished women, convincing them that voluntary
servitude in the kitchen was the secret of their liberation.

At last count, I have cooked Thanksgiving dinner in seven
countries, starting with Morocco. The year was 1968. The
city was Meknes. The bride—me—was cooking without
benefit of silver, recipes, or a table. And the groom, deep in
fieldwork with a brotherhood of hospitable Sufi curers and
musicians who danced their patients into trance in amiable,
if occasionally bloody, exorcistic rituals, had decided, by way
of reciprocation, to introduce them to Thanksgiving. Our
larder, when I got this news, consisted of bread, Boulaouane
wine, and several sacks of eggplants, Meknes being some
months into an eggplant season that threatened to last all
winter—and did. I had never tasted an eggplant in Providence,

or for that matter at Vassar, where I went to college. My first experience with eggplants was in New York, at graduate school, and they were still as exotic to me as my mother's stuffing was to the Europeans at *her* Thanksgiving table. I had already made grilled eggplant, tagine with eggplant, couscous with eggplant, soup with eggplant, and even eggplant stuffed with eggplant, and whenever I was tired of eggplant we would drive to Rabat for a steak smothered in pizzaiola sauce—the specialty of a restaurant called La Mama, which was frequented that fall mainly by diplomats who were also tired of eggplant but not, in my experience there, by Sufi exorcists. So I made do.

I concocted an eggplant flan so thick with onions, cheese, and spices that the taste of the eggplant faded, though not, I have to admit, into the taste of red cabbage or sweet potatoes or Brussels sprouts. Everybody said they liked it. They said they liked my chicken, too—the only poultry within a hundred miles was chicken—and even my stuffing, which I had put together with onions, dates, and flatbreads from the local market. We sat in a circle on the floor (around a large brass platter that, along with a rug, two cushions, and a straw-filled mattress, amounted to the family furniture) and scooped up everything with our fingers, just like Pilgrims and Indians, and drank a good deal of mint tea and told stories. I would count that Thanksgiving as my first success. If the Sufis were a bit bewildered by my household arrangements—men and women eating together, sharing the best parts—they were too kind to say so. I was known thereafter, and not without affection, as the woman who chopped up bread and put it inside her chickens instead of leaving it on the platter, to wrap around the eggplant and sop up the sauce.

Over the next several years, I managed to cook some

semblance of Thanksgiving dinner whenever I was off reporting, trying to win the hearts and minds of unlikely
people. The worst was a dinner I put together in Södertälje,
Sweden, in the fall of 1975, for the families of three Yugoslav
workers from the local Saab-Scania factory. It wasn't the food
that failed. My cranberry (well, lingonberry) sauce was good,
and the turkey, fresh from my babysitter's boyfriend's mother's
oven, across the street, even better. But my guests, as history
soon showed, didn't really think of themselves as Yugoslavs.
They thought of themselves as Serbs, Slovenes, and Croats,
and while they had always been agreeable and even effusive
when we talked alone, they were not in the habit of breaking
bread together. The conversation was, putting it nicely,
strained; it flowed with the slivovitz that the men had brought,
and each of them brought two bottles. They were close to
brawling when the Slovenian's wife opened a box of homemade pastries—flaky, buttery mille-feuilles layered with
thick whipped cream. Peace returned to the kitchen table
in my borrowed flat and lasted until, flushed with compli-
ments and brandy, she smiled at the Serbs and Croats and
said, "Slovenians make the best cakes."

Then there was the Thanksgiving dinner I cooked for a
family of Ugandan-Asian refugees in Southhall, an outlying
London neighborhood where, in the early seventies, tens of
thousands of South Asian immigrants lived. I shopped with
the lady of the house—who, having vetoed a turkey of suspicious provenance (Harrods), had ordered her own from a
halal butcher—and cooked in her tidy kitchen, monitored by
her son, an excruciatingly pious eleven-year-old who, on his
imam's instructions, had stayed home from school to glare
into my pots and pans, hoping to catch his mother and me
in some unpardonable dietary indiscretion. (I repressed the

urge to sneak some bourbon into his mother's roasting pan, to capture the last sticky bits, and then into the pot of gravy, where all the alcohol would have evaporated in eleven minutes at a brisk simmer: a trick I had learned from a New York neighbor who had learned it in AA.) My daughter, who was in London with me—"missing a whole month of important peer experience," her nursery school teacher had protested—still remembers the perfume of Gujarat spices rubbed into turkey skin, and I came home with the recipe that transformed my dull creamed spinach into a marvelous saag paneer that I still serve, though not, admittedly, with Thanksgiving turkeys.

But none of my foreign Thanksgivings were as strange as the one I cooked in 1990, on the Rue du Cherche-Midi in Paris, where I kept an apartment-cum-office for seventeen years. It wasn't the food. I had shopped for a week. There were no mice sheltering behind the stove, as there had been the Thanksgiving before. (They roasted, sadly, with the turkey.) And I had discovered a table leaf in the *cave*, which gave me the space to invite fourteen people, if some of them brought chairs. The problem was my guests and their finicky European palates. The teenage son of some French friends sat down, announced that he ate only "white things," and helped himself to the lion's share of turkey breast and mashed potatoes. My daughter's boyfriend of the moment, a German student she had acquired on her last vacation, explained that *he* ate only "separate things"; he tackled his dinner dish by dish, disappearing into the kitchen after each one to wash his plate. My husband insists that the banker at his end of the table actually divided his meal into three mysterious sections—on the same plate but not touching—and ate them separately. I hadn't noticed. By then I was at the *glacier* on the rue du Bac, buying vanilla ice cream.

The problem with cooking Thanksgiving dinner away from home is never just the shopping, though that can drive you crazy: buttermilk (for cornbread) in Italy? chipotles in France? fresh pecans in Germany? The problem is what I would call the local culinary aesthetic. (Reinold Kegel, who cooked at the American Academy in Berlin when I was a fellow there, read up on the big feast, and inspired by the idea, and perhaps by the availability, of pumpkins, produced a Thanksgiving dinner that, barring the turkey, was almost entirely orange: pumpkin soup, pumpkin purée, pumpkin pie.) The fact is that a lot of Europeans are like my daughter's friend. They find it at best peculiar and at worst revolting to be expected to sit down to a groaning board of Thanksgiving dishes and, more to the point, to eat them smushed together into one big glorious taste—preferably under enough gravy to ensure that no food, as it were, sits alone. They like their tastes one at a time. Try going to a Chinese restaurant with a Frenchman or an Italian; he will order separately, guard his plate, and refuse to share his lemon chicken in exchange for a helping of your Hunan beef. One Frenchman I know even cleans his chopsticks with an alcohol wipe between courses, and I remember a Thanksgiving in Umbria where the same neighbors who had chucked the noodles I once served with rabbit paled when I handed them pumpkin ravioli and turkey on the same plate. Last month, thinking about that Thanksgiving, I called up Ron Suhanosky, who owns the restaurant Sfoglia, across the park from me in New York, and asked him how he cooked "Italian" Thanksgivings for his customers. He said he didn't. He took his family to Nantucket;

brined a turkey for four days; stuffed it with hazelnuts, "drunken prunes," and sweet Italian sausages; and generally "put a spin on Thanksgiving that's Italian." Homemade mostarda. Raw-kale salad. Brussels sprouts with crispy mortadella. A crusted sweet-potato sformata (he described it as "kind of a sweet-potato quiche") with béchamel, bread crumbs, Parmesan, and cream. And for dessert, his wife's department, Italian bread pudding or a panna cotta. It sounded good—all but the part about "no gravy, just a drizzle of olive oil."

Then, there is the problem of whose turkey you are cooking. A good French turkey is either a wild turkey, shot on the wing, or a turkey raised especially for Christmas—which amounts to the same thing: eight or nine pounds at most. And in Paris those eight pounds can set you back a hundred and fifty dollars, because your butcher knows that at Christmas the French will spend as lavishly on fish, fowl, caviar, foie gras, and champagne as we do on stocking stuffers and prime ribs. Last summer I asked my friend Catherine McGurn, a French dentist married to an American lawyer, if she had ever found a turkey big enough to satisfy the Americans in the Paris office of her husband's firm. She consulted a notebook in which she had recorded the menus and travails of her Paris Thanksgivings, and told me, "Once. 1991. Seventeen pounds." She said that the Americans ate everything in sight, down to the last cranberry and sweet potato, while the French friends whom she'd invited "took these little plates" and nibbled politely at everything except her stuffing, which they wolfed down, recognizing it as the same stuffing (known grandly as La Farce) they eat at Christmas: pain de mie mixed with pork sausage, ground veal, crumbled chestnuts, foie gras, and truffles. The McGurns live in

Rome now, a city that, from the point of view of Thanksgiving, makes Paris seem like Plymouth. Last winter, finding herself in Paris the day before a belated holiday dinner, she flew home with a hundred Belon oysters in an ice bag in her suitcase, along with some good French cheeses, rillettes, pâté de campagne, and a couple of blocks of foie gras from Les Landes. The lawyers in Rome loved it. No one noticed that there was no bird.

Last summer I decided to try another Thanksgiving dinner in Italy. Don't ask why I was even thinking about Thanksgiving—in Italy, in the heat, with a deadline looming and the garden outside my windows full of tomatoes, peppers, eggplant, zucchini, basil, garlic, arugula, baby lettuce, and a dozen other fresh, ripe, lovely Italian things that I can only dream about at home in New York in November. Or how I was going to cook it, given that my Italian stove is even more temperamental than my New York stove ever was. True, it also has two ovens, and the bigger one—call it the turkey oven—also stopped working in 1997; the difference is that my Italian oven still sits there, twelve years later, waiting for the technician who can figure out how to fix it. As for my stovetop, it is made entirely for pasta. There is a huge burner in the middle—which ignites with a whoosh of flame that laps at the handles of even the tallest pots and has to be coaxed down into submission before you can turn around—surrounded by four tiny burners whose only possible purpose is simmering pasta sauces that have already taken an hour or two to heat.

Still, it would be my first summer Thanksgiving anywhere. I was determined to cook it. The only summer Thanksgiving I had ever been to, let alone cooked, had taken place in 1974, at Mary McCarthy's house in Castine, Maine, to celebrate Richard Nixon's resignation. Mary was a serious hostess and a splendid cook, and more to the point, the only other person I knew who served Thanksgiving dinner out of season. Even her stuffing was splendid, despite the fact that there wasn't a trace of cornbread in it. On the other hand, she was not given to sharing recipes. (Years later, when we were neighbors in Paris, I ate it again at one of her November Thanksgivings and asked her to write it down. She smiled sweetly and said, "No, I don't think so.") But the thing I remember most about her Castine Thanksgiving was how easy she said the marketing had been: she had called a farmer, ordered a sixteen-pounder, and three days later it was there.

The bad thing about good memories is how cheerful and optimistic they can leave you feeling. I was going to find the finest turkey in Italy—or at least a turkey as good as Mary's—and with that in mind I got in the car, drove two hours from my house to a parking lot under the Borghese Gardens, and made my slow way, by taxi and foot, through Rome to the Via della Maddalena, where I asked Angelo Feroci, arguably the city's best meat and poultry purveyor, to find me a sixteen-pound turkey for July or August. Feroci looked astonished. "Impossible," he said. His turkeys were not only Christmas turkeys—"come back in December," he told me—they were *Italian* Christmas turkeys, which is to say, "younger and smaller and better" than anything the French ate. Then I remembered: most good butchers in Italy frown on large turkeys; it is a matter of reputation. They call them "poor food," because birds like that are usually raised in feed yards—not to sixteen pounds but to fifteen or sixteen kilos, which translates as thirty-five pounds of old tom turkey—after which they are sliced thin, packaged, and sold cheaply in

supermarkets as *petti di tacchino.* (Those slices are so ubiquitous that even the peasants who refuse to distinguish between
a duck and a goose, at least if they happen to be selling one—
or for that matter, who refer to all squash, from pumpkins to
zucchini, as *zucca*—admit that turkey is turkey.) They are the
kinds of turkeys my husband remembers from the army, which
may be why turkey is not his favorite food. The farmers who
supply places like Feroci's would never raise one; the farmers
competing with feed yards to supply my local co-op, in Todi,
would never consider anything smaller. Their feeling, which
dates from centuries of poverty, is "the bigger the bird, the
more people it can feed." (They feel the same way about
vegetables. Last year, I rescued a twenty-inch cucumber
from the back of my vegetable garden. I had thought it was a
skinny watermelon until our old gardener, now replaced,
said, "Cucumber, almost ready to eat.")

I asked Feroci what he told the Americans in Rome who
wanted Thanksgiving turkeys. He told them, laughing, "Invite fewer people, or order two." He allowed that he had been
ordering "Christmas turkeys" for November since the early
sixties, when Burt Lancaster, who was filming the interiors
for *The Leopard* at Cinecittà, walked in and asked for one.
There was some discussion. Feroci won the first battle—seven
pounds, no bigger—but he couldn't persuade the actor to let
him bone the bird and stuff it with, among other good things,
prunes and pistachios, ready to be cooked and cut across into
"pretty slices, full of colors inside." Now, he says, his customers get "pretty" or none at all.

That was June. I was still searching for a sixteen-pounder
in July, when an old Paris friend and fellow journalist named
Merete Baird decided to fly to Italy with her husband for a
long weekend. She asked if I needed anything from Paris, and

I heard myself saying, "Yes, a turkey." My husband was horrified, but Merete is Danish—which is to say, exuberant in the face of a challenge—and she said, "Of course." Her turkey traveled, like Catherine's oysters, in a thermos bag in the luggage hold, and despite its hours in airport taxis, French security checks, and Italian baggage claims, smelled fine when I unwrapped it. I set the table on the porch for eight people and began to cook. At seven and a half pounds, it just fit into the little oven where I had been doing my roasting for thirteen years, and I had thought to buy a bottle of bourbon for the gravy. Sadly, there were no pumpkins in my garden yet, or even canned pumpkin at the co-op, and, given the refrigerator-life expectancy of a bird that had just emerged from the hold of an Air France jet, there was certainly no time to persuade a dairy farmer to ferment a couple of cups of milk into latte acido, or soured milk, which, I had just discovered, was close enough to buttermilk for a cornbread stuffing.

I searched my memory for the tastes in Mary McCarthy's stuffing. I spent the morning trying to reconstruct it. It was not a success. But I managed to transform my sweet-potato purée into a carrot purée—there were young carrots in the garden—with molasses that someone had brought from New York years earlier standing in for the maple syrup, red peperoncini for the chipotles, and fresh cream from the dairy for the crème fraîche. I brightened some local spinach with beet-root greens. I made grits, with Sardinian Pecorino—the nearest thing I could find to a sharp Cheddar—using the last bag of stone-ground cornmeal that I had brought from New York, since, for reasons I have never pierced, Umbrians stop cooking with cornmeal at the summer solstice, and it virtually disappears from the market shelves. But I couldn't claim credit for the apple and frutti di bosco crumble, steeped in maraschino liqueur—my friend Lin Widmann, an Anglo-Argentine painter from a long line of English pudding fanatics, made that—or even for the French turkey, which I have to admit had been born delicious.

Given the success of my little July Thanksgiving—I thought of it as a trial run—I scheduled a big Thanksgiving for my birthday, on August 7. I looked for a new oven. I visited poultry farmers. I tried to negotiate the slaughter of one of the sixteen-pounders I would always see, strutting like teenagers, in their backyards. I held out ridiculous sums of money, but I could not shake the farmers' conviction that you don't slaughter a bird that will double in size, and yield, in a matter of four months. Their answer was always the same: "Too small. Not ready." Marketing is not what I like to do in Umbria. Unless I am off somewhere on a story, I don't do much of anything that can't be done within a mile of home. I sit on the porch steps and watch the sun rise. I smile at sunflowers. I sit at my desk and write. Toward the end of the afternoon, I check out my figs and my pots of basil and marjoram—Umbrians love marjoram and will not touch oregano—thyme and parsley, and then I tap my way through the vegetable garden with a big stick (Umbria is viper country) and a basket, and head for the kitchen to chop and slice whatever I've carried back. At night I cook it. Once in a while, I will drive north to Todi and pick up a chicken or a guinea fowl at the co-op, or south to Avigliano for mussels or *spigola* at the local fish store. But if you had asked me in July where in Perugia or Terni to find a big new oven that would fit between the counters that flank my stove, I wouldn't have been able to say. And if you had asked me where to find a farm-raised sixteen to eighteen-pounder I would probably have cried.

By then, I had exhausted two Italian provinces in my turkey quest. So I crossed the Monti Martani (a massif best known as the epicenter of the earthquake that toppled the ceilings of the Basilica of Saint Francis of Assisi in 1997) to consult with my friends Joanna Ross and Bruce Adgate. The Rossgates, as they are sometimes called, have been an Umbria resource since the day they decided to quit their jobs in New York—Joanna was a theater agent and Bruce an actor with Ellen Stewart's La MaMa theater company—to move with their ten-year-old son to Eggi, a village near Spoleto (where Bruce had spent three summers performing Euripides in the mid-seventies). They went to work restoring a fifteenth-century village house, best described at the time as a pile of stones, and in the process unearthed a bread-and-pizza oven just outside the wall of their son's bedroom. The oven was falling apart, but they peered into its cavernous beehive chamber and immediately thought Thanksgiving, or, as Bruce puts it, "Getting it back in shape went right up there with plumbing and heat as one of my high priorities." He worked on the oven all summer, making pizzas. By November of 1993, he was able to roast a Thanksgiving turkey for ten people. (His biggest turkey, to date, weighed thirty-seven and a half pounds, and thirty-five people spent the better part of two days polishing it off.) In July of 2009, he volunteered his oven for my next Thanksgiving, and more to the point, his services at the oven, because just firing it up— feeding it wood until the embers turn red and the bricks lining it white hot—takes four or five hours of skilled hard labor and leaves you drenched, even in November. In August, you *start* drenched.

So I moved Thanksgiving across the mountain. I stopped looking for an oven, and a few days later, when Joanna called with the news that she and Bruce had prevailed on their butcher to find a farmer willing to part with a turkey for fifteen or sixteen people, I stopped looking for a bird, too. We made a guest list of American friends who lived in or around Spoleto and would be spared having to cross a mountain after a feast that, according to Bruce, promised to last past midnight. We made a shopping list. Bruce, whose Thanksgiving specialty is pumpkin pie, came home that night with the first pumpkin of the season. Joanna discovered a dusty bottle of maple syrup at the back of a shelf in a discount supermarket called Sabatini, which didn't surprise me; she can find anything, and what she doesn't find, she grows. We were in countdown mode when Naomi Duguid, the Canadian food scholar and cookbook writer I had got to know on assignment last year, e-mailed to say that she was flying to Italy that week. I invited her to Thanksgiving and, of course, gave her the rest of my shopping list. She arrived at night, on August 5, and emptied a suitcase full of rapidly defrosting cranberries on my kitchen table, along with a sack of pecans, two jars of chipotles, three cans of organic pumpkin, and homemade crackers for the cooks. Dinner was pasta al pesto (my basil pots) and salad (my garden) tossed with oil from my olive trees, and it left me thinking how much simpler life would be if the Pilgrims had been Italian.

The next morning, we drove to a farmers' market for spinach and dandelion greens, and then to my favorite Todi salumeria to discuss with the salumerista's wife the pros and cons of faro or chestnut flour for my stuffing bread. It was our *festa del ringraziamento*, I told her, only a little early. She considered my problem for a minute, disappeared into the stockroom, and emerged with a two-pound sack of local cornmeal, stamped "To be eaten by June 21, 2009," which she had been saving for herself. ("Of course you can use it," she said.) By lunchtime, I had started a pumpkin purée, and Naomi, having discovered three plum trees on the hill behind my kitchen door, had managed to bake two plum cakes and a loaf of bread and to produce a mysteriously spiced and soured cranberry sauce, which, she assured me, was much prized in its original incarnation as a sour-plum sauce in Georgia (the republic, not the state). Lunch was salami, prosciutto, creamy Campania mozzarella, garden tomatoes, and cucumber salad; it emptied the fridge. The afternoon meant cornbread. The recipe I had found, tearing through cookbooks, seemed a little off—six eggs, for one thing—but it looked easy, and, more to the point, it was the only one without buttermilk. I should have known better. When Bruce and Joanna crossed the mountain that afternoon with maple syrup for my purée, giblets for my gravy, fenugreek seeds for Naomi's cranberries, and fresh pumpkin for Bruce's pies, they found us crumbling burnt cornmeal goo onto a cookie sheet to dry.

Eggi is a walled medieval village tucked into one of the Apennine foothills, with a road that winds up to the church and then turns into a path—which is to say that to get to the Rossgates' house you walk. We were three people, a very large dog, my grandmother's turkey roaster, which I had carried on a plane from New York ten years earlier (turn-of-the-twentieth-century pans were made to last) and six big and extremely heavy Le Creuset pots, bought on the last day of a going-out-of-business sale in Todi and one of them filled with what was left of my gravy stock, which had splashed and splattered all over the back of the car by the time we parked. Ullie, the dog, licked up the gravy. The climb, pot by pot, in the August sun, took twenty minutes. The first

thing I saw, walking up the steep stone steps to the Rossgates' house, was a fiendish circle of flames leaping out of the
enormous mouth of the pizza oven, and Bruce, with a bottle
of cold white wine and a pair of long iron tongs, waiting for
me in a deck chair.

I fled up to the house, where Naomi was already at work,
doctoring our greens with spices from Joanna's larder, and
Joanna herself, an inspired cook, was slipping a paste of pancetta, garlic, and rosemary under the skin of a perfect turkey
that covered most of her kitchen table. Her mother had just
arrived, bearing a case of prosecco, and she and her husband
were sitting in the garden, filling glasses for the first guests.
They came, like Indians, with offerings—everything from ca-
ponata and olives to platters and decorations. Big cardboard
turkeys were soon perched on the garden tables, their tails
unfolding into a kaleidoscope of crepe-paper pleats. The trees
were draped with the Rossgates' Christmas lights, and a string
of big gold letters—HAPPY THANKSGIVING—was dangling between two pergola poles, waiting for a breeze.

The bricks turned white by the end of the afternoon. The
turkey slid into the oven. Bruce covered the mouth with an
iron sheet, to seal in the heat, and the two of us settled into
the deck chairs, poured some wine, and told Thanksgiving
stories. (I have to admit that Bruce's were better, given that
in the past five years he and Joanna had managed to pull off
credible Thanksgiving dinners in Mexico, Vietnam, and Ar-
gentina and were planning to do it again this year in Laos.)
From time to time, he would pull on the thickest mitts I had
ever seen, lift the sheet with his tongs, prod the roasting pan
into a half-turn, and from a safe distance, fling some wine
over the bird to baste it. People drifted down from the garden,
watched for a while, and disappeared back up the garden

steps. It has to be said that I was not much use that evening as a sous-chef. My one attempt at flinging wine into the fiery maw of the pizza oven fell at least a foot short of the roasting pan. On the other hand, Bruce was spared all my Thanksgiving in New York anxieties: should the bird be lying on its back in the pan, or upside down, or on one side and then the other? Should it be falling apart from "slow cooking," or turning crisp from a quick run, legs and wings akimbo, under a blast of electric heat? Should it be basted with butter, or wrapped in a cloak of wet cheesecloth, or left to smolder under a paper bag? Our eighteen-pounder—roasting, by Bruce's calculations, at somewhere between seven hundred and eight hundred degrees—was golden-brown, tender, and on its platter in not much more than an hour. The pots of pumpkin purée and doctored stuffing went into the oven to reheat. I poured some bourbon into the roaster. It sizzled into a juicy sauce, which brought my gravy pot close to brimming, and ready to carry upstairs.

It turned into a fine night. A soft breeze blew in from across the Spoleto Valley and set the HAPPY THANKSGIVING fluttering; the chimes in the garden trees came to life. I forgot the work of the past few weeks and joined the party. The best thing about Thanksgiving is that it is always worth it. Everyone agreed on that. In fact we decided to do it again next summer. We toasted Thanksgiving at midnight with what was left of the wine and a bottle of Jack Daniel's that the Rossgates had stashed for the occasion. I fell asleep in the car and dreamed of leftovers, going home.

RITES, RITUALS, AND CELEBRATIONS

⚜

DECEMBER 2016/FEBRUARY 2017

In January of this year, when the Metropolitan Museum's medievalists Melanie Holcomb and Barbara Drake Boehm were five years into researching and assembling the exhibit "Jerusalem 1000–1400: Every People Under Heaven," they called Yotam Ottolenghi in London to talk about holding a period celebration soon after their show opened in the fall. Ottolenghi was born and raised in Jerusalem. And given that his cookbooks, restaurants, and documentaries have been largely responsible for our millennial obsession with the tastes and colors and textures of the Eastern Mediterranean, it isn't surprising that Holcomb and Boehm—having spotted an eleventh-century brass lentil pot and brazier in a cache of metalwork long buried in a huge clay fenugreek jar in Caesarea—decided to throw a medieval Jerusalem dinner at the museum, and said to each other "Ottolenghi!" (*Jerusalem* was the third of Ottolenghi's six cookbooks.) "We travel together, we love to eat, it's part of what we do," Holcomb told me, describing their first trip to one of Ottolenghi's London restaurants, and their decision to celebrate Jerusalem's cultural heritage and its historic diversity with a feast that would evoke civility and amity in what is arguably a politically toxic present.

A few weeks later, Ottolenghi flew to New York for meetings with the two curators and with Limor Tomer, the director of the Met's Live Arts program, and in the course of them, suggested bringing on board the food writers Maggie Schmitt and Laila El-Haddad, whose cookbook *The Gaza Kitchen* was for him an eloquent reminder of the fact that, however potent its symbolic status and however many armies fought to control it, medieval Jerusalem was a dusty provincial town, with little to offer by way of a great culinary tradition of its own, whereas Gaza, at the time, was a prominent trade-route port and cultural center where the classic Indian spices—galangal, ginger, cloves, and cinnamon, to name a few—had transformed the local cuisine into a repository of flavor, fit for what you might call high-end feasting.

Back in London, Ottolenghi started researching Arabic texts of the period, which, he says, introduced him to the "richly thick dining history" of the Abbasid dynasty, whose decline had opened the door to the First Crusade at the end of the eleventh century, ushering in ninety years of Christian rule, but whose glory years had long since defined the sumptuous and extravagant potlatch style of the high court celebrations that resumed during the Ayyubid Caliphate, when Saladin's armies took back Jerusalem from the Europeans. It was, as Ottolenghi puts it, "a period notably obsessed with the culinary arts."

A few weeks later, he went to work in his London test kitchen, transforming the arcane clues and measurements gleaned from hundreds of medieval recipes into dishes adapted to the Met's vast basement kitchen, not to mention his own. El-Haddad, a Gazan who lives in Maryland, and

Schmitt, a New Yorker who lives in Spain, are scholars of the Abbasid high-court banquets, which in the dynasty's heyday involved as many as two or three hundred dishes, and they kept in touch with Ottolenghi for the next six months, sharing research and results, until together they had worked out what Ottolenghi calls "the significant flavors" that you would have found in any one of those feasts. Most notable, he says, were the combinations of sweet and sour—of fruits, say, cooked with meat. Then came the flavors of preserving—pickling fish, for instance, in the white-pomegranate vinegar known as "Babylonian vinegar" and honey. But the most surprising delicacies of all were bananas. "The Europeans who arrived in the eleventh century were bananas about bananas," Ottolenghi told me, his point being that for every period of crusaders gnawing bones at dinner there were periods of great gastronomic surprises and sophistication and even a certain amount of monotheistic mingling. (In Hebron, for instance, an ancient Abrahamic tradition of hospitality ensured that any stranger entering the town was welcomed and fed.)

The daily staples of medieval Jerusalem were bread and lentils. Lentil pots like the one the two Met curators found were the sine qua non of every Jerusalem kitchen, from the humblest to the most elaborate. So, too, was the battery of tools with which wheats and grains were pounded and refined in very distinct and various ways to produce whiter, lighter flours and hence more delicate breads and pastries. Europeans, accustomed to heavy, unrefined breads—especially rye-flour breads—took to them instantly, as well as to the unaccustomed taste of cane sugar, which came from the marshes of Iraq, in their desserts. Ottolenghi and his young test-kitchen cook, Esme Howarth, spent the better part of six months translating the instructions and ingredients in

scores of ancient recipes into their contemporary equivalents, or near equivalents—their job being to create new
dishes that would still be unmistakably medieval.

El-Haddad and Schmitt say that they dreamed of serving
a hundred of those dishes at the banquet, passed and shared
at long, low, communal tables, with everyone sitting on the
floor eating with their fingers, making the celebration a lesson in historical authenticity. Their dreams were dashed, not
only by the impossibility of sourcing and cooking all those
exotic dishes (for one thing, there are no armies of slaves in
the Met's kitchen), but by the strong likelihood that the kind
of people willing to spend a hundred and twenty-five dollars
to sit on the floor for a forkless three-hour meal would be
too old or simply too stiff to get up from the floor once they
finished eating. After some negotiation, and a test run
through the famous multicultural shelves and counters of the
purveyor Kalustyan's, fifty blocks south of the Met on Lexington Avenue, the menu was fixed at thirteen courses. As
for the proper libations, Ottolenghi ordered local Cremisan
wines—red and white—from vineyards in the Judean Hills
that Salesian monks have been cultivating for the last eight
hundred years (and that are now threatened by an Israeli
government attempt to claim the land for new settlements,
as well as for a new wall pushing back the Palestinians who
still live there). The irony was not lost on the diners when
on the second of two sold-out nights of feasting, he told the
vineyard's story and El-Haddad talked about visiting her
parents in Gaza but being unable to cross into Israel and visit
the city whose celebration she was helping to plan.

In the end, though, there was something inspiring, even
hopeful, about a meal served in the wing of a great museum at
a couple of tables so long that a hundred and twenty people,

most of them strangers, could sit down together, passing platters of arguably odd, unfamiliar food, chatting to each other
about it and then about themselves and, by the end of the
evening, exchanging e-mail addresses and phone numbers
while, at the front of the room, Ottolenghi, El-Haddad, and
Schmitt, holding microphones, explained the courses as they
appeared. I learned from Ottolenghi that when he was a boy,
his parents liked taking him to the Cremisan cellars "to see
how the monks did it"; and from El-Haddad that alcohol is an
Arabic word, and is also the word for kohl; and from Schmitt
that the sweet-and-sour marinade from the halibut we were
about to eat—and from which Europeans derived seviche
and escabeche—has practically disappeared from Arab cuisine; and from all three of them that an abundance of sugar,
when it came to sweets, was a sign of wealth, generosity, and
refinement.

The next day I avoided the scale and ate vicariously by
reading and rereading the menu I had saved. The first course
included, along with the halibut, platters of wine-poached
quinces with spices, blue cheese, and walnut brittle; braised
fennel, capers, and olives in verjus; burnt aubergine, tahini
sauce, cucumber, pomegranate, and Urfa chili; chicken meatballs with melokhia, garlic and coriander; and sambousek
root-vegetable pies with cardamom and lime yogurt. The main
course involved slow-cooked lamb shoulder with figs, apricots,
and an almond-and-orange-blossom salsa; sweet-and-sour
leeks, goat's curd and currants; green beans with pistachio and
preserved lemon; and harak osbao, a lentil dish of such irresistible complexity that its Arabic name means "he burnt his
fingers," perhaps because the cook couldn't wait to try it. Dessert was kataifi (shredded filo) nests filled with feta-and-saffron
cheesecake; and pomegranate granita, with mint and roses.

"Something light, after all that food," Ottolenghi had said.

That night I e-mailed him asking what, exactly, went into harak osbao, figuring that it must have been the one dish on the menu with too many ingredients to list. The next morning, this was in my inbox:

Harak Osbao

This is a dish for a feast, yet it is extremely comforting and delicious with all the toppings mixed in. Serves eight to ten.

> 40g tamarind, soaked with 200ml boiling
>   water
> 250g fettuccine, broken up roughly
> 60 milliliters olive oil
> 2 red onions, thinly sliced (350g)
> 1.5 litres chicken stock
> 350g brown lentils
> 2 tbsp pomegranate molasses
> 6 garlic cloves, crushed
> 30g coriander, roughly chopped
> 20g parsley, roughly chopped
> 90g pomegranate seeds
> 2 tsp sumac
> 2 lemons cut into wedges
> Flaky sea salt and black pepper

1. Mix the tamarind with the water well to separate the pips. Strain the liquid into a small bowl, discarding the pips and set aside.

2. Place a large saucepan on a medium-high heat, and once hot, add the broken-up fettuccine. Toast for 1 to 2 minutes until the pasta starts to brown, then remove from the pan and set aside.

3. Pour 2 tablespoons of oil into the pan and return to a medium-high heat. Add the onion and fry for 8 minutes, stirring frequently until golden and soft. Remove from the pan and set aside.

4. Add the chicken stock to the pan and place on a high heat. Once boiling, add the lentils, reduce the heat to medium, and cook for 20 minutes, or until soft. Add the toasted fettuccine, tamarind water, 150 millilitres water, pomegranate molasses, 4 teaspoons of salt, and lots of pepper. Continue to cook for 8 to 9 minutes until the pasta is soft and almost all of the liquid has been absorbed, and set aside for 10 minutes. The liquid will continue to be absorbed, but the lentils and pasta should remain moist.

5. Place a small saucepan on a medium-high heat with 2 tablespoons of oil. Add the garlic and fry for 1 to 2 minutes until just golden brown. Remove from the heat and stir in the coriander.

6. Spoon the lentils and pasta into a large shallow serving bowl. Top with the garlic and coriander, parsley, pomegranate seeds, sumac and serve with the lemon wedges.

It's safe to say that good food is, and probably always was, what separates celebrations from rites and rituals, where the food is prescribed and, in the case of rites, ingestion tends to be more symbolic than tasty. (Think communion wafer.) I confess to being an avid drop-of-a-hat celebrator, so it stands to reason that after years of marriage to an anthropologist and a working life of travel, I have also become something of an *amateur* of the history and ethnography of celebration, of how different people celebrate and why they celebrate, whether it's a couple of hungry museum curators inspired by the discovery of an ancient lentil pot or Ed Koch presiding over a groaning board at Gracie Mansion or, as he once put it, "celebrating not being poor anymore." And what's amazing to me is that until food became a respectable field of social and cultural history, you could read the most exhaustive studies of people and their celebrations and find so little about the food those people ate and where it came from, who grew or raised it, how it was prepared and cooked, and what made it special—or, you could say, celebratory.

Four years after we got married, my husband and I took our baby daughter to a village called Bonnieux, in southern France, for the summer, and when I wasn't busy sweeping scorpions out the door of our cellar kitchen or laying foam rubber over the stone floors in the rest of the house we'd rented—a primitive form of babyproofing, or more accurately, baby-saving, on the order of plastic socket blockers—I started reading Laurence Wylie's famous study *Village in the Vaucluse*, about the people of a nearby village named Roussillon, which he called Peyrane. Wylie, who taught anthropology at Harvard when my husband was studying there, had lived in Roussillon during the first two winters of the 1950s, and six years later had produced his book, which remains a classic in the field of French rural studies. It was in most ways a wonderfully rich portrait. Every aspect of life in Roussillon—all the rivalries and feuds and infidelities and secrets—seemed to be covered, or so I'd thought when I lived in Bonnieux, twenty years later, thrilled to be so close to such a legendary place. But when I took down the book again, six years ago, in the course of writing a talk about celebration that I was due to give at Oxford, I was stunned to discover that there wasn't a word about what most people in Roussillon ate, celebrating—or pretty much what they ate at all, beyond the chestnuts that one ingenuous housewife roasted in a worn-down skillet into which she had punched holes. More distressing, the one chapter purportedly *about* celebrating was mainly confined to the menu for the village's yearly banquet—"our firemen's banquet," the villagers called it—a desultory affair which no one but Roussillon's six firemen and the mayor attended, because it was so expensive. Here's what the firemen ate and drank, five years after the end of the Second World War:

- Choice of hors d'oeuvre
- Lobster à l'américaine
- Civet of hare du Ventoux
- Hearts of artichoke peyrannais
- Canapé of Alpine thrush
- Homemade pastries
- Local red wine, rosé wine reserve, sparkling wine, coffee and liqueurs

That was it: less a menu, actually, than a list, given that it lacked any of the intimations of color, taste, and texture that a great menu would evoke. I thought, "Wait a minute, Professor Wylie! Where did the firemen get their lobsters?" This was a question of keen reportorial interest to me, since, at the time of their banquet, Roussillon was dirt poor, postwar dirt poor—like Koch's boyhood Bronx neighborhood—not to mention *literally* dirt poor, since it stood in precipitous dirt-road isolation in the Luberon mountains, hours from a paved road, let alone a seacoast. It was also of some gastronomic interest to me—a New Englander stripped down at her computer in the sweltering heat of an Umbrian summer, picturing the thousands of lobster pots bobbing in the cool Atlantic, off the Maine coast, and getting hotter and hungrier by the minute. I also wanted to know what besides thrush went into a canapé of Alpine thrush, and who had actually baked those homemade pastries, and how much time did it take the women—I assumed it was women—to make them and, more to the point, what kind of pastries were they. I wanted to know what kind of wood the women of Roussillon fed into their centuries-old stone ovens for the different dishes on that menu. I wanted to know who caught the hare for the lepre du Ventoux, and what went into the sauce, and what did *it* taste like. What in fact did a lugubriously bourgeois menu like the firemen's mean in Roussillon? What did *food* mean? And most of all, why and what were those firemen celebrating? For me, rereading Wylie was like reading my first biography of Edith Wharton, a passionate decorator, and learning nothing at all about what her living room in Newport looked like, or what colors she preferred, and what kind of fabric she used for curtains.

There is, of course, plenty of celebration in fiction. Emma Bovary transformed herself from farmer's daughter to respectable bourgeois doctor's wife in the course of one copious wedding dinner. The oozing charcuterie and reeking cheeses in Zola's *Le Ventre de Paris* were emblems of the greedy potlatch feasts of Louis-Napoléon's ascendancy. Balzac—who himself went from months of famine (self-inflicted while writing a novel) to a day of feasting (when the novel was finished), which, as the writer Anka Muhlstein tells us in her enchanting book *Balzac's Omelette*, always began with an order for a hundred oysters and four bottles of white wine, followed by lamb chops, duckling, roast partridge, and Normandy sole, topped off with dessert and Comice pears—raised the possibility that the most satisfying celebration of all was a solitary one. And in this, Balzac had something in common with Mad King Ludwig of Bavaria, who built himself a castle for one called Linderhof, with a single bedroom and, more to the point, a single chair for feasting alone in his small mirrored dining room, surrounded by endless refractions of perhaps the finest collection of Meissen on the planet. But even Balzac's attention to cookery in celebration could flag when it came to the upstairs-downstairs Paris of the banquets he describes in *Illusions Perdues*, which had mainly to with adjustments and readjustments of favor by way of table seating; it's hard to imagine the guilefully ingenuous Lucien de Rubempré venturing into anyone's kitchen to watch the pastry chef spin sugar or ask the cook at the fireplace where to buy a proper roasting spit.

It took Virginia Woolf, in *To the Lighthouse*, to lead us from vegetable garden to kitchen to dinner table for the Sunday boeuf bourgignon prepared and served by the sublime Mrs. Ramsay at her summer house on the Isle of Skye. Mrs. Ramsay regarded Sunday dinner as a celebration—a coming together of family and friends, an occasion for matchmaking, for an embrace of lonely, solitary people (call it a gathering of strays) and for the courtesies that a prescribed occasion involves. Children bathed and behaving. Interesting, agreeable conversation. Time out of time, or what we call liminal time—a passage from the ordinariness of daily life into the next round of daily life by way of a salubrious diversion that restores connections, renewing affection for that life and for the people in it. All celebrating is, in that sense, liminal, and it has been more and more obvious to me, as a reader, that I owe my fascination or, more accurately, obsession, with the part food plays in the experience of celebration to (as with so much else) Woolf and her luminous creation. Mrs. Ramsey literally changed the way I see, and the questions I ask, and the conclusions I draw whenever I sit down at my desk to write.

Last summer in Italy, my husband and I went to the penultimate night of our local sagra—a two-week-long celebration during which the women of the village of Sismano prepare nightly dinners for the hundreds of people who come from similar villages in the area to eat, dance, drink, and play. In larger towns—towns with a few thousand rather than fifty or a hundred people—the sagra used to include a pageant or a historical reenactment. In one sagra, in a town off the mountain road we take to Spoleto, you can still wander through narrow streets, from tableau vivant to tableau vivant, with a paper cup of terrible red wine and your plate heaped with local specialties, and the most popular of those tableaux is always the one with a witch burning at the stake. Girls from the town compete to play her, and the winner each year is always the prettiest girl who can scream and groan the loudest.

In most towns, the sagra used to be political. The Christian Democrats had one, the Communists had one, and the Socialists had one. They were a way of reinforcing, with an eye to the next election, what you could call communities of ideology, through food, music, and regrettably, long speeches.

But Sismano, which is literally tucked into a castle close, was part of a feudal estate until the 1950s, and politics were not encouraged by the local nobility—the result being that our sagra had none of those ideological diversions: no oompah bands playing "The Internationale"; no tipsy bishop telling you to vote for the party of God; no posters of a perennially renascent Berlusconi. It did use to include a procession honoring the Madonna on the last of its fourteen nights, but a few years ago the local priest rescheduled it for the following Sunday, saying that he didn't want to spoil the fun with too much piety—meaning, of course, that there was a limit to mixing the sacred and the profane. The result is that no one in Sismano actually knows anymore what it is they're celebrating or why, only that "that's what we do in June, and in July, we'll go to the sagra in Castel dell' Aquila, and then the one in Avigliano, and before you know it will be September."

Here's what happens at the Sismano sagra. All the otherwise unbridgeable differences between castle and contadini break down (though, this being a nighttime celebration, they are certainly preserved during the day). Our local marquesa, a beautiful and very sexy woman who is usually regarded with longing from a deferential distance, dances with all the men. The village children sit on her lap and wipe their hands on her designer dresses. (I should explain that the local specialty is stinco di maiale, a roasted pork shank you can polish off with your fingers at a sagra, though presumably with a knife and fork at home. The men get drunk and air old quarrels, and end the evening the best of friends. Everybody embraces. Our gardener, a man of such exquisite decorum that he insists on knocking whenever he carries a pail of vegetables to the kitchen, planted a kiss on both my cheeks, and so did the ironsmith who made our lanterns and the base for our porch table.

Here's what our sagra is not. It's not a harvest feast, to mark the end of the trebbiatura. The harvest is at least a month away. It's not the birthday of Sismano's patron saint; that's in August. When I ask my neighbors why they're celebrating, the best they can think of to say is, "It's time," and to prove it they go on eating. A lot of celebrations are like that. When the Navajo celebrate the slaughter of a sheep, it's not for one of the incantational ceremonies known as ways—an enemy way, say, or a ghost way, or a supplication for rain. They don't even say, "We're killing the sheep because we're celebrating." They say, "We're celebrating because we've killed the sheep; it was time." The age and readiness of the sheep—that's the determinant. The Navajo are herders. They were once a nomadic people and their homesteads today tend to be far apart. When a sheep is slaughtered, they come together from all over to celebrate—and of course to eat it. And a far-flung community is rearticulated.

Whether you eat a sheep or a pork shank, you do the same thing, celebrating—even if it's just two people celebrating an anniversary. You get together, you do something transformative, something that renews the group or the family or the couple. Celebration is civilizing. It deepens the bonds that can keep people who have no choice but to live together from killing each other—and as often as not, it does this with food that's special to the occasion. On New Year's Eve in Italy, it's lentils and sausage. In China, it's noodles. In France, it's foie gras; you save for a year to buy the best. What's more, you tend to get dressed up—a dinner jacket or a slinky gown is enough to transform most people into glamorous, romantic strangers, even if they go to the same dinner with the same old people and eat the same old thing every year. In fact, the most satisfyingly transgressive way to celebrate the New Year may be to stay home in your sweats and eat something different.

On Christmas Eve, the menu is seven courses, and if you're doing it right in a Catholic country like Italy, it's fish. On birthdays, by now almost universally, it's a cake with candles. At Pagan weddings, as I discovered when my friend Margot Adler, who was a Wicca priestess, married, it's a symbolic display and tasting of a lamb shank and bitter herbs, just like Passover. (I often wonder how many of America's Pagans grew up in secular Jewish families.) At christenings, in much of Europe, it's a symbolic mix of salty and sweet, and the rules are strict. I am godmother to two French children, and the instructions presented to me for sweet and savory were as clearly defined as the kind of the gold cross I was supposed to buy for the Catholic baby to wear on a gold chain—solid and plain—as opposed to the one for the Calvinist baby, which, contrary to my expectations, was uncommonly elaborate and came with a little gold bird (which is to say the Holy Spirit) hovering on top. In Morocco, when you break fast at sundown during the month of Ramadan, the celebratory meal always begins with a special soup called harira. Next door in Algeria, the harira is different, but the imperative is the same. In Whatcom County, Washington, at a time when rural poverty was driving people out of their houses and into trailers, they celebrated payday with potluck dinners, the rule for which was explicitly, and defiantly, "Bring trailer-trash food." At baseball games in New York, everybody eats hot dogs and drinks beer in the bleachers—a ritual you could call "Yankee fans are one people" or "Mets fans are one people." In Boston, you also eat hot dogs, but there it means, "Red Sox fans are one people, in teams and taste." After high school proms, it's twelve kids and a carton of pizza in a stretch limo. At American movies, the celebratory food is popcorn. You are out of the house in a dark room with a couple of hundred strangers, all noisily munching on the same thing. This is a ritual I embrace. I cannot watch a movie without a bag of popcorn on my lap; it would be a kind of blasphemy. I know this because my husband prefers the little gummy candies called Dots, and the looks he always gets from the people in our row are killing.

In 1967, when I was writing a book about Allen Ginsberg and his friends, we made a ritual climb of Mount Tamalpais, near San Francisco—a mountain sacred to the tribes that had first settled Northern California. We were celebrating "being." The climb was arduous, made more so by the fact that we were chanting Sanskrit mantras as we climbed. Our goal was to make a joyous circumambulation of the mountaintop. No one could say whether the Native Americans ever did that, or whether the Tibetan guru with us did the same thing, back home in the Himalayas. But the love generation was very syncretic—so we just did it. I sprained my ankle crossing a rocky stream on my way down, and was "healed" with a joint, accompanied by a mudra to take the pain away. At the bottom of the mountain, we trooped to an ice-cream store in our beads and boots and sweaty clothes. I ordered a cone of fudge ripple. Allen stopped me. "The flavor has to be rocky road," he said. "It's part of the celebration. We eat it every time." The ritualized repetition of a menu is part of what makes celebrating so satisfying. Every year, on my husband's birthday, I make linguine alle vongole, which started out as a simple dish with Manila clams steamed open in a white wine and garlic sauce, but has become incrementally tastier and more elaborate, for which I credit Mario Batali's sublime addition of diced pancetta, red onions, and hot pepper flakes to the recipe, not to mention my own self-appointed license to double the amount of whatever ingredients I like best, especially the clams. On our anniversary, we go out. At first it was always to the modest (okay, cheap), bring-your-own-bottle Afghan restaurant on St. Mark's Place where we spent what could be called our first date, meaning that he paid my half of a bill which, as friends, we had always split. Thankfully, the restaurant closed before I could deliver an ultimatum. We went to Le Bernardin, and I never looked back.

Every year, I wait for Easter, Passover, and the Muslim holiday I knew in Morocco as Eid al-Kabir to fall in the same week (the odds are astronomically high) so that for once the three monotheisms could be celebrating a feast whose origins they in many ways share—food rituals involving the sacrifice of a lamb which over time have morphed into celebrations. The difference lies in how we celebrate and why and what our celebrations symbolized in a past that we will never know completely. The Torah says that the Hebrews sacrificed a lamb to commemorate their exodus from Egypt—a moment when their firstborn sons were spared death at the hands of an avenging angel by the trick of marking their doors with the blood of a slaughtered sheep. There is always a lamb shank on display at a Passover seder, just as there was at my friend's Pagan wedding—celebrated, by the way, on Martha's Vineyard—but the food of choice at American seders, at least today, is chicken. The question is why? Is it for the broth of the boiled chickens, which can then be used for matzo ball soup. That is, for thrift. Or is it simply that for centuries Jews have preferred chicken, and it eventually became their go-to holiday dish? The early Christians celebrated Easter with lamb because Jesus is said to have eaten it at the Last Supper, which was a Passover feast, and because, sacrificed and resurrected, he became "the lamb of God." The Catholics and Orthodox Christians of Southern Europe still eat lamb at Easter, but in the north of Europe, ham is the dish of choice. Why again? Ham was a symbol of luck in the Pagan north, so perhaps it's that. But it's worth noting that early Christians in the Middle East were also said to have preferred ham, because it proved that they were Christians, celebrating the resurrection of the Messiah, and thus no longer bound by Hebrew food proscriptions. Muslims, on Eid al-Kabir, slaughter a lamb, have always eaten it, and still do. Each family who can afford to does this, but they do it to commemorate the story of Abraham and Isaac. Theirs is the one "why we do this" meal that has never been contested by, say, a chicken—or, understandably, by a ham.

There are probably as many theories of celebration as there are writers or academics to invent them. Mine is that people often celebrate because they're bored. "It's time," as the Navajo say. But given that my favorite celebration is Thanksgiving, and that I write about our national holiday at every chance I get, I should add that what I love most about it is the ritual discipline it instills in most of us, the guilty feeling when we have to miss it, even the excuses I make to myself when I'm happily celebrating it at the "wrong" time in the "wrong" country, and the recitation I feel compelled to offer of all the authentic dishes I would be cooking at home in New York. In this, our Thanksgiving dinner has somehow become a sacralized celebration, the binding agent in the secular melting pot of the republic, which may in fact be why it continues to fascinate me as a subject—a theological puzzle I can never solve. Who, for instance, are we supposed to be thanking at Thanksgiving—God? Country? Mother? The harvest? The turkey? The Pilgrims who were feckless enough to climb into three creaky boats and make the trip to Plymouth? The answer remains a delicious mystery. My husband, who endures nights of terrible takeout dinners while I'm cooking my way through Thanksgiving week, thinks that I should be thanking him. So I have begun to call it the feast of the First Forgiveness. His. There is in fact a strong element of forgiveness involved in the run-up to our national groaning board, given that something inevitably goes wrong, starting with the quality of the pad thai and the soggy tempura and the oily mopu tofu and the cartons of cold greasy pizza sped by kamikaze cyclists to just about every apartment in every building in New York that week. Or the turkey is undercooked, the turkey is overcooked, the white meat is dry, the dark meat is raw, the Brussels sprouts are burned, the sweet potato purée is lumpy. And worse, the Indian pudding, three or four hours in the oven, has failed to firm.

In the course of my research into Thanksgiving eight years ago—the part that wasn't in the kitchen—I consulted a book called *Readings in Ritual Studies*, which included an essay with the title "Consumption Rituals of Thanksgiving Day." Out of kindness, I will keep the authors—there were two—nameless. Their first theory was that over the centuries, Thanksgiving had gone from being a harvest celebration to being a celebration of "consumerism," a celebration of—this is a quote—"not just a moment of bounty, but a culture of enduring prosperity." The thought was interesting, in a kind of mean-spirited Marxist way. And in any event, the professors were wrong about harvest celebration. The first Thanksgiving, at least, was a hunt celebration; the Pilgrims caught the wild turkeys, and a party of Wampanoag braves went into the woods with bows and arrows and supplied the deer. I would add, *pace* Cardinal Richelieu, that sitting down to a feast with your real or imagined enemies can go a long way toward keeping the peace. (Still, it's worth remembering that the cardinal did take the precaution of banning daggers from his dinner table.)

But the idea of Thanksgiving as a consumer sport was nothing compared to the Freudian hypotheses that the authors offered next: Thanksgiving, they said, being "mythically connected to the infancy of the nation," represents the "oral stage of development, allowing each participant to return to the contentment and security of an infant wearing comfortable soft clothing who falls asleep after being well fed." In fact, they likened the smushing and mashing of food around on your plate—that tasty American Thanksgiving habit—to a return to baby food. Christmas, they said, was the "anal stage"—a "cultural negotiation of greed and retentiveness." New Year's Eve, which from their arid perspective— they lived in Arizona—must have looked like a bacchanal, was a time of "hedonic sexual fulfillment." The genital stage. After which, they said, Americans returned to "the everyday world of adult instrumentality." Whatever that is.

Lately, I have come to the conclusion that celebrating Thanksgiving is about affirming and reaffirming a connection between generations past and future, and especially generations of women, about a continuity of family—my mother's Thanksgivings, her mother's—that now includes my daughter, presiding over her own Thanksgiving table and extends into the future with her son grown up and *his* children smushing their food around. I don't think it's a stretch to say that even our most secular ceremonies involve a kind of magical thinking, in the way of prayers.

Weddings, of course, are the universal ritual celebration, and perhaps the most magical, in that prayerful sense that Pascal called a *pari*, a wager—and it doesn't matter if they're royal marriages with three billion people inexplicably tuned in, or the boy and the girl down the street. What's universal, among other things, is the presence of food that's somehow attached to one's idea of the people getting married. I remember the wedding of two Chinese friends—they were married at the groom's parents' house in Greenwich (the Connecticut Greenwich)—and how odd it seemed when the dinner began with trays of deliciously briny oysters on the half shell and went on to hot boiled lobsters from Long Island Sound. The groom, a linguistic anthropologist, was properly speaking Chinese-American. The bride, a well-known writer from Beijing, had done her graduate work in New York. They were a worldly, sophisticated couple. He loved lobster. She loved oysters. So why was the menu bewildering? Perhaps because the celebration was otherwise quite traditional. The bride wore a red Chinese wedding robe, and the groom's father, a master of classical Chinese poetry—which exists, calligraphically, on several levels of reference and meaning—wrote the epithalamium. (On one level of the poem, the newlyweds went out in a boat, and the bride fell in the water and presumably drowned; but a few levels deeper, there they were, living happily together ever after.) What I mean to say is that the guests expected a Chinese banquet, not the truly delicious New England seafood feast they got. It was like the shock of pork chops at a Thanksgiving dinner.

I can't think of any weddings that don't include eating—from the potlatch feasts of the hedge-fund billionaires who get married in places like Phuket or Patagonia or Patmos to a champagne and finger food reception in the backyard to the restaurant lunch after a quick trip to the marrying judge at city hall. And the magical thinking behind most of them, especially the truly excessive ones, are the hedged bets that they involve—the wagers, as Pascal would say, that the more elaborate they are, the more enduring the marriage bond will be. Hindu weddings can last for days and feed hundreds of people, many of whom were not invited. Muslim weddings, too. The elaborateness is considered propitious. I was once—I guess you could say—a bridesmaid at the marriage of a thirteen-year-old Berber girl from a tribe in the Middle Atlas. It was arranged as an exchange, because the groom's village had been losing its young men to the bride's village, and needed to replenish its supply of girls in order to earn back the animals it had been paying out in bride's prices. The wedding itself was a three-day celebration. It began in the bride's village, with the bride sequestered and decorated with henna, and course after course of food for the male guests, each course cooking while they ate the one already on the platter. The etiquette was that the men ate until, literally, they dropped. The second day was taken up with the bride's ceremonial trip to, and arrival in, the groom's village, where she would be taking up residence in his mother's house. The third day was spent in preparation for her deflowering, followed by the presentation of a bloody cloth on a copper plate, and then another feast. The bride was missing from the feast, though I was the only person who seemed to have noticed that. When I found her, she was passed out on the floor of the wedding room, still tied up for her initiation into wedded bliss. I was horrified. The first thing she said to me when I managed to revive her by burning incense was "Go eat. It's over, and they'll be serving dinner." I often wonder if it would have all gone better if the dinner had been served first.

The collapse of that particular marriage began at the dinner, when the men of the two clans started fighting, and the bride's family fled to avoid being killed. The bride, of course, stayed. A few weeks later, when a goat that was being saved for another wedding died, she was accused of bringing bad magic to the village and became a pariah in her new family. The marriage itself survived. The feasts had cost too much to bear repeating.

In the West, the order of food and sex at a wedding is, of course, reversed. The tribal wedding I just described didn't involve Islam. It was a thoroughly secular economic exchange of what you could call goods and services. The Western wedding, whatever the reality, is a pointedly religious exchange of vows if a priest or pastor or rabbi officiates. A couple is joined "under God" with all the attendant promises of fidelity, longevity, and devotion, not to mention its admonitions to "bear fruit" and to "let no man put asunder." And never mind that, at least traditionally, a wedding was mainly what you needed to go through to have sex. That's clearly not necessary now, but it's my guess that in those late, unlamented days of blushing virginal brides and horny, anxious grooms, the unspoken function of the wedding feast, with its cheerfully leering toasts and endless courses, punctuated by an exhausting amount of dancing, was an even more liminal ritual than the ceremony itself. It linked, eased, and extended a fairly flagrant transition from sacred to profane—in time, distraction, and alcohol. It wasn't so different, in this, from the Sismano priest calling a week's respite between the sagra and the procession of the Madonna. Or for that matter, from the long Last Supper in Xavier Beauvois's beautiful film *Des Hommes et des Dieux* (translated backward, in English, as *Of Gods and Men*). The film—set in Algeria during the violence of the early nineties—is about a small, remote community of French Trappist monks, a doctor among them, who have peacefully taught and treated and farmed with their Arab neighbors until the fighting reaches them and everyone's lives are abruptly shattered. Actually, it's about the monks waiting to die, knowing they are marked by Islamists for assassination and celebrating life—and the things of this world—in the face of death. They spend their last day working, chanting, praying, and most satisfyingly, as the sun sets, at their kitchen table, feasting. They open two bottles of rare French wine, prepare a last supper, and calmly and silently await the attack, nodding, tearing, and even at times smiling to the music of an old, scratchy record of Tchaikovsky's *Swan Lake*. Their last supper has all the joy and solemnity and futility of ritual. With its intimations of sacrifice, it is as liminal—and as transformational—as human beings can get.

Twelve years ago, in England, I went to the Beaufort Hunt, which I have to admit found an extremely civilized affair, perhaps because you can't eat a fox and so your celebratory ritual is the hunt breakfast—a propitiatory feast known and coveted across the pond as the English breakfast, served before the men and women of the hunt get on their horses and begin to gallop after their baying hounds. It is a warming and inevitably delicious banquet and how not, given that it comes with kippers, sausages, rashers of bacon, scrambled eggs, fried eggs, grilled mushrooms, tomatoes, and potatoes, and plenty of jam, marmalade, and butter for your toast. In France, though—as I discovered over my years of commuting to a Paris office—the celebratory hunt ritual is a wild boar hunt, after which you eat the boar. (You can't count birding as a hunt; on the continent, it's likely to be a slaughter on the order of Sarah Palin knocking off moose from a helicopter or stuffing turkeys into a decapitating machine.) In the Sologne, the traditional boar hunt opens with an alarming dance—a pas de deux, you might call it, or an attack, or if you were Bill O'Reilly, in court on harassment charges, just a "seduction"— in which a hunter advances on a young girl, a thrusting boar tusk in each hand, and the girl, naturally, twists away and tries to flee. The dance is atavistically macho, but so is the hunt itself and the consumption of the boar's flesh.

The best account of a boar hunt I have ever read was written, not surprisingly, by an amused, interested, and somewhat less than enthralled woman—a wonderful French ethnologist named Claudine Fabre-Vassas. It's about the ritual of boar hunting and what you could call transformative boar feasting in the Languedoc in southwestern France, as told by the men who hunt—and by one of the hunter's wives, who cooks whatever share of the beast her husband brings home after the hunters castrate and divide it. The men are interested less in the boar itself than in the boar's testicles— in the hunter who earns them for the kill and in what the others get when they dig in and divide the rest. They castrate the boar very quickly, almost furtively, Fabre-Vassas says, in what could be called a private ritual. They stand in a circle around the animal; they use a knife to castrate it while telling apocryphal stories about hunters who have bit the testicles off—impossible feats of mastery, given that a boar in his prime weighs some four hundred pounds. They say that the power of the boar's balls—they call it "the iron" or "the force," using the Latin word *ferum*—enters the hunter who makes the kill.

In some hunts, the hunting party divides the ferum. In others, they use the French word—*couilles*—to describe what happens once the force has entered the hunters. The testicles are worthless then; the hunters purge them in running water and vinegar, cook them, taste a symbolic morsel, and throw them to the dogs. Some hunters make a celebratory meal in the woods, and prepare it themselves. They take the heart, the lungs, the windpipe, the spleen, and the liver, purge them in the same way, chop them up, cook them over a fire with onions, tomatoes, thyme, laurel, vinegar, and red wine—while drinking as much of the wine as they can handle—call it a civet, and eat it. Most often, they divide the meat and the organs and bring them home for their wives to purge and preserve or cook. Fabre-Vassas says that either way, the name of the game is virility, and given the news lately, it's safe to say that in matters of virile preening, it doesn't matter if the men are old hunters or old politicians, or if they're three-star restaurateurs scalping the cockscomb off a soon-to-be capon at the capon festival in Bresse, or if they're worshiping the force of the ferum in Languedoc. The celebration, in any event, belongs to men, like the firemen's feast in Roussillon.

The truth is that when men "celebrate" without women, the fare is often far more crudely challenging than celebratory, or even tasty. No woman I know would trade one taste of the heartbreak, love, and longing that flavor the wedding banquet Tita cooks in *Like Water for Chocolate*, or one bite of the French delicacies in *Babette's Feast*—the sherried turtle soup, say, or the blinis with caviar, or the quail in puff pastry with foie gras and truffle sauce—with their power to enchant even the dour Pietists of Jutland, for a taste of the ferum at what could be called a stag party in the woods. When that lone Languedoc woman speaks, at the end of the Fabre-Vassas's account, the blood rites in the woods are over and she is about to cook her husband's share of scraps of meat and organs from the mutilated boar. We are back to the everyday and family dinner, back to cookery and domestication and its own kind of transformations: "Moi, I make a farcis of sausage meat," she says. "I stuff the heart with it, and then I cook it, slowly, with petits onions. It's the only way that they will ever get me to eat it." That's life, and she's not celebrating.

Acknowledgments

So many remarkable people have helped me in the course of the fifteen years since I sat down to write the first essay in this collection: at the *New Yorker*, David Remnick's valiant team of editors, fact checkers, grammarians, and OKers who shepherded me through these pieces, plus years of cumulative gratitude to Pat Keogh, in Makeup, who could glance at the huge line-overflow in every one of them and in minutes find the space to restore the words I was suddenly so desperately attached to; at St. Martin's Press, Elizabeth Beier's gracious and efficient publishing staff, with special thanks to the unflappable Nicole Williams; at home and in Italy, my husband, Vincent Crapanzano, and the family and friends who gamely worked their way through every recipe I tried, and most of the plants and animals I mentioned, with the understandable exception of *Amanita phalloides*, and especially my grandson, Garrick, an inspirational eater since, at the age of six or seven, he ordered nettle soup at a fancy country restaurant and asked for seconds; and most of all the huge cast of characters in this book—people who welcomed me into their lives and kitchens, answered what must have seemed a bewildering if not relentless barrage of questions—it was—and became my friends.

These essays began as a food-issue break from my usual *New Yorker* beat covering people and politics in Europe. They quickly became not only an annual respite from the rest of the year's bad news but the source of a deepening appreciation of the table, and of the people who grow and cook and share the gifts of their talent and dedication whenever the rest of us sit down together to break bread. Somewhere along the line, my agent, Eric Simonoff, said, "This is your next book." Food, like music, is civilizing—balm for the soul, really—and I am grateful to him, and grateful to them all, not least to the friends at Oxford and Yale who invited me to give the talks that in time grew into the long essay that ends this book.

New York, May 2017